# A PECULIAR TREASURE

# A PECULIAR TREASURE

## Brent L. Top

Bookcraft
Salt Lake City, Utah

Library of Congress Catalog Card Number: 97-72958
ISBN 1-57008-332-0


First Printing, 1997


Printed in the United States of America

# Contents

# Acknowledgments

Ｏne of the choicest blessings associated with my work in Religious Education at Brigham Young University is the opportunity to rub shoulders with men and women who possess not only significant academic credentials but, more important, real strength of character and personal spirituality. I express my sincere appreciation to all of them, as well as to my students, who often teach me more than I teach them.

I have received significant help from several of my colleagues who possess specific skills and knowledge that I needed for this project. Specifically, I wish to acknowledge the contributions of Richard Draper, Andy Skinner, Richard Holzapfel, and Dana Pike, who put up with my steady stream of questions and unselfishly helped me to better understand the meaning of Hebrew words and Old Testament history and cultural practices, as well as discussing doctrinal matters with me. I also extend my appreciation to Robert Millet, dean of Religious Education, who served as a sounding board for many of my ideas and who also shared with me important insights into the scriptures that I hadn't seen before. I appreciate his taking the time to teach me. In this book I have tried to include much of the help, insights, and ideas I gained from all of these colleagues. I believe it is a better work because of their contributions.

I also wish to express appreciation to all my friends at Bookcraft. They have treated me with the utmost kindness, respect, and professionalism through many years and several books. I am always grateful (and somewhat amazed) each time they agree to publish one of my books. I express specific thanks to Cory Maxwell for being so supportive of my projects and encouraging me to continue to write even when I vow to never do another book. This book has also been greatly enhanced by the careful editing of Rebecca Taylor. Having been one of my students at the Jerusalem Center, she had to listen to me teach these concepts. As a result, she was able to assist me in allowing the spirit of the Old Testament to shine through on every page. I greatly appreciate her time and efforts on this project.

סְגֻלָּה

# Introduction

Unlike President Spencer W. Kimball, who as a twelve-year-old boy read the entire Bible cover to cover, I did not read the Bible until I was much older. In fact, I had not read the entire Old Testament until I was a teacher in the Church Educational System—and even then I probably skimmed over much of it. Like many members of the Church, however, I was somewhat familiar with the Old Testament through a smattering of familiar stories that I had heard from my youth. My superficial knowledge was probably due in part to a couple of attitudes I had unconsciously embraced which seem to be prevalent among many members of the Church.

First, there is the view that because the Old Testament deals so much with the ancient law of Moses, which was fulfilled in Christ's atoning sacrifice, it has no relevance for us today. Since the Mosaic law was a lesser law, some unwittingly view the Old Testament as a lesser scripture. I was once told by an acquaintance, an evangelical Christian, that we didn't have to read the Old Testament or believe its doctrines or live the commandments given therein (including the Ten Commandments), because "it was all done away with Christ." While I would hope that no Latter-day Saint would dismiss the Old Testament like that, I am afraid that sometimes we unintentionally denigrate its significance in our lives when we speak of the God of the Old Testament as a "God of vengeance" and then we speak of the same divine being in the New Testament as a "God of love and mercy." Likewise, we minimize the Old Testament's profound scriptural stature when we emphasize it as an account of destruction and punishment and the New Testament as the story of redemption and deliverance. Neither characterization is accurate. The Old Testament is filled with as much love, mercy, and redemption as is the New Testament. The law of Moses may have been done away with or fulfilled in Christ, but the Old Testament is also God's "eternal word, which cannot pass away" (2 Nephi 9:16). As the Psalmist declared: "The counsel of the Lord standeth for ever, the thoughts of his heart to *all generations*" (Psalm 33:11; emphasis added).

The second attitude that became a major obstacle to my greater understanding of an appreciation for the Old Testament was the mistaken notion that the Old Testament is impenetrable because it is an ancient book filled with unfamiliar customs and cultures. Even Nephi understood this challenge. In the Book of Mormon he explained why some of his brethren had a hard time understanding the prophecies of Isaiah: "For they know not concerning the manner of prophesying among the Jews" (2 Nephi 25:1; see also verse 6). Readers may confront this cultural challenge throughout the Old Testament. Perhaps because of this I have said myself and also heard others make comments like: "Oh, I just can't understand the Old Testament. It's way above my head." "It's just so boring." "It was written for a different people and different time and so it has no meaning for me." My natural tendency was to just put the Old Testament on the shelf, thinking I could never really understand it. I was content to glean a little "gold dust" from its pages if something jumped out at me, but I didn't realize that there was a "gold vein" deep within the book that I could find if I would just exert myself.

I had to face these attitudes and seek to overcome my Old Testament illiteracy when I was appointed to teach at the Brigham Young University Jerusalem Center for Near-Eastern Studies. I loved the land of Israel and had at least some degree of knowledge of the sites where I would be taking the students. While I was still somewhat apprehensive about leading field trips, my greatest worry was regarding teaching the Old Testament. *What if the students know more than I do?* I wondered. I was more concerned about knowing enough about the Old Testament to properly teach it than I was about bus bombs, terrorists, or even unfamiliar Middle Eastern foods. I had never even learned the cute Primary song that teaches the books of the Bible in their sequential order. I didn't know the difference between Zephaniah and Zechariah or Kings and Chronicles, and I didn't know a psalm from a proverb. I only knew about Isaiah because I had encountered him so much in the Book of Mormon—and every time I did I had to start the book over because I couldn't wade through the Isaiah chapters. (As is typical with many adolescent boys, I had some exposure to the Song of Solomon. I could find that in my Bible.) I may be facetiously exaggerating my Old Testament ignorance—but not by much. I recognized that my most important preparation for teaching in Jerusalem would be to seriously study the Old Testament and to become absorbed with and excited by it.

As I began this most intimidating task, I started to find things in this volume of scripture that I had never heard of before—ideas and words that profoundly affected me. My initial reaction was "They must have put that in just recently; I've never seen it before!" The ancient book that I thought boring and difficult to understand was quickly becoming a new book that was speaking not only about ancient peoples but directly to me and about my day. I began to understand, as Nephi taught his brethren, that the key to understanding the scriptures is "likening" them to ourselves (see 1 Nephi 19:23). I became excited about what I learned from the Old Testament and was grateful that the Lord inspired prophets and scribes to record his words, however imperfect or incomplete their records, so that I could thereby be spiritually fortified today. I came to recognize that I had been too long viewing it as a dry old history book rather than an intimate diary of my own ancestors who speak to me and mine "out of the dust."

Living, studying, and traveling in the Holy Land only enhanced my love for the scriptures in general and the Old Testament specifically. I wanted the students to share in my love and excitement. The fruits of that serious study, commenced initially out of my own fear of professional humiliation but developing into my own love affair with the Old Testament, were evidenced in what my students came to experience in their own studies. I was thrilled with their excitement in finding a new friend—the Old Testament. It was music to my ears to hear comments like these: "I never knew that the Old Testament could be so exciting." "I thought I would find Christ only in my study of the New Testament. Little did I know that Christ can be found on almost every page of the Old Testament." "When I have been struggling with my own challenges or problems, I have been surprised at how something I was reading in the Old Testament answered my prayers and spoke right to my soul. The peoples and their challenges may have been different, but the principles of the gospel are the same."

From my own study of the Old Testament, and the experiences I had while teaching it in the most intensive way I had ever known, came the idea for this book. I did not want to write a doctrinal commentary or an exhaustive treatment of the historical, cultural, or linguistic aspects of the Old Testament. There are many good books written by far more educated and capable people than I am that accomplish that. I merely want to share my excitement for this great book by likening it to our times, our needs, our challenges, and our day. Just as Mormon declared that the Book of Mormon was written for us in the last days, so too can the teachings, examples, doctrines, and spirit of the Old Testament speak to us today. My desire is to share some of those timeless themes and timely teachings that can, as the Apostle Paul declared, "make thee wise unto salvation through faith which is in Christ Jesus. All scripture is given by inspiration of God, and is profitable for doctrine, for reproof, for correction, for instruction in righteousness: that the man of God may be perfect, throughly furnished unto all good works." (2 Timothy 3:15–17.)

How grateful I am that, as Ezekiel prophesied, the stick of Judah and the stick of Joseph would "become one in thine hand" (Ezekiel 37:16–17). Our lives can be enriched by both the Bible and the Book of Mormon. The Book of Mormon prophets testified that if one would believe the words of the "stick of Judah" they must also believe the words of the Book of Mormon; similarly, we cannot love, read, and cherish the teachings of the "stick of Joseph" while ignoring the Old Testament's vital messages for our day. Making them one in our hands is more than just putting them together in our modern leather-bound scripture covers—they must become one in our hearts.

I have not intended to include here every theme that has relevance and personal application or meaning for us today, for that, I hope, is subject to ongoing revelation. I am sure that some readers will say, "Why didn't he include this or that theme?" I probably will say that myself and kick myself in the pants for leaving something out, but hopefully I will continue to find more gold nuggets as I continue my study of the Old Testament. I have merely tried to share those messages that are deeply personal and relevant to me and that have been most helpful in strengthening my faith and renewing my resolve to live the gospel. It is my utmost desire that the chapters that follow will inspire and, more important, will serve as a catalyst to greater study of, excitement about, love for, and application of the Old Testament in your own life.

It was the Old Testament that Jesus admonished all to "search" (John 5:39). It was the Old Testament that Nephi was referring to when he declared, "My soul delighteth in the scriptures" (2 Nephi 4:15). As we study and feast upon the Old Testament we will get a glimpse into why it was so important to Lehi that he would not continue his journey to a new land without the brass plates, which contained much of the Old Testament. And from those scriptures Nephi and numerous other Book of Mormon prophets quoted.

We often think of the Book of Mormon being written "for our day" but fail to remember that much of it contains significant passages and prophecies from the Old Testament. The book may be called the *Old Testament*, but it is certainly not archaic. It can be new each time we read it and find those messages that perhaps are needed as much now as ever before. Elder Neal A. Maxwell said to religious educators, "I would hope that the students, as well as members of the Church whom you teach, will be able to discover for themselves that the Old Testament is new—new in the sense that its antiquity is filled with relevancy" ("The Old Testament: Relevancy Within Antiquity," address given at the Third Annual Church Educational System Religious Educators Symposium—Old Testament, 16–18 August 1979, Brigham Young University, Provo, Utah, p. 8). That is the purpose of this book—to illustrate the modern messages found in an ancient volume of scripture, or in other words, to discover relevancy within antiquity.

*Now therefore, if ye will obey my voice indeed, and keep my covenant,*
*then ye shall be a peculiar treasure unto me above all people:*
*for all the earth is mine: and ye shall be unto me*
*a kingdom of priests, and an holy nation.*
*—Exodus 19:5–6*

CHAPTER ONE

# A Covenant People: God's Peculiar Treasure

When I was a senior in high school I received a remarkable Christmas present from my parents. While it may not seem so remarkable to anyone else, it was one of the best gifts I have ever received. I was playing on the varsity basketball team, and I ate, drank, dreamed, and lived basketball at that time in my life. My mother found a porcelain figurine in a gift shop and then had someone sand off the colors and repaint it in our school colors—complete with my jersey number, my name on the back, and our high school insignia on the ball the player was holding. (I have to admit that the artist made the figure much more handsome than me.) Mom then had it gift-wrapped in my high school colors. I don't know how much it cost, but no amount of money could have made this present more valuable to me.

As the years passed this simple Christmas gift became even more special—not because I had had a great basketball career, but because it represented my parents' deep love for me. I have received many Christmas gifts through the years, most of which I can't even remember. The majority I used for a short time and then discarded. Perhaps today some of those gifts that I once thought were so important lie rusting and eroding in some landfill. But this special gift is different. I put this little figurine in a prominent place—first in my room and then later, after I was married, in our home, and finally, when I became a teacher, in my office. People coming into my office would often comment on how unique it was. Truly it was unique because no one else in the world had a figurine just like mine, and certainly it was unique because it came from my parents, especially for me. It was a priceless possession, an irreplaceable heirloom.

I have thought often of this precious gift and my parents' love for me when I read in the Old Testament of ancient Israel being characterized as a "peculiar" people. In our modern English vernacular the word *peculiar* is interpreted to mean "different," "strange," or even "weird." But that is not the intended meaning in the Old Testament.

After Jehovah had miraculously liberated the Israelites from their bondage in Egypt, he led them in a marvelous manner so that they would know that he was indeed with them—in a cloud by day and a pillar of fire at night (see Exodus 13:20–22; Numbers 14:14). At the base of Mount Sinai Moses commanded the Israelites, as instructed by the Lord Jehovah, to prepare themselves to be in the Lord's holy presence. Because of his great love for them, God was renewing his covenant with them if they would keep their covenants with him.

> And Moses went up unto God, and the Lord called unto him out of the mountain, saying, Thus shalt thou say to the house of Jacob, and tell the children of Israel;
>
> Ye have seen what I did unto the Egyptians, and how I bare you on eagles' wings, and brought you unto myself.
>
> Now therefore, if ye will obey my voice indeed, and keep my covenant, then ye shall be a *peculiar treasure* unto me above all people: for all the earth is mine:
>
> And ye shall be unto me a kingdom of priests, and an holy nation. (Exodus 19:3–6; emphasis added.)

The Hebrew word for *peculiar* is *segullah*, which signifies a property or treasure that is exceedingly precious and is diligently cared for and painstakingly preserved. In a modern context, God is offering to make us his prized possession that he will lovingly look after and protect if we will keep his covenant. Segullah means that Israel, both ancient and modern, can become a treasure endeared unto the Lord, unlike anything else in the world, if we will keep the covenant. What is the covenant that, if kept, transforms ordinary men and women into *segullah* or "a peculiar treasure" and a "holy nation"?

## THE ABRAHAMIC COVENANT

A gospel covenant is an agreement between God and man. Man promises obedience to the Lord's will and dedicates his life to the Lord's service; in turn, God promises glorious blessings, even unto "all that [the] Father hath" (D&C 84:38; see also vv. 34–39). The Old Testament repeatedly refers to the "covenants of the fathers," and we generally think of the covenants and blessings associated with Abraham, Isaac, and Jacob, but the covenant predates even these ancient patriarchs. The Lord made great promises to Enoch and Noah based on their faithfulness (see Genesis 6:18, 22; JST, Genesis 13:14). Undoubtedly Adam and his seed made similar covenants (see Moses 6:53–68). These covenants and blessings are merely mortal extensions of the "everlasting covenant" that was also extant in the premortal realm. Just as ancient Israel became the chosen people through their faithfulness to the covenants of their fathers, those who kept the everlasting covenant of the gospel in their premortal existence became *segullah*, God's peculiar treasure on earth. "There was a group of souls tested, tried, and proven before they were born into the world, and the Lord provided a lineage for them," Elder Marvin J. Ballard taught. "That lineage is the house of Israel, the lineage of Abraham, Isaac and Jacob and their posterity. Through this lineage were to come the true and tried souls that had demonstrated their righteousness in the spirit world before they came here." (*Melvin J. Ballard—Crusader for Righteousness* [Salt Lake City: Bookcraft, 1966], pp. 218–19.)

On earth the prototype of covenant-keeping was Father Abraham. In the Old Testament he is the focal point of the covenant; all subsequent references to it and to the blessings for obedience and curses for disobedience grow out of Father Abraham's righteous example. He was faithful in keeping his covenant to do all that God commanded, even being willing to offer his only son as a required sacrifice (see Genesis 22:1–18; Hebrews 11:17–19). Because of his faith and righteousness, the Lord promised to provide certain blessings and opportunities for him and all his lineal and adopted descendants who would likewise faithfully adhere to the everlasting covenant. Four great blessings were promised to the covenantal seed of Abraham:

1. *A promised land.* "Lift up now thine eyes, and look from the place where thou art northward, and southward, and eastward, and westward: for all the land which thou seest, to thee will I give it, and to thy seed for ever" (Genesis 13:14–15).

2. *A great posterity.* "I will bless thee, and in multiplying I will multiply thy seed as the stars of the heaven, and as the sand which is upon the sea shore; and thy seed shall possess the gate of his enemies" (Genesis 22:17).

3. *The everlasting priesthood and the blessings of the gospel.* "I will establish my covenant between men and thee and thy seed after thee in their generations for an everlasting covenant, to be a God unto thee, and to thy seed after thee" (Genesis 17:7).

4. *A responsibility to share the gospel of salvation.* "And I will make of thee a great nation, and I will bless thee above measure, and make thy name great among all nations, and thou shalt be a blessing unto thy seed after thee, that in their hands they shall bear this ministry and Priesthood unto all nations; . . . and in thy seed after thee . . . shall all the families of the earth be blessed, even with the blessings of the Gospel, which are the blessings of salvation, even of life eternal" (Abraham 2:9, 11).

These aspects of the Abrahamic covenant have both a temporal and a spiritual application. While much of the Old Testament deals with the literal fulfillment and eventual loss of the blessings of seed, land, and priesthood, there is a much greater spiritual meaning of the covenant. In their fullest sense, these promises are realized only through the blessings of the fulness of the gospel. Inheriting the "promised land" eternally is realized by inheriting the millennial lands of promise (see 2 Nephi 6:11; 10:7–8) and ultimately by inheriting the celestialized earth (see D&C 130:9).

Millions on earth can claim Father Abraham as their great progenitor, yet the only way that those who inherit the blessings of Abraham, Isaac, and Jacob can have seed as numerous as the stars is through the covenant of celestial marriage. As the Lord declared unto the Prophet Joseph Smith:

> Abraham received promises concerning his seed, and of the fruit of his loins—from whose loins ye are, namely, my servant Joseph—

which were to continue so long as they were in the world; and as touching Abraham and his seed, out of the world they should continue; both in the world and out of the world should they continue as innumerable as the stars; or, if ye were to count the sand upon the seashore ye could not number them.

This promise is yours also, because ye are of Abraham, and the promise was made unto Abraham; and by this law is the continuation of the works of my Father, wherein he glorifieth himself.

Go ye, therefore, and do the works of Abraham; enter ye into my law and ye shall be saved.

But if ye enter not into my law ye cannot receive the promise of my Father, which he made unto Abraham. (D&C 132:30–33.)

This is the covenant that God has made with his people—the everlasting covenant which, if obeyed, results in his people being *segullah,* or a peculiar treasure that is blessed of the Lord and which blesses the world (see Abraham 2:9–11; see also Kent P. Jackson, "The Abrahamic Covenant: A Blessing for All People," *Ensign*, February 1990, pp. 50–53).

## "Ye Are Bought with a Price"

One of the interesting connotations of the Hebrew word *segullah* is that of a special possession or treasure that has been purchased. The idea is even more evident in the Greek word *peripoiesis,* from which the word *peculiar* is translated in the New Testament. This Old Testament theme takes on added significance when the Apostle Peter teaches in the New Testament that through the blood of Christ "ye are a chosen generation, a royal priesthood, an holy nation, *a peculiar people*; that ye should shew forth the praises of him [Christ] who hath called you out of darkness into his marvellous light" (1 Peter 2:9; emphasis added). Becoming a peculiar people, or a precious treasure unto God, comes through the everlasting covenant and the Atonement of Jesus Christ. "For ye are bought with a price," the Apostle Paul declared (1 Corinthians 6:20).

All of the commandments associated with the covenants of the fathers described in the Old Testament are designed to lead people to the salvation that is to be found only in Christ and his everlasting gospel. The great blessings of being *segullah* are not found merely in possessing promised lands or having numerous seed, but in being safeguarded in the protection of God's loving covenant. "I will save them out of all their dwellingplaces, wherein they have sinned, and will cleanse them: so shall they be my people, and I will be their God," Jehovah declared to covenant Israel. "Moreover I will make a covenant of peace with them; it shall be an everlasting covenant with them: and I will place them, and multiply them, and will set my sanctuary in the midst of them for evermore.

My tabernacle also shall be with them: yea, I will be their God, and they shall be my people.

And the heathen shall know that I the Lord so sanctify Israel, when my sanctuary shall be in the midst of them for evermore." (Ezekiel 37:23, 26–28.)

## BEING DIFFERENT FROM THE WORLD

Unlike my basketball figurine, a "peculiar treasure" is not for display purposes only. God doesn't have a chosen people to keep in a trophy case. The blessings of the covenant are inseparably linked to its responsibilities. Being *segullah* requires being peculiar—not weird or strange, but unique, different from those who reject God's covenant. For this reason the Lord instructed Moses to teach the Israelites not to wear their hair or clothes in the same style and manner as their pagan neighbors or to engage in many of the same practices and traditions of those not of the covenant (see Leviticus 19:26–32). "Ye are the children of the Lord your God: ye shall not cut yourselves, nor make any baldness between your eyes for the dead," the Lord declared. This was not just a matter of taste or style. In order for Israel to perform its sacred responsibilities as part of the Abrahamic covenant—to bless all nations of the earth—they must maintain higher standards. "For thou art an holy people unto the Lord thy God, and the Lord hath chosen thee to be a peculiar people unto himself, above all the nations that are upon the earth" (Deuteronomy 14:1–2). Ancient Israel was often reminded that they could not remain *segullah* and be like everyone else. Such practice turns an object that is unique and special, or peculiar, into one that is common and cheap.

One of the ways that ancient Israel was reminded of their covenantal role as *segullah* was through an interesting element associated with the many sacrificial rites of the law of Moses and the carnal commandments. The Lord had instructed that on every sacrifice, regardless of its type, the officiating priest would sprinkle salt. From time immemorial salt has been a preservative and as such has served as an important symbolic reminder to the Israelites. The salt represented the preservation of the covenant throughout the world. It was this familiar symbol that the Savior spoke of when he said to his disciples: "Ye are the salt of the earth: but if the salt have lost his savour, wherewith shall it be salted? it is thenceforth good for nothing, but to be cast out, and to be trodden under foot of men." (Matthew 5:13.) Just as salt loses its savor only through contamination by impure, foreign elements, the covenant people lose their *segullah* status and power to "bless the nations of the earth" by becoming impure and unworthy and by abandoning the protective covenants of the Lord.

One of the best Old Testament examples of the results of such contamination is the account of ancient Israel's desire to have a king. Such a desire was not based on public policy or governmental efficiency but rather on the Israelites' expressed desire "that we also may be like all the nations" (1 Samuel 8:20). Despite the prophet Samuel's explicit warnings to them of all of the terrible consequences that would come upon them, they no longer desired to be different, or *segullah*, but instead wanted to be like others. Samuel took this rejection of their covenantal status personally and felt rejected by his own people, to which the Lord declared, "They have not rejected thee, but they have rejected me, that I should not reign over them" (1 Samuel 8:7). The Old Testament is replete with accounts of hardships, droughts, plagues, and destruction that befell the Israelites because they had rejected the covenant and were no longer worthy to be blessed and protected by the Lord. Such a theme is a relevant warning for us today.

Elder Neal A. Maxwell has spoken of the need to "be different in order to make a difference in the world" ("Why Not Now?" *Ensign*, November 1974, p. 13). To make such a difference *in* the world, then, we need to be different *from* the world. In order for us as modern covenant Israel to fulfill our obligation to the world as the "salt of the earth," we must remain *segullah*, a unique, untainted treasure that has been blessed and sanctified by the Lord so that we, in turn, can bless and sanctify the world. To the Prophet Joseph Smith the Lord declared:

When men are called unto mine everlasting gospel, and covenant with an everlasting covenant, they are accounted as the salt of the earth and the savor of men;

They are called to be the savor of men; therefore, if that salt of the earth lose its savor, behold, it is thenceforth good for nothing only to be cast out and trodden under the feet of men. (D&C 101:39–40.)

But inasmuch as they keep not my commandments, and hearken not to observe all my words, the kingdoms of the world shall prevail against them.

For they were set to be a light unto the world, and to be the saviors of men;

And inasmuch as they are not the saviors of men, they are as salt that has lost its savor, and is thenceforth good for nothing but to be cast out and trodden under foot of men. (D&C 103:8–10.)

Just as Moses and other prophets reminded ancient Israel that, because they were *segullah*, they must not become contaminated by the evil practices of the world around them, modern prophets continually remind us that we too must remain peculiar to receive the blessings of the Lord and to achieve our covenantal destiny. President Gordon B. Hinckley admonished:

Peter speaks of "an holy nation." He does not refer to a political entity. He refers to a vast congregation of the Saints of God, men and women who walk in holiness before him and who look to Jesus Christ as their Savior and their King. . . . What a treasured privilege to have citizenship in this holy nation. Never belittle the rights, privileges, and responsibilities that flow therefrom.

Peter's final description—"a peculiar people."

Of course you are peculiar. If the world continues its present trend, and if you walk in obedience to the doctrine and principles of this Church, you may become even more peculiar in the eyes of others.

To each of you I say this: As members of The Church of Jesus Christ of Latter-day Saints, you have been taught many values of divine origin. These values are based on the commandments which the finger of the Lord wrote upon the tablets of stone when Moses spoke with Jehovah upon the mountain. You know them. You are familiar with them.

The values you have been taught likewise are based upon the beatitudes which Jesus spoke to the multitude. These, with others of His divine teachings, constitute a code of ethics, a code of values, a code of divine doctrine familiar to you and binding upon you.

To these have been added the precepts and commandments of modern revelation.

Combined together these basic, divinely given principles, laws, and commandments must constitute your value system. You cannot escape the consequences of their observance. If you will shape your lives according to their pattern, I do not hesitate to promise that you will know much of peace and happiness, of growth and achievement. To the degree that you fail to observe them, I regretfully say that the fruits will be disappointment, sadness, misery, and even tragedy.

You of this generation, this chosen generation, this royal priesthood, this holy nation, you of this peculiar people—you cannot with impunity follow practices out of harmony with values you have been taught. I challenge you to rise above the sordid elements of the world about you. (In Conference Report, April 1992, p. 99.)

## A Covenant of Love

Just as the basketball figurine was a priceless gift of love from my parents to me, so too is God's covenant with us a matchless gift of infinite love. God does not bestow the designation *segullah* randomly, like drawing names from a hat, but out of love for his children. Because of that love, the covenant is designed to protect his children from those things of the world that will destroy happiness and bring misery and heartache in their wake. The greatest manifestation of that love is found in Christ and his infinite sacrifice (see John 3:16). The stipulations of his covenant, therefore, are not burdensome or capricious but instead are loving, protective, and merciful. It is this call to be his chosen people that underlies all the Lord's teachings and dealings with his people that we read in the Old Testament. Though the circumstances and culture are different today, the covenant remains the same and the spiritual quest to become and to remain God's peculiar treasure is as vital for us today as it was for those in the days of Adam, Abraham, Moses, or Malachi.

For thou art an holy people unto the Lord thy God: the Lord thy God hath chosen thee to be a special people unto himself, above all people that are upon the face of the earth.

The Lord did not set his love upon you, nor choose you, because ye were more in number than any people; for ye were the fewest of all people:

But because the Lord loved you, and because he would keep the oath which he had sworn unto your fathers, hath the Lord brought you out with a mighty hand, and redeemed you out of the house of bondmen, from the hand of Pharaoh king of Egypt.

Know therefore that the Lord thy God, he is God, the faithful God, which keepeth covenant and mercy with them that love him and keep his commandments to a thousand generations. . . .

Thou shalt therefore keep the commandments, and the statutes, and the judgments, which I command thee this day, to do them.

Wherefore it shall come to pass, if ye hearken to these judgments, and keep, and do them, that the Lord thy God shall keep unto thee the covenant and the mercy which he sware unto thy fathers:

And he will love thee, and bless thee, and multiply thee: he will also bless the fruit of thy womb, and the fruit of thy land, thy corn, and thy wine, and thine oil, the increase of thy kine, and the flocks of thy sheep, in the land which he sware unto thy fathers to give thee.

Thou shalt be blessed above all people. (Deuteronomy 7:6–9, 11–14.)

Several weeks after I had taught this important concept in connection with the book of Deuteronomy to my class of Old Testament students at Brigham Young University, a young woman shared with me a letter she had written her parents. The message of the book of Deuteronomy as God's covenant of love had had such a profound impact on her that she felt compelled to express her feelings to her parents. That kind of spiritual impact, as evidenced in her letter, illustrates how the Old Testament can truly demonstrate "relevancy within antiquity."

Dear Mom and Dad:

What a day!!! I just had a wonderful experience in my Old Testament class. I knew that if I tried to call and tell you about it that I'd just be one big blubberpuss.

We just studied Deuteronomy—a covenant of love. Moses is sort of giving his farewell address to the Israelites. As I thought to myself what I would say to these stupid, murmuring, slow-to-remember, quick-to-sin people, Deuteronomy became more like a message of fear rather than a covenant of love. I thought, If I were Moses I wouldn't waste my time reminding them of all that the Lord had done for them—the manna, the quail, the pillar of fire that lit their way, their indestructible clothes, etc. No, I'd remind them of my rage at Sinai, drinking the melted golden calf, the earth swallowing up the rebels, all the plagues, etc. I'd scare them into obedience. Well, I thought that would be a good idea. So, why didn't Moses do it? Maybe it had something to do with Moses' connections; maybe he knew something I didn't. Seriously, why did Moses use his last words to remind Israel of the incredible love God had for them? Brother Top, in our class discussion, helped me answer my own questions.

First of all, fear is not a lasting motivation. We read in the scriptures that we're supposed to "fear" God. Well, I was right on top of that one. "'Fear' means to respect," I thought to myself. Right? Well, sort of. It actually means to revere. It means adoration. It means love—and love inevitably leads to obedience, service, and righteousness. In fact, it is only through love that these actions are not burdensome. Brother Top gave an example in class of this concept of a husband who cleans the house and makes dinner for his wife who has spent the whole day teaching their three daughters how to ski. His point was that the husband doesn't do the work begrudgingly. In fact, he was glad to do it, because he loved her so much. You see, it's imperative that the covenant between God and Israel that is being renewed in Deuteronomy be based on God's perfect love for his children. If we knew how much Heavenly Father really loves us, we would give up all our sins and be totally righteous. Now this is the part where I started to bawl.

I don't think I've voiced this concern at any time in my life, but I've always had this nagging little question as to why I've always been such a goody-goody. I don't mean to say that I've lived a sin-free life, but the fact is I have passed up a lot of tempting opportunities to mess up. Why have I been such a good girl? I remember, even as a little kid, passing up some mischievous little crime with my friends and hearing them honestly say, "No way, I can't do that; my parents would kill me." . . . But I was never afraid of you. Then today in our Old Testament class, the answer came to me. It just overwhelmed me. If ever I have made a truly righteous decision, it has been only because I have wanted to. And I've only wanted to because I love you so much because you loved me first. It's not that I feel obligated to be righteous, I *want* to honor you. Even away from you I never wanted to do anything that would dishonor you. Every aspect of my testimony stems from your love for me. Families are so important.

Mom and Dad, how can I ever thank you enough? I love you so much. Today as we talked about the love Heavenly Father had for the Israelites, I feel like I caught a glimpse for the first time of how much he loves me, because it's like the love you have for me. That love helps me want to do good and be righteous. What an important lesson from Deuteronomy. Look what the Old Testament has done to me—I'm a wailing wreck now. Man, who would have thought those Israelites could play such a big part in teaching me one of the most important lessons of my life?

*And Esau said, Behold, I am at the point to die: and what profit shall this birthright*
*do to me? And Jacob said, Swear to me this day; and he sware unto him:*
*and he sold his birthright unto Jacob. Then Jacob gave Esau bread*
*and pottage of lentils; and he did eat and drink, and rose up,*
*and went his way: thus Esau despised his birthright.*
*—Genesis 25:32–34*

CHAPTER TWO

# Selling the Birthright

One of the stories in the Old Testament that most intrigues me is the story of Esau selling his birthright to his younger brother, Jacob, for a meal of bread and lentil soup. There are many things associated with this story that I don't fully understand, and there are many questions raised by the way the account makes Rebekah look as though she tricked or deceived Isaac, the patriarch. Much has been said and written concerning Rebekah's actions to ensure that Jacob received the birthright, but to focus merely on that part of the story really misses the point. I believe this story was included in the scriptural text not just because it is fascinating reading, but because there is a major message or spiritual lesson to be learned from understanding not only Esau's selling of his birthright, but what that action symbolized in the Old Testament and what it means to us today.

Unfortunately, many today find Esau's trading of his inheritance for food because of his immediate hunger to be extremely short-sighted. Yet today there are those just like Esau all around us who, in their desire for some source of immediate gratification, sometimes knowingly and other times unwittingly trade an inheritance of eternal significance for something that fades and flees.

## WHAT IS THE BIRTHRIGHT?

On the surface the birthright appears to be just a temporal inheritance of land or property that is bequeathed to a firstborn son. According to ancient custom, the firstborn son inherited a double portion of the estate. The Old Testament, however, gives many accounts of someone other than the firstborn son who inherited the birthright. Because of these emphasized exceptions one must not overlook the spiritual dimension of the birthright blessing. If this inheritance were only temporal in nature—dealing only with lands and flocks—then Rebekah's insistence that Jacob be granted the birthright would appear to be motivated out of self-serving greed. However, she understood that the birthright was as much a spiritual responsibility and blessing, if not more so, than merely a temporal inheritance.

The birthright involved spiritual leadership of the family and an obligation to act in harmony with the conditions of the covenant. The birthright blessing was the right of presidency and included the keys of the priesthood. "It appears that anciently under the Patriarchal Order certain special blessings, rights, powers, and privileges—collectively called the *birthright*—passed from the father to his *firstborn son* (Genesis 43:33)," wrote Elder Bruce R. McConkie. "In later ages special blessings and prerogatives have been poured out upon *all* the worthy descendants of some who gained special blessings and birthrights anciently (3 Nephi 20:25–27)." (*Mormon Doctrine*, 2d ed. [Salt Lake City: Bookcraft, 1966], p. 87; emphasis in original.) One of the underlying themes of the Old Testament is that inheritance of the birthright was based more upon the son's worthiness than just birth order. This is evidenced later in the Old Testament when Reuben, the eldest son of Jacob (Israel), forfeits the birthright when he is immoral with his father's wife (see Genesis 35:22; see also Genesis 49:3–4).

With this spiritual dimension of the birthright in mind, Esau's selling of his birthright takes on new meaning. The scriptural phrases "what profit shall this birthright do to me?" (Genesis 25:32) and "Esau despised his birthright" (Genesis 25:34) give us a glimpse into how Esau really sold his birthright. It was not the financial gain he could have expected that he despised. It was the spiritual conditions attached to the covenant of Father Abraham that meant nothing to him. The birthright that he sold was in fact *segullah*, or the power and privilege to be God's "peculiar treasure" and inherit all the blessings of

Abraham both in time and in eternity. To Esau the spiritual aspects of that covenant meant nothing, and so it was easy to settle for a single portion of land and possessions as an inheritance—a temporal inheritance alone with no spiritual strings attached and no covenantal conditions to meet.

## DESPISING THE BIRTHRIGHT: MARRYING OUT OF THE COVENANT

The literal event of Jacob willingly trading a bowl of his delicious soup to Esau for his birthright is symbolic of how not only Esau but others before him and even in our day "despise" the birthright, trading it away for something of considerably lesser value. Esau's selling of the birthright had actually been done previous to the literal bartering with Jacob. *Despise* means not only "to abhor" or "to reject" but also "to look down upon," "to have little regard for," "to regard as beneath one's notice or unworthy of one's consideration or interest." Esau had "despised" the spiritual aspects of the covenant when he had chosen not to live a life of righteousness, not to maintain his *segullah* or treasured status before the Lord. His despising of the covenant became even more pronounced when he later married out of the covenant (see Genesis 26:34; 28:8–9). His actions brought terrible heartache to both Isaac and Rebekah (see Genesis 26:35). Far more painful to them was his "selling out" or abandonment of the Abrahamic covenant than was his literal selling of his temporal birthright for bean soup, a morsel of venison, and pita bread.

All throughout the Old Testament but particularly in Genesis, the sacredness of marriage within the everlasting covenant of the gospel is powerfully portrayed. When Isaac became of age to marry, Abraham made arrangements for his servant to journey to Haran and find a wife for Isaac. So important was this task and the impending marriage that Abraham made his servant take a solemn vow. "And Abraham said unto his eldest servant of his house, that ruled over all that he had; Put forth I pray thee thy hand under my hand, and I will make thee swear by the Lord, the God of heaven, and the God of the earth, that thou shalt not take a wife unto my son, of the daughters of Canaanites among whom I dwell; but thou shalt go unto my country, and to my kindred and take a wife unto my son Isaac." (JST, Genesis 24:2.)

I don't think that Abraham sent a servant hundreds of miles away to secure a wife for his son because the women in Haran were the best-looking or had more bounteous dowries. Abraham did not want his son to marry a Canaanite woman, not because they couldn't be good wives or mothers or make for happy homes and fulfilling lives. Almost any wife and husband can provide those things. What was of utmost importance to Abraham was the eternal glory and the "continuation of the seeds forever and ever" (D&C 132:19) that can be obtained only through faithful adherence to the covenants of the gospel—including eternal marriage.

A generation later Esau took wives from among the people of Heth, a Hittite. Like the Canaanites, the Hittites were not of the covenant—not *segullah*. "And Rebekah said to Isaac, I am weary of my life because of the daughters of Heth: if Jacob take a wife of the daughters of Heth, such as these which are of the daughters of the land, what good shall my life do me?" (Genesis 27:46.) Once again the patriarch commanded his son, "Thou shalt not take a wife of the daughters of Canaan" (Genesis 28:6), and again it is sealed with a sacred vow. Jacob returned to the land of Haran to find a wife from among the "household of faith" (see Genesis 28–30; Galatians 6:10). More important than romance or riches was a common commitment to the covenant; a shared faith in the God of Abraham, Isaac, and Jacob; and an understanding of his promises to the faithful.

One of the most troubling parts of the Old Testament for the modern reader is the account of Joshua entering the promised land and commanding his men to "utterly destroy" all of its inhabitants. Why would the Lord command such destruction anciently when today he expects us to love our enemies and to live by our neighbors in peaceful coexistence? The answer is found within the very command that Jehovah gave to the Israelites through Moses:

> When the Lord thy God shall bring thee into the land whither thou goest to possess it, and hath cast out many nations before thee, the Hittites, and the Girgashites, and the Amorites, and the Canaanites, and the Perizzites, and the Hivites, and the Jebusites, seven nations greater and mightier than thou;
>
> And when the Lord thy God shall deliver them before thee; thou shalt smite them, and utterly destroy them; thou shalt make no covenant with them, nor shew mercy unto them:

Neither shalt thou make marriages with them; thy daughter thou shalt not give unto his son, nor his daughter shalt thou take unto thy son.

For they will turn away thy son from following me, that they may serve other gods: so will the anger of the Lord be kindled against you, and destroy thee suddenly.

But thus shall ye deal with them; ye shall destroy their altars, and break down their images, and cut down their groves, and burn their graven images with fire.

For thou art an holy people unto the Lord thy God: the Lord thy God hath chosen thee to be a special people unto himself, above all people that are upon the face of the earth. (Deuteronomy 7:1–6.)

The preservation of the covenant and the eternal blessings associated exclusively with it were so important that the Lord even commanded that some people's lives be taken rather than the eternal souls of the Israelites be destroyed. Unfortunately, ancient Israel wasn't very obedient. Much of the tribulation, bondage, and destruction that ultimately befell them came because of their "selling of the birthright" through intermarriage and the forsaking of gospel covenants. Some of the most notorious characters in the Old Testament that followed this tragic pattern were King Ahab, an Israelite, and his Phoenician wife, Jezebel, who promoted and perpetuated the illicit worship of pagan gods, resulting in drought, famine, and much bloodshed (see 1 Kings 16:30–33; 17–22.)

Even in the golden age of Israelite history, marriage out of the covenant brought about the decline and ultimate destruction of the kingdom of Judah. One of Israel's most important figures, King Solomon—the same Solomon who had been blessed by the Lord with "wisdom and understanding exceeding much, and largeness of heart, even as the sand that is on the sea shore" (1 Kings 4:29) and who had built the Lord's house and received personal visitations from the Lord Jehovah (see 1 Kings 3:5; 9:2)—disobeyed the Lord's command and married many wives not of the covenant.

And he had seven hundred wives, princesses, and three hundred concubines: and his wives turned away his heart.

For it came to pass, when Solomon was old, that his wives turned away his heart after other gods: and his heart was not perfect with the Lord his God, as was the heart of David his father.

For Solomon went after Ashtoreth the goddess of the Zidonians, and after Milcom the abomination of the Ammonites.

And Solomon did evil in the sight of the Lord, and went not fully after the Lord, as did David his father.

Then did Solomon build an high place for Chemosh, the abomination of Moab, in the hill that is before Jerusalem, and for Molech, the abomination of the children of Ammon.

And likewise did he for all his strange wives, which burnt incense and sacrificed unto their gods.

And the Lord was angry with Solomon, because his heart was turned from the Lord God of Israel, which had appeared unto him twice,

And had commanded him concerning this thing, that he should not go after other gods: but he kept not that which the Lord commanded.

Wherefore the Lord said unto Solomon, Forasmuch as this is done of thee, and thou hast not kept my covenant and my statutes, which I have commanded thee, I will surely rend the kingdom from thee. (1 Kings 11:3–11.)

Just as Solomon and his Israelite seed ultimately lost their kingdom due to their marrying out of the Abrahamic covenant, so too will we lose our "thrones, kingdoms, principalities, and powers" (D&C 132:19) if we, like the ancients, despise or set at naught the only covenant of marriage that can produce kings and queens, priests and priestesses. In our dispensation the Lord has reiterated the infinite importance of marriage in the covenant. It isn't a matter of mere marital happiness or family stability here on earth, "for marriage is ordained of God unto man" (D&C 49:15), but it is about an eternal birthright that will remain long after the brick and mortar of earthly homes have become so much dust. "For whatsoever things remain are by me," the Lord declared; "and whatsoever things are not by me shall be shaken and destroyed."

Therefore, if a man marry him a wife in the world, and he marry her not by me nor by my word, and he covenant with her so long as he is in the world and she with him, their covenant and marriage are not of force when they are dead, and when they are out of the world; therefore, they are not bound by any law when they are out of the world.

Therefore, when they are out of the world they neither marry nor are given in marriage; but are appointed angels in heaven, which angels are ministering servants, to minister for those who are worthy of a far more, and an exceeding, and an eternal weight of glory.

For these angels did not abide my law; therefore, they cannot be enlarged, but remain separately and singly, without exaltation, in their saved condition, to all eternity; and from thenceforth are not gods, but are angels of God forever and ever. (D&C 132:14–17.)

Several years ago as I taught at the BYU Jerusalem Center, my class was studying the great emphasis that the ancient patriarchs placed upon covenant marriage. We discussed the meaning of those Old Testament passages for us today. I didn't think anything of our class discussion; it seemed pretty normal and uneventful. But as I made the statement that marrying out of the temple was like Esau selling his birthright for a mess of pottage—eternally shortsighted—there was an obvious hush in the class, and one young woman became red in the face and then began to cry.

As class ended, all of the students left the room except for this young woman. Her eyes were full of tears, and also anger. She was angry with me for being so forceful in my declarations concerning the importance of marriage in the covenant. She accused me of being unrighteously judgmental and too dogmatic.

I was somewhat taken aback by her anger and accusations. Then the rest of the story came to light. What the other students knew, but I didn't, was that she had just become engaged while in Israel. (I should have figured something was up when her boyfriend wired her a large and beautiful flower arrangement that she proudly displayed to all.) Others in the class were engaged but didn't react to my lesson the way she did. It was because, of course, she was not marrying in the temple. I tried to talk with and comfort her and ease some of her anger, but I couldn't revoke the Lord's law.

"He promised me that he would get his life in order and take me to the temple someday," she told me. "He is such a good man, and he makes me happy. We can still have a happy marriage and a strong family."

My heart certainly went out to her. Her words were touching, but not convincing. I think she was trying to convince herself, but she too began to realize that the romance, the bouquets of flowers, and the glittering engagement ring looked more and more like cold lentil soup when compared to the promised birthright.

> And again, verily I say unto you, if a man marry a wife by my word, which is my law, and by the new and everlasting covenant, and it is sealed unto them by the Holy Spirit of promise, by him who is anointed, unto whom I have appointed this power and the keys of this priesthood; and it shall be said unto them—Ye shall come forth in the first resurrection . . . and shall inherit thrones, kingdoms, principalities, and powers, dominions, all heights and depths . . . and they shall pass by the angels, and the gods, which are set there, to their exaltation and glory in all things, as hath been sealed upon their heads, which glory shall be a fulness and a continuation of the seeds forever and ever.
>
> Then shall they be gods, because they have no end; therefore shall they be from everlasting to everlasting, because they continue; then shall they be above all, because all things are subject unto them. Then shall they be gods, because they have all power, and the angels are subject unto them.
>
> Verily, verily, I say unto you, except ye abide my law ye cannot attain to this glory. (D&C 132:19–21.)

Our discussion ended. The class went on. The semester ended. She and the rest of the students returned home and I remained behind in Jerusalem. I received a wedding invitation a few weeks later. After several years, back at BYU in Provo, she enrolled in one of my classes—it was the first time I had seen her since that class in Israel. Almost afraid to know the answer, I asked how her marriage was doing and if she was happy. I was saddened but not totally surprised when she told me that she was in the process of obtaining a divorce. "He just didn't want to live the gospel," she replied.

Several months later she once again visited me in my office seeking my advice. She had met a young man who was extremely nice and good to her, and a romance had bloomed. "He wants to marry me," she said. "But I don't know whether I should marry him before he joins the Church or wait until after his baptism. He is taking the missionary lessons right now."

She didn't need my advice. She already knew how I felt about the subject. I just wished her well, and as the door to my office closed I whispered to myself, "One in seven."

That phrase had become significant to me and my students, including this young woman, while we were living and studying in Jerusalem. I was far more afraid of traffic in Jerusalem than I was of any potential terrorist threat. I came to believe that riding in a New York City taxi or in a giant roller coaster in a popular amusement park was tame compared to the "thrill" of driving or walking in Jerusalem. When we prayed in our family prayers for safety in the mornings, it was more heartfelt in Jerusalem than in Utah. As we walked to places in the city of Jerusalem and as we crossed streets, often without the aid of streetlights or crosswalks—as if that would have mattered to most of the motorists—I would often yell out to the scrambling students, "Remember, one in seven."

Because the students often commented on the "crazy" drivers in the Holy Land, I used that situation as a teaching tool in class. As we talked about the importance of covenant marriage as taught in the Old Testament, I asked the students, "Would you dare to cross the street or jaywalk or run between oncoming cars if you knew that six out of seven of you would be killed in doing so?" It immediately got their attention, and they agreed that with those odds, the risk was too great to take. That graphic imagery and the daily challenge of dodging traffic in Jerusalem served as a powerful springboard for my introducing to the class these poignant sentiments expressed by President Spencer W. Kimball:

> Over the years many times women have come to me in tears. How they would love to train their children in the Church, in the gospel of Jesus Christ! But they were unable to do so. How they would like to accept positions of responsibility in the Church! How they would like to pay their tithing! How they would love to go to the temple and . . . be sealed for eternity, and to have their own flesh and blood, their children, sealed to them for eternity!
>
> But the doors are locked! They themselves have locked them, and the doors have often rusted on their hinges. Someone did not teach these individuals sufficiently, or they did not study the scriptures and they did not understand, or they ignored the warnings which came to them. They married out of the Church. Perhaps he was a good man. Maybe he was handsome. He may have been cultured and well trained; but he did not have the qualification that he needed most and which they overlooked. He did not have membership in the kingdom; he did not have the priesthood, the ordinances, and the righteousness that would carry them to exaltation.

No implication is here made that all members of the Church are worthy and that all nonmembers are unworthy, but eternal marriage cannot be had outside of the temple, and nonmembers are not permitted to go into the temple. Of course, they can become members if they are interested enough and prove that interest. . . .

Yes, a small minority are finally baptized. Some good men and women have joined the Church after the interfaith marriage and have remained most devout and active. God bless them! We are proud of them and grateful for them. These are our blessed minority.

Others who do not join the Church are still kind, considerate, and cooperative, and permit the other spouse to worship and serve according to the Church pattern. God bless them also!

Many others join the Church ostensibly for the marriage, then fail to live the commandments. Many of them are later divorced. Others, though not divorced, continue to have friction, particularly in religious matters in the home.

The majority, however, do not join the Church. Surveys have indicated that *only one of seven* finally join the Church—the odds are against the others. And nearly half of those who marry out of the Church become inactive. As parents give up their religion, an increasing number of their children are brought up without any religion.

So you are taking a desperate chance if you say, "Well, maybe he will join after we are married. We will go ahead and try it and see." It is a pretty serious thing to take a chance on.

Frequently people think, "Oh, that doesn't matter. We'll get along all right. We'll adjust ourselves. My spouse will permit me to do as I please or I will make adjustments. We'll both live and worship according to our own pattern." This is not broad-mindedness, but even if it were, to be broad-minded with the Lord's eternal program is somewhat like being generous with other people's money. (*The Teachings of Spencer W. Kimball* [Salt Lake City: Bookcraft, 1982], pp. 298–300; emphasis added.)

## SELLING THE BIRTHRIGHT:
## TRADING ETERNITY FOR IMMEDIATE GRATIFICATION

A nationally televised documentary aired a few years ago that dealt with the unwillingness of people in modern society to have deferred gratification. One of the most fascinating parts of the program portrayed an experiment conducted with young children. Using a hidden camera to record each child's behavior, the experts told the children that if they would not eat a marshmallow that was placed in front of them for five minutes, they would then be rewarded with five marshmallows. The child was then left all alone in the room with the one marshmallow on the table facing him or her "eyeball to eyeball." It was interesting and humorous to watch each of the children deal with this challenge in his or her own unique way. Some tried to look in a different direction, others would sing or talk to themselves, and yet others would squirm around in their seats, struggling with the urge to reach out and pick up the marshmallow. Some would pick it up and look at it and even smell it. Those who reached that point almost invariably would lick the marshmallow, then take small bites, and soon pop the whole thing into their mouths. One little boy didn't even hesitate. As soon as the door was closed, he gobbled down the marshmallow and sat back in his chair with a contented smile. Some struggled mightily against the temptation and were justly rewarded for holding out. Others, however, made no attempt whatsoever to resist—they wanted that marshmallow, and they wanted it *now*!

As I watched this program I was immediately reminded of Esau. Like the children who couldn't wait even five minutes, Esau declared unto Jacob: "Feed me, I pray thee, with that same red pottage; for I am faint" (Genesis 25:30). (That almost sounds like me on Fast Sunday: "I've got to eat. I can't hold out any longer. I've got a headache.") When Jacob offered the pottage to his twin brother in exchange for the birthright, Esau responded with his classic statement: "I am at the point to die: and what profit shall this birthright do to me?" (Genesis 25:32.)

I wish I had a dollar for every time I have said, like Esau, "I'm so hungry I think I'm going to die" or "If I don't have dinner right now, I will surely starve to death." Somehow I've always seemed to survive, even if I've had to wait awhile or fast for two meals. As I have read this story, I have often been left to wonder if Esau, after having enjoyed a satisfying meal of red pottage and bread and after a refreshing night's sleep, didn't arise the next day and, when his empty stomach growled and was hungered again, realize that he had made a really bad trade. The scriptures are silent regarding his immediate reaction, but we do learn that after a while Esau came to realize, at least to some degree, what he had forfeited. He then hated Jacob and sought by force to regain his inheritance. (See Genesis 27:30–41.)

Satan loves to put "eternity blinders" over our eyes and make us shortsighted by downplaying the eternal rewards for those who resist temptation and overemphasizing the gratification of here and now. He often seeks to convince us that we can "have our cake and eat it too." Lucifer, the father of lies, delights when we embrace attitudes such as, "I can still have what I want right now, because I can always repent later." We sell our birthright each time we fall prey to the temptation to gratify our carnal desires, pride, and vain ambitions at the expense of obedience to those covenants that guarantee a far greater reward. "Deny yourselves of all ungodliness," the prophet Moroni admonished (Moroni 10:32). Denying oneself means to give up, look away, and avoid those actions and attitudes that are like pottage, which gratify hunger now but leave us empty on the morrow and stripped of our birthright—the right and power to be kings and queens forever.

A grandfather did something that helped his grandchildren understand this concept in a very practical way. For birthday or Christmas presents, Grandpa gave the children a choice: he would give them cash that could be used to buy things at the mall, or he would take the money and buy them a share of a blue-chip stock that could be saved for their college and mission funds. The concept of a long-term stock portfolio or bonds that mature at a later date was too abstract for some of the kids, whereas cash in hand was something concrete. They understood that dollar bills could buy clothes or toys, but they could not quite grasp the notion that something they could not even see could actually be far more valuable. Eventually the toys, clothes, or cassette tapes purchased with birthday money will be long gone, whereas the stocks could someday buy them a house. Only then will they fully understand deferred gratification.

Similarly, we sell our birthright, or trade away the blessings of Abraham, Isaac, and Jacob, if we fail to live up to the covenants attached to those blessings because of the desires of the flesh. How foolish it is to satisfy carnal desires by committing fornication or adultery now while losing the right to eternal companionship and the "continuation of the seeds forever and ever" hereafter. How shortsighted to abandon spouse and children for supposed greater fulfillment in mortality, yet then to be destined to remain "single and separate" for eternity. What mortal mess of pottage can compare in any way to the inheritance promised to those who faithfully cleave unto their covenants—that "all that my Father hath shall be given unto him"? (D&C 84:38.)

In the Old Testament there is an interesting parallel to the story of Jacob and Esau and the selling of the birthright. Although separated in time by many centuries, Joseph who was sold into Egypt and King David provide us an interesting contrast in resisting temptation and cleaving unto the covenant.

When Potiphar's wife sought to seduce the handsome young Joseph, I am sure there was a part of him that desired physical gratification. Like Esau, he could have said, "I'll just die if I don't satisfy this hunger" or "What will it matter if I do this? I can still repent later." But instead, even at the expense of his safety and freedom, Joseph declared, "How then can I do this great wickedness, and sin against God?" The account continues: "And it came to pass, as she spake to Joseph day by day, that he hearkeneth not unto her, to lie by her, or to be with her. And it came to pass about this time, that Joseph went into the house to do his business; and there was none of the men of the house there within. And she caught him by his garment, saying, Lie with me: and he left his garment in her hand, and fled, and got him out." (Genesis 39:9–12.)

Although Joseph was falsely accused and unjustly imprisoned, "the Lord was with Joseph, and shewed him mercy" (Genesis 39:21). The rest of the story is familiar to us all: "The Lord was with him, and that which he did, the Lord made it to prosper" (Genesis 39:23). After rising to great authority in the Pharaoh's court, Joseph became the means for blessing Egypt greatly as well as for providing for the temporal redemption of his own family (see Genesis 41–48).

> And Jacob said unto Joseph when the God of my fathers appeared unto me in Luz, in the land of Canaan; he sware unto me, that he would give unto me, and unto my seed, the land for an everlasting possession.
>
> Therefore, O my son, he hath blessed me in raising thee up to be a servant unto me, in saving my house from death;
>
> In delivering my people, thy brethren, from famine which was sore in the land; wherefore the God of thy fathers shall bless thee, and the fruit of thy loins, that they shall be blessed above thy brethren, and above thy father's house. . . .
>
> For thou shalt be a light unto my people, to deliver them in the days of their captivity, from bondage; and to bring salvation unto them, when they are altogether bowed down under sin. (JST, Genesis 48:7–9, 11.)

Because he would not, in a matter of speaking, sell his birthright for a mess of pottage, even if the pottage were in the guise of the beautiful and seductive wife of Potiphar, not only did Joseph inherit the blessings of Father Abraham, but through him we as his lineage are bounteously blessed today.

> And Joseph said unto his brethren, I die, and go unto my fathers; and I go down to my grave with joy. The God of my father Jacob be with you, to deliver you out of affliction in the days of your bondage; for the Lord hath visited me, and I have obtained a promise of the Lord, that out of the fruit of my loins, the Lord God will raise up a righteous branch out of my loins; and unto thee, whom my father Jacob hath named Israel, a prophet; (not the Messiah who is called Shilo;) and this prophet shall deliver my people out of Egypt in the days of thy bondage.
>
> And it shall come to pass that they shall be scattered again; and a branch shall be broken off, and shall be carried into a far country; nevertheless they shall be remembered in the covenants of the Lord, when the Messiah cometh; for he shall be made manifest unto them in the latter days, in the Spirit of power; and shall bring them out of darkness unto light; out of hidden darkness, and out of captivity unto freedom.
>
> A seer shall the Lord my God raise up, who shall be a choice seer unto the fruit of my loins.
>
> Thus saith the Lord God of my fathers unto me, A choice seer will I raise up out of the fruit of thy loins, and he shall be esteemed highly among the fruit of thy loins; and unto him will I give commandment that he shall do a work for the fruit of thy loins, his brethren.
>
> And he shall bring them to the knowledge of the covenants which I have made with thy fathers. (JST, Genesis 50:24–28; see also 2 Nephi 3.)

In striking contrast to the faithfulness of Joseph is the sellout by King David. This same man who in his youth had delivered the Israelites from the Philistines with one stone slung into the forehead of Goliath (see 1 Samuel 17)—this man who would not harm nor speak evil of the Lord's anointed (see 1 Samuel 26:13–25)—this man who had conquered the Jebusites and secured Jerusalem as his capital and who brought the sacred tabernacle to a permanent home (see 2

Samuel 5–7)—this talented and mighty man who had done so much good and had so much potential sold his spiritual birthright for an illicit affair with another man's wife.

> And it came to pass, after the year was expired, at the time when kings go forth to battle, that David sent Joab, and his servants with him, and all Israel; and they destroyed the children of Ammon, and besieged Rabbah. But David tarried still at Jerusalem.
> And it came to pass in an eveningtide, that David arose from off his bed, and walked upon the roof of the king's house: and from the roof he saw a woman washing herself; and the woman was very beautiful to look upon.
> And David sent and enquired after the woman. And one said, Is not this Bath-sheba, the daughter of Eliam, the wife of Uriah the Hittite?
> And David sent messengers, and took her; and she came in unto him, and he lay with her; for she was purified from her uncleanness: and she returned unto her house.
> And the woman conceived, and sent and told David, and said, I am with child. (2 Samuel 11:1–5.)

When David first saw Bathsheba bathing on her rooftop he could have turned away and gone back into his house. But instead of running away as Joseph had done, he looked and lusted and acted upon his physical impulses. Not only did David sin with Bathsheba but also his attempts to cover his sin led to the death of Uriah, Bathsheba's faithful husband (see 2 Samuel 11:6–27). The pottage was temporary pleasure, but the birthright that was lost was David's exaltation. The Lord revealed, "David's wives and concubines were given unto him of me, by the hand of Nathan, my servant, and others of the prophets who had the keys of this power; and in none of these things did he sin against me save in the case of Uriah and his wife; and, therefore he hath fallen from his exaltation, and received his portion; and he shall not inherit them out of the world, for I gave them unto another, saith the Lord." (D&C 132:39.)

The significance of this scripture took on a special meaning to me in a powerful, personal way. As I walked out of my graduate statistics class many years ago while I was working on my doctorate, I was overwhelmed with discouragement. I felt as if my academic career were going down the tubes because I didn't have a clue what was

going on in the class, which was required for my Ph.D. program.
Every day I would leave the class with my head spinning. I would try
to do the homework, and I studied hard for the exams, but nothing
seemed to click. My daughter Tiffany, who was about three at the time,
would comment to her mother when I huffed and puffed in frustration while doing my homework, "Mommy, Daddy is doing his sadis-
tics again." Out of the mouth of babes!

As I walked to our apartment that day my head was in a fog of sta-
tistical equations, when something remarkable happened. I had a "revelation." I think the Lord was mindful of my discouragement and frustration, and out of his mercy he blessed me with a glimpse of eternity
that helped me put things in the proper perspective. I didn't hear
God's voice, nor did angels attend, nor did I visually see anything out
of the ordinary, but I was overwhelmed with what I felt. It was as if my
whole being—my spirit and body and every sense—absorbed a divine
message. Words cannot do justice to what I felt, but suffice it to say
that I was so overcome and surprised by the experience that it almost
took my breath away. I had to sit down on a large rock in the botanical
gardens to get my wits about me, and I just sat there and wept. I am
sure that the other students who walked by thought to themselves,
*There is another graduate student flunking statistics!*

What I was feeling was divine love—the love of the Lord for me as
well as a divine love for my wife and family, a love that transcended
any earthly emotion and defied mortal description. For a brief moment I experienced something akin to what Nephi described: "He
hath filled me with his love, even unto the consuming of my flesh" (2
Nephi 4:21). I think the Lord gave me a small glimpse of the kind of
eternal love that can prevail in the celestial kingdom. I had a new perspective of what it really could mean to be an eternal family.

After I regained some composure, I walked the few blocks to our
apartment. When I walked in the door, Wendy noticed my red and
puffy eyes, and I could tell she was deeply concerned as to why I had
been crying. I just took her in my arms and held her and told her how
much I loved her, and then we wept together. When our children saw
Mommy and Daddy crying they came to us and hung on our legs and
cried with us. "Did you wreck the car?" was Wendy's immediate concern. "No," I assured her. "I just want you and the kids to know how
much you mean to me. I don't ever want to be without you."

From that experience I learned that no mess of pottage—no earthly possession, no prestige, no physical gratification, no other mortal relationship—could ever be worth exchanging for my birthright, or the eternal association with my wife and family and the inheritance of all the blessings of Father Abraham. I could think of no greater hell than to lose my exaltation and have my wife and children taken from me, as happened to King David: "For I gave them unto another, saith the Lord" (D&C 132:39). With all that is at stake both here and hereafter, none of us can afford to despise the birhtright or to sell its blessings by our disobedience in any way. As President Ezra Taft Benson declared:

> Don't trifle away your happiness by an involvement with someone who cannot take you worthily to the temple. Make a decision now that this is the place where you will marry. To leave that decision until a romantic involvement develops is to take a risk, the importance of which you can't calculate now.
>
> I would urge you further to pray about this matter. Obtain the testimony of the truth of these things before a romantic involvement can take root. Covenant with your Heavenly Father that you will do His will. Live a clean, moral life, and be worthy of His spirit to bless you.
>
> No sacrifice is too great to have the blessings of an eternal marriage. To most of us, a temple is easily accessible, perhaps so conveniently that the blessing is taken too casually. As with other matters of faithfulness in gospel living, being married the Lord's way takes a willingness to deny yourself ungodliness—worldliness—and a determination to do our Father's will. By this act of faith, we show our love to God and our regard for a posterity yet unborn. As our family is our greatest source of joy in this life, so it may well be in the eternity. ("This Is a Day of Sacrifice," *Ensign*, May 1979, pp. 33–34.)

*Ye shall diligently keep the commandments of the Lord your God, and his testimonies,*
*and his statutes, which he hath commanded thee. And thou shalt do that which*
*is right and good in the sight of the Lord: that it may be well with thee. . . .*
*And the Lord commanded us to do all these statutes, to fear the Lord*
*our God, for our good always, that he might preserve us alive,*
*as it is at this day. And it shall be our righteousness,*
*if we observe to do all these commandments before*
*the Lord our God, as he hath commanded us.*
*—Deuteronomy 6:17–18, 24–25*

CHAPTER THREE

# The Timeless and Timely Ten Commandments

The young man looked me squarely in the eye and declared, "Those commandments have no meaning to me today. They are fulfilled in Christ, and so I don't have to live them. When I accepted Jesus as my personal Savior, I no longer had to live the Ten Commandments."

I wasn't sure that I heard him correctly, and so I inquired, "Are you saying that if you have accepted Jesus you can commit adultery or steal or lie?"

He was somewhat taken aback by my question. He paused and seemed to squirm a little in his seat, but then he responded: "Yes, I guess that is what I am saying. All old things are done away, and all that matters is accepting Christ."

This young man was a self-professed born-again Christian and had emphatically declared to me that Mormons are not Christians, yet

I felt he was confused and misguided as to not only the role of the Ten Commandments and the Old Testament in Christian theology, but also what it means to accept Christ. (His views concerning the Ten Commandments certainly did not fully reflect the beliefs of many of my devout Christian friends.) As he had previously peppered me with questions and arguments about Mormon beliefs concerning the need to keep the commandments, or what he falsely characterized as the Mormon belief that salvation comes only from works, I was reminded of an event recorded in the New Testament. The Pharisees, in their attempts to entrap Jesus in his words, asked the Master, "What is the greatest commandment?" The Savior's enemies wanted to see if he would contradict or criticize the ancient law that God had revealed unto Moses. In no way did the Savior's teachings indicate that the Ten Commandments were out of date, irrelevant, unnecessary, or fulfilled. In fact, his response validated their divine origin and endorsed them as principles that permeate all other commandments and teachings. He said, "Thou shalt love the Lord thy God with all thy heart, and with all thy soul, and with all thy mind. This is the first and great commandment, And the second is like unto it, Thou shalt love thy neighour as thyself. On these two commandments hang all the law and the prophets." (Matthew 22:37–40.)

Jesus did not make up this statement right then and there on the spur of the moment. He was reminding his critics that his teachings only confirmed the very commandments and law that had been delivered to Moses on Mount Sinai (see Deuteronomy 6). They knew exactly what he was referring to: loving God and putting him first in our lives, and loving our family and fellowmen, is the very essence of the Ten Commandments.

In our dispensation the Lord also reiterated the timelessness of these commandments when he included them in the law of the restored Church as revealed to the Prophet Joseph Smith (see D&C 42:18–29; see also D&C 59:5–23). In a letter written by the Prophet while in Liberty Jail, he said of the Ten Commandments, "We most cordially embrace [them], and consider them binding on us because they are adapted to our circumstances" (letter to Isaac Galland, 22 March 1839; published in *Times and Seasons*, February 1840, p. 54). The great filmmaker Cecil B. DeMille, who produced the classic film

*The Ten Commandments*, expressed a similar thought: "Today some people are inclined to look upon those Commandments as a bit archaic. But they are not. They are more modern than today's newspaper—because they are timeless." (Commencement address at Brigham Young University, 31 May 1957, typescript, p. 5.)

Several years ago I was intrigued by a radio program that featured a debate between two prominent Bible scholars regarding the modern relevance of the Ten Commandments. One of the scholars insisted that there really were no tablets of stone and that the scriptural account was nothing more than myth. That religious myth served a necessary function anciently, the scholar explained, in providing some sort of civil order to a lawless people. He contended that "black and white" prescriptions or absolutes could not apply in our modern society, which is so complex and advanced that it is composed almost exclusively not of black and white but varying shades of gray. The other scholar, however, explained that the problem with modern society was not its absence of laws and regulations, but its absence of absolute values—black and white values like those thundered forth from Mount Sinai. He made a valid point in stating that the complexities and entanglements of modern society, along with all the so-called gray areas, have resulted from society's turning its back on Mount Sinai, thinking it has outgrown the Ten Commandments.

As I listened to the program I was surprised that there could even be such a debate. Although the Ten Commandments were given to an ancient people and served as the backbone of their legal code, modern society seems to be crying out for the simple solutions found in those timeless values. "The Ten Commandments are not rules to obey as a personal favor to God," Cecil B. DeMille stated. "They are the fundamental principles without which mankind cannot live together. They make of those who keep them faithfully, strong, wholesome, confident, dedicated men and women. This is so because the Commandments come from the same Divine Hand that fashioned our human nature." (Ibid.)

The timelessness and the personal relevance of the Ten Commandments is reinforced in an interesting statement made by Moses after the Israelites had wandered in the wilderness for forty years. Only three Israelites were of the original Camp of Israel who were present when Moses received the stone tablets at Mount Horeb, or Sinai—Moses, Joshua, and Caleb (see Numbers 26:65; 32:12; Deuteronomy 1:36–38). A new generation had been raised up, a generation that either was too young to remember the remarkable events of Sinai or had not yet been born when Israel covenanted to obey the Ten Commandments. Yet before they entered the promised land, Moses declared unto them: "The Lord our God made a covenant with us in Horeb. The Lord made not this covenant with our fathers, but with us, even us, who are all of us here alive this day. The Lord talked with you face to face in the mount out of the midst of the fire." (Deuteronomy 5:2–4.)

Moses' message is exactly the same for us today. The significance of what happened on Mount Sinai is not that a law was given to our ancient forefathers, but that God covenanted with and gave a law to us, "even us, who are . . . alive this day." It is for each of us individually, as if God spoke to us face to face and personally delivered into our hands the stone tablets declaring the Ten Commandments. Like the two great commandments upon which the Savior declared "hang all the law and the prophets," the Ten Commandments are not only a simple solution to society's complex ills but also the prescription for personal righteousness. Why? Because the Ten Commandments deal with our greatest obligations to loving God, our families, and our fellowmen.

## Exclusive Devotion to God

"Thou shalt have no other gods before me," the Lord declared. "For I the Lord thy God am a jealous God." (Exodus 20:3, 5.) At first glance the phrase "for I . . . am a jealous God" makes God's commandments regarding exclusive devotion to and worship of him look like the selfish, arrogant demands of a tyrannical despot paranoid that someone else may dethrone him. However, the Hebrew word for jealous is qannah, which implies something much different from our typical understanding of jealousy as a selfish and negative emotion. Qannah means "possessing deep, sensitive feelings." God does not command mankind to have "no other gods before me" to fill an ego need. Then why does he demand our exclusive allegiance and devotion?

The answer is found in another definition of the Hebrew word qannah as used in Exodus 20:5—"the zeal of God in striving to achieve his goal." Our Father in Heaven possesses such "deep, sensitive feelings," or such profound love for his children, that he is zealous in his efforts "to bring to pass the immortality and eternal life of man" (Moses 1:39). His is the only power that can save man, and therefore he is "jealous" of any false worship or allegiances that take us away from the only power and love that can exalt us. He does not demand our devotion for his sake, but rather for our sake. "Whatever God requires is right," declared the Prophet Joseph Smith.

> Everything that God gives us is lawful and right; and it is proper that we should enjoy His gifts and blessings whenever and wherever He is disposed to bestow; but if we should seize upon those same blessings and enjoyments without law, without revelation, without commandment, those blessings and enjoyments would prove cursings and vexations in the end, and we should have to lie down in sorrow and wailings of everlasting regret. But in obedience there is joy and peace unspotted, unalloyed; and as God has designed our happiness—and the happiness of all His creatures, He never has—he never will institute an ordinance or give a commandment to His people that is not calculated in its nature to promote that happiness which He has designed, and which will not end in the greatest amount of good and glory to those who become the recipients of His law and ordinances. (*Teachings of the Prophet Joseph Smith*, comp. Joseph Fielding Smith [Salt Lake City: Deseret Book Co., 1976], pp. 256–57.)

## *"Thou Shalt Have No Other Gods Before Me"*

While serving as a bishop several years ago I noticed a young wife and mother who would bring her children to church meetings without her husband. His attendance had been quite regular in the past, but then it became somewhat sporadic. At first I didn't think much of it, but as this pattern progressed I became concerned. When I talked with the wife she assured me that there was no serious illness or other obvious problem that was preventing him from attending church with his family. Her comment, however, was most revealing. "Oh, his favorite professional football team is playing on television at the same time as our meeting schedule," she reported. "He said he'll be here next week."

The next week he was there, but then he was absent again for the few weeks that followed. When I checked with his wife I was met with a perturbed shrug of her shoulders and the simple response, "Playoffs." Of course, his favorite team couldn't win without his support—or so he thought. Then there was the Super Bowl—he certainly couldn't miss that, even if his team wasn't playing.

After the football season ended I expected that he would once again be active. His attendance was regular for a while but then dropped off again. His wife informed me that now it was basketball season and he "just had to stay home to watch the NBA All-Star game." Then it would be the playoffs and the championship series; then it would be time for baseball season. There was always something that he "just couldn't miss."

If I were to ask this young man what was most important to him, he undoubtedly would have responded that God and family were his top priorities. His actions, however, indicated otherwise. He could not see that he was worshipping a false God, just as surely as the ancient Israelites worshipped the golden calf. His idolatry was not in the form of a graven image of stone or gold. He was worshipping at the modern-day altar of sports and entertainment.

"Ye shall have no other Gods before me," the Lord declared. The Hebrew word for *before* is *alpanai,* which means "in front of," "in hostility to," or "in preference to." The Mosaic law prescribed death as the penalty for worshipping or sacrificing to pagan gods (see Exodus 22:20; Leviticus 19:4; 20:1–5). Modern-day idolatry, however, is harder to identify, for often we don't think we are worshipping false gods just because our "hearts are set so much upon the things of this world" (D&C 121:35). Sports, money, hobbies, professional pursuits, popularity, recreation, or any other object or attitude that causes our devotion to God to be lessened can be a type of false god that we worship.

Modern-day idolatry comes most often in the form of divided loyalties. It is a matter of having one's priorities out of balance. It is the placing of things of lesser importance before those things that matter most. "Ye cannot serve God and mammon," the Savior declared (Matthew 6:24). Divided loyalties inevitably lead to the dilution of our devotions. It is for this reason that the Lord declared: "Thou shalt love the Lord thy God with all thy heart, and with all thy soul, and with all thy mind. This is the first and great commandment." (Matthew 22:37–38.)

When our love for and devotion to God is first and foremost in our lives, no other false god can find place in our hearts. "The breadth, depth, and height of this love of God extend into every facet of one's life," President Ezra Taft Benson taught.

> Our desires, be they spiritual or temporal, should be rooted in a love of the Lord. Our thoughts and affections should be centered on the Lord.
>
> Why did God put the first commandment first? Because He knew that if we truly loved Him we would want to keep all of His other commandments. . . .
>
> We must put God in the forefront of everything else in our lives. He must come first, just as He declares in the first of His Ten Commandments: "Thou shalt have no other gods before me" (Exodus 20:3).
>
> When we put God first, all other things fall into their proper place or drop out of our lives. Our love of the Lord will govern the claims for our affection, the demands on our time, the interests we pursue, and the order of our priorities. (In Conference Report, April 1988, p. 3.)

I heard my wife on many occasions say while teaching youth in the Church or counseling our own children, "Marry someone who loves the Lord more than he or she loves even you." At first the youth or my children would often react with, "No, I want him to love me more than anyone or anything else." They would see the point when Wendy would explain, "When he or she loves God first and foremost, then you will automatically always come next, but if anything or anyone else is more important than God there is no guarantee that you will always be held in proper priority."

That seems to be the very essence of the first commandment. Every aspect of our lives and all of our relationships is affected by our devotion, or lack of it, to God. When nothing or no one has greater importance to us than God, a "spiritual sifting" occurs, as President Benson explained. Those things of lesser importance fall back to their proper places or out of our lives completely, and those things of eternal significance rise to the top of our priorities. This prioritization, induced by the first commandment, therefore directs all of our other decisions, desires, devotions, and deeds.

## "Thou Shalt Not Make unto Thee Any Graven Image"

Many pagan religions of the ancient world involved worshipping graven images of various gods and goddesses. It was not just the statues or figurines that offended God, but rather the fact that his children would ascribe power to or willingly put their trust in such inanimate objects. Today we may view falling down and worshipping idols of stone or brass "which see not, nor hear, nor know" (Daniel 5:23) as superstitious at best, perhaps even downright silly, like ascribing supernatural power to a rabbit's foot. Yet despite the pseudo-sophistication of modern society, idolatry not only exists today but actually flourishes all around us. The idols have a different form and substance, and the "worship" may not be a religious endeavor, but the end product remains the same—a heart turned away from God, and a path of life "whose image is in the likeness of the world, and whose substance is that of an idol" (D&C 1:16). "Modern idols or false gods can take such forms as clothes, homes, businesses, machines, automobiles, pleasure boats, and numerous other material deflectors from the path of godhood," wrote Elder Spencer W. Kimball.

> What difference does it make that the item concerned is not shaped like an idol? . . . Intangible things make just as ready gods. Degrees and letters and titles can become idols. Many young men decide to attend college when they should be on missions first. The degree, and the wealth and the security which come through it, appear so desirable that the mission takes second place. Some neglect Church service through their college years, feeling to give preference to the secular training and ignoring the spiritual covenants they have made.
>
> Many people build and furnish a home and buy the automobile first—and then find they "cannot afford" to pay tithing. Whom do they worship? Certainly not the Lord of heaven and earth, for we serve whom we love and give first consideration to the object of our affection and desires. . . .
>
> Many worship the hunt, the fishing trip, the vacation, the weekend picnics and outings. Others have as their idols the games of sport, baseball, football, the bullfight, or golf. These pursuits more often than not interfere with the worship of the Lord and with giving service to the building up of the kingdom of God. To the participants this emphasis may not seem serious, yet it indicates where their allegiance and loyalty are.

Still another image men worship is that of power and prestige. Many will trample underfoot the spiritual and often the ethical values in their climb to success. These gods of power, wealth, and influence are most demanding and are quite as real as the golden calves of the children of Israel in the wilderness. (*The Miracle of Forgiveness* [Salt Lake City: Bookcraft, 1969], pp. 40, 41–42.)

"Graven images" represent all the things of the world that are shaped, fashioned, manufactured, or thought up by mortal man. They are those things that are not eternal and that by their very nature are temporary. Whatever their attractions, whatever temporary pleasures or powers they provide man, they pale in comparison to the omnipotent arm of the Almighty and the enduring rewards that accompany his approbation. Just as a stone statue has no power to save or bless, neither can any other worldly graven image to which we vainly expend our energies. Ancient worship of graven images is merely a cousin of modern-day "relying on the arm of flesh," or trusting in man's ways and mortal learning and seeking satisfaction in the lifeless adornments of a telestial world (see Mormon 8:39). "Do not spend money for that which is of no worth, nor your labor for that which cannot satisfy," Jacob declared. "Hearken diligently unto me, and remember the words which I have spoken; and come unto the Holy One of Israel, and feast upon that which perisheth not, neither can be corrupted, and let your soul delight in fatness" (2 Nephi 9:51; see also Isaiah 55:2).

## *"Thou Shalt Not Take the Name of the Lord Thy God in Vain"*

Profaning the name of God was also indicative of a lack of reverence for the Lord. The Mosaic law specifically outlined many different ways that Jehovah's name could be taken in vain. They included sorcery (see Exodus 22:18), divination (see Leviticus 19:26, 31; Deuteronomy 18:9–14), speaking of God contemptuously (see Exodus 22:28), blasphemy (see Leviticus 19:12), and taking oaths in the name of pagan deities (see Exodus 23:13; Joshua 23:7). Each of these various acts of contempt toward God was punishable by death.

In our day, however, taking the name of God in vain is more commonly associated with swearing. Such foul speech reflects a lack of love and reverence for God, for one would not speak of someone else in such blasphemous and profane ways if love and true worship were at the heart of their relationship. Instead there would be words of praise and adoration. Irreverent speech almost always precedes harsh, crude, and unholy behavior. In contrast, loving God and holding his sacred name in cherished reverence safeguards us from unworthy and unholy behavior.

While this common interpretation of taking God's name in vain is important and should not be overlooked or minimized, there is another meaning that has relevant application for us today. The Old Testament also relates profaning the name of God to taking upon oneself an oath or covenant in the name of God and then failing to uphold that covenant (see Leviticus 19:12). "This prohibition applies strictly to perjury or false swearing, the breaking of a promise or contract that has been sealed with an oath in the name of God," one eminent Bible scholar wrote. "He will not allow His name to be associated with any act of falsehood or treachery. His name must not be taken in vain, i.e. lightly or heedlessly." (J. R. Dummelow, *A Commentary on the Holy Bible* [New York: Macmillan Publishing Co., 1936], p. 67.)

Each of us has taken upon us the name of Christ through covenants and ordinances. As we do so, we promise to "always remember him and keep his commandments" (see D&C 20:77). In the temple, we make additional covenants in the name of God. Far worse than even profaning the name of Deity in our speech is to take lightly our solemn and sacred covenants. To take God's name upon us in sacred ordinances and then pretend to be faithful to those covenants when in reality our hearts are impure and our lives unclean is a far more serious form of profanity and irreverence. Through the prophet Isaiah the Lord said, "With their lips [the people] do honour me, but have removed their heart far from me" (Isaiah 29:13). Those covenants, promised in his holy name, thus become vain, empty, and meaningless, and the blessings for total devotion to our God "who is mighty to save" are forfeited (see 2 Nephi 31:19).

## "Remember the Sabbath Day, to Keep It Holy"

Perhaps the key word in the fourth commandment is *remember*. We are to remember to keep the Sabbath holy in order to remember God and our relationship with him. To keep our heartstrings firmly fastened to the Lord, he gave the Sabbath (the Hebrew word *shabbat* means "rest") as a regular reminder of our need to be exclusively devoted to God. "Sabbath observance was a sign between ancient Israel and their God whereby the chosen people might be known," Elder Bruce R. McConkie wrote (*Mormon Doctrine*, 2d ed. [Salt Lake City: Bookcraft, 1966], p. 658). It was to serve as a continual reminder that real, lasting rest is not found in the world and worldly ways, but only through true worship of the Almighty. So important was this day that all work was to cease both by master and servant (see Exodus 23:12), and even seemingly small tasks requiring little or no effort were forbidden (see Numbers 15:32–36). The violation of this sacred commandment was death (see Exodus 31:15), the same punishment as for idolatry, because failing to honor the Sabbath was a form of infidelity toward God and a form of worshipping the false gods of the world. The death penalty also served as a symbolic reminder that failure to remember God in all aspects of life constitutes a kind of death—a spiritual death in which one is cut off from the life-giving powers of God. In contrast, obedience and devotion to God, as symbolized by Sabbath observance, means life—the abundant life.

I must admit that as I was growing up, whenever I would hear the phrase "keep the Sabbath day holy" my mind immediately focused on the "thou shalt nots." Like the Pharisees of Jesus' day, I had a long mental list of all of the "can't dos" that that command imposed upon me. Viewing the Sabbath this way caused me to think of the commandment as a form of punishment, kind of like being grounded. Instead of looking forward to it as a day of spiritual rejuvenation and a reminder of my covenantal relationship with God, I dreaded the day and often found myself counting the minutes until real life could resume.

Even as I grew older and had many responsibilities in the Church, I often felt frustrated on the Sabbath, thinking that the only reason the Sabbath kept me close to God was that I was so busy and in so many meetings that I didn't have time to sin. Even when I was not blatantly breaking the fourth commandment, I still couldn't fully understand why the injunction to "remember the sabbath day, to keep it holy" (Exodus 20:8) was so closely akin to "thou shalt have no other gods before me" (Exodus 20:3). Then several years ago I caught the vision in a remarkable yet unusual way. I came to see the Sabbath truly as evidence of God's special blessing of love for his chosen people. I saw strict obedience to that commandment as a sign of one's deep love for God and gratitude for his bounteous blessings. I saw that the

Sabbath was not burdensome or to be resented, but rather could be a much anticipated and celebrated respite from not only the labors but the ways of the world. I learned this profound lesson not while attending priesthood meeting, serving as a bishop, or attending high council meetings (even though I could have learned it there if I had been more spiritually attuned). I learned it while witnessing an orthodox Jewish rabbi and his family not merely observe but truly celebrate the Sabbath.

I became acquainted with Rabbi David Rosen while teaching at the BYU Jerusalem Center for Near-Eastern Studies. David taught classes on Judaism at the center, and I came to appreciate him as a friend, colleague, and wonderful human being. Each semester David would bring his family to the center to celebrate a Jewish Sabbath with the students and staff there. We became his "family" for that Shabbat. While it was designed to be a cultural and educational experience for the students, it became a profound, life-changing spiritual experience for me. As we sang traditional Jewish Sabbath songs at the Shabbat meal, I could see the utter joy and delight on Rabbi Rosen's face. He and his family actually enjoyed the Sabbath—they loved being together, singing together, eating together, and worshipping God together. There were no complaints of what they couldn't do, such as drive the car or use the electric stove to prepare their food. There was just pure delight in remembering the Lord their God. Each of the various Sabbath activities, and even some of the food partaken at the meal, was symbolic of spiritual matters. Truly, their Sabbath was not just something to get over with but was a celebration of remembering God and basking in the light of his goodness and grace.

I would be moved to tears when Rabbi Rosen and his wife, Sharon, would take their children into their arms as part of their weekly Sabbath observance and give them Sabbath blessings or *Kiddush*. "God make thee as Ephraim and Manasseh," states the blessing to the sons; and to the daughters, "God make thee as Sarah, Rebekah, Rachel, and Leah." The words that the Rosens spoke to their children also included these blessings that are uttered each Sabbath in the synagogue: "The Lord bless thee, and keep thee: The Lord make his face shine upon thee, and be gracious unto thee: The Lord lift up his countenance upon thee, and give thee peace. And they shall put my name upon the children of Israel; and I will bless them." (Numbers 6:24–27.)

Rabbi Rosen explained that the Jews view the Sabbath as a queen coming to visit their homes. It is a joyous event, a covenantal sign "that ye may know that I am the Lord that doth sanctify you" (Exodus 31:13). A spice box is also used to represent the sweetness of the Sabbath and the refreshment it is to the soul. At the conclusion of the Sabbath, a special candle, or *havdalah*, is lit; the light and then the darkness that comes when the candle is extinguished represent the conclusion of something that is sacred (Shabbat) and the beginning again of the mundane and profane. Hence, the Sabbath sanctifies one *from* the world and strengthens and prepares one to live *in* the world.

As I watched Rabbi Rosen and his family observe the Sabbath, I came to realize how I had actually cheated myself out of much joy and strength that could help me in meeting the challenges of a new week. I had cheated myself by viewing the command to keep the Sabbath as a burdensome chore requiring a composite list of "don'ts" rather than as a "day of delight."

> If thou turn away the foot from the sabbath, from doing thy pleasure on my holy day; and call the sabbath a delight, the holy of the Lord, honourable; and shalt honour him, not doing thine own ways, nor finding thine own pleasure, nor speaking thine own words;
>
> Then shalt thou delight thyself in the Lord; and I will cause thee to ride upon the high places of the earth, and feed thee with the heritage of Jacob thy father: for the mouth of the Lord hath spoken it. (Isaiah 58:13–14.)

It shouldn't have taken a trip to Israel and the observing of a Jewish family's Sabbath to learn this valuable lesson. I just needed to spiritually understand better what the Lord has revealed in our day. "And that thou mayest more fully keep thyself unspotted from the world," the Lord lovingly prescribed, "thou shalt go to the house of prayer and offer up thy sacraments upon my holy day; for verily this is a day appointed unto you to rest from your labors, and to pay thy devotions unto the Most High" (D&C 59:9–10.)

As the false gods of this world—materialism, recreation, vanity, entertainment, professional ambitions, and all the others—press ever more suffocatingly around us, the Lord's command seems more loving and merciful than ever. In today's fast-paced, idolatrous society, Sabbath observance can be viewed as an outward manifestation of inward devotion to God. When the Lord's holy day becomes just another day, so our relationship with God becomes just another of the many mundane demands upon us instead of a sanctifying, ennobling relationship.

Sabbath observance is not merely a matter of not doing certain things or doing other things. It involves our attitudes and our innermost desires and feelings—our whole being—and our love, devotion, and appreciation for God. It reminds us that there is no rest, no peace, no salvation in the world or in the following after its many false gods. The Sabbath is our constant reminder to "always remember him" and to walk not after the idols and images of the world, but to love God first and foremost in our lives. "Our observance or nonobservance of the Sabbath is an unerring measure of our attitude toward the Lord personally and toward his suffering in Gethsemane, his death on the cross, and his resurrection from the dead," Elder Mark E. Petersen declared. "It is a sign of whether we are Christians in very deed, or whether our conversion is so shallow that commemoration of his atoning sacrifice means little or nothing to us." (In Conference Report, April 1975, p. 72.)

## HONORING PARENTS AND BEING HONORABLE PARENTS

"Honour thy father and thy mother," the Lord declared, "that thy days may be long upon the land which the Lord thy God giveth thee" (Exodus 20:12). Why does the Lord place this commandment right after those dealing with exclusive devotion to and reverence for God, but ahead of serious things such as murder, stealing and adultery? The placement of this commandment teaches us about the proper priority of our relationships: first God, then family, then fellowmen. It points us both to God and to others. "The commandment to honor our parents has strands that run through the entire fabric of the gospel," taught Elder Dallin II. Oaks.

> It is inherent in our relationship to God our Father. It embraces the divine destiny of the children of God. This commandment relates to the government of the family, which is patterned after the government of heaven.
>
> The commandment to honor our parents echoes the sacred spirit of family relationships in which—at their best—we have sublime

expressions of heavenly love and care for one another. We sense the importance of these relationships when we realize that our greatest expressions of joy or pain in mortality come from the members of our families. ("Honour Thy Father and Thy Mother," *Ensign*, May 1991, p. 15.)

The Apostle Paul prophesied that "in the last days perilous times shall come. For men shall be lovers of their own selves, covetous, boasters, proud, blasphemers, *disobedient to parents,* unthankful, unholy, without natural affection, trucebreakers, false accusers, incontinent, fierce, despisers of those that are good, traitors, heady, highminded, lovers of pleasures more than lovers of God" (2 Timothy 3:1–4; emphasis added.) I have always found it interesting that right smack-dab in the middle of the list of evils of the last days, Paul throws in "disobedient to parents." Why? I believe that we are seeing in modern society, more clearly than perhaps even Paul or Moses could see, that infidelity toward God and loss of love for family inevitably lead to all other vices. All around us today, shouting, as it were, from housetops, we see evidence of increased violence, crime, and moral decay. The disintegration of the family and the dissolution of time-honored family values contribute immensely to the chaos and contention of today's world. The command "honor thy father and thy mother" that was thundered anciently from Sinai is more relevant and needed today than ever before.

While some may say that the divine directive to submit to, obey, and honor parents is old-fashioned, it has not been revoked but rather reiterated and reemphasized. "Children, obey your parents in all [righteous] things," declared the Apostle Paul, "for this is well pleasing unto the Lord" (Colossians 3:20; see also Ephesians 6:1–4). It is not just pleasing unto the Lord, it is also for our benefit, like all of God's commandments. The Lord commanded us to "honor thy father and thy mother: that *thy* [not their] days may be long upon the land." Honoring and obeying parents not only affects *them* but, more important, affects, shapes, and protects *us.* Our lives are enriched, strengthened, and even preserved both physically and spiritually through faithful obedience to this commandment.

"If we truly honor [our parents]," President Spencer W. Kimball counseled, "we will seek to emulate their best characteristics and to fulfill their highest aspirations for us. No gift purchased from a store can begin to match in value to parents some simple, sincere words of appreciation. Nothing we could give them would be more prized than righteous living." (*The Teachings of Spencer W. Kimball*, ed. Edward L. Kimball [Salt Lake City: Bookcraft, 1982], p. 348.) Honoring our parents is closely related to true devotion to God. We honor both our heavenly and earthly parents in much the same way: with love, respect, and appreciation, and above all else, by seeking to faithfully follow their counsel in righteousness and by patterning our lives after the commandments of God.

Now that I am a parent as well as a grandparent, I understand that there is another way that I honor my parents, and that is by being an honorable parent myself. I want my children to honor me not out of compulsion or a sense of begrudging duty, but because they love me and appreciate the example I have set for them and how I have tried to teach them to honor their Heavenly Father. I can teach them to honor their mother by honoring her myself with love, respect, courtesy, and appreciation. In this manner I also repay in a small way my own parents for the love, devotion, time, and resources they invested in me. My children in turn can honor me and show appreciation for my parental efforts, however feeble they may have been, by striving to be devoted, loving, righteous parents to their own children. I would be most honored, even thrilled, if each of my children becomes an even better parent than I have been.

Living the fifth commandment involves not just honoring and obeying parents but also striving to model all of our earthly family relationships after the heavenly pattern provided us. President David O. McKay declared, "Let us cherish in our homes as we cherish the lives of our children themselves that word *honor* with all the synonyms—respect, reverence, veneration; honoring mother, honoring father, having them honor us as we honor and revere God our Eternal Father. Let the element of honor, devotion, reverence permeate the home life." (*Gospel Ideals* [Salt Lake City: Improvement Era, 1953], pp. 483–84.)

## LOVE FOR FELLOWMEN

"Thou shalt love thy neighbour as thyself," the Savior declared (Matthew 19:19). His Golden Rule states, "Therefore, all things whatsoever ye would that men should do to you, do ye even so to them"

(3 Nephi 14:12). Each of these divine declarations synthesizes and encapsulizes all of the rest of the Ten Commandments.

The Mosaic law was a civil and criminal code of law for the ancient Israelites, specifically defining all different kinds of criminal and delinquent behavior and specifying punishments for each crime. "Thou shalt not kill." "Thou shalt not commit adultery." "Thou shalt not steal." "Thou shalt not bear false witness against thy neighbour." Each of these commandments deals with our relationships and associations with one another. Although modern society has no dearth of criminal and civil code books, these basic commandments adequately address human behavior and could solve most societal ills if faithfully observed. In fact, one statement could even replace these four great commandments: "Love thy neighbour as thyself." If each of us truly loved our fellowmen, viewing them in the light of the restored gospel as literal sons and daughters of God and our literal brothers and sisters, there would be no stealing from another, destroying another's family through adultery, or maliciously lying about another. There would be no domestic violence, no hatred or anger that would lead one to injure or kill another. With love for and devotion for God foremost in our hearts, and with divine concern, compassion, and love for our fellowmen, there would be little or no need for a litany of "thou shalt nots," for "every man [would be] seeking the interest of his neighbor, and doing all things with an eye single to the glory of God" (D&C 82:19). If lived today the Ten Commandments would be more vital to us, individually and to the world as a whole, than all the laws governments can enact, all the punishments that justice can impose, and all the so-called solutions that "experts" can propose. Each of these timeless yet timely commandments is simply summarized by the Golden Rule: "Therefore, all things whatsoever ye would that men should do to you, do ye even so to them."

## "Thou Shalt Not Kill"

There isn't a lot of commentary needed concerning this commandment. It is pretty straightforward and awfully difficult to misunderstand. Even in a modern world with its sometimes mixed-up values and upside-down view of right and wrong, we are usually quite united—with a few exceptions concerning some controversial social issues—on the taboo against murder. As a bishop I counseled ward members with a wide variety of problems and encountered almost every kind of sin, but I never had to deal with a murder. Neither have I heard many talks in general conference or other Church settings on this subject. So, generally speaking, we've got this one down pretty well. Yet there are other aspects of this commandment that, though stated in the scriptures, often are overlooked and unlived.

To the modern Church the Lord reiterated the four commands I have mentioned, adding an important phrase. "Thou shalt love thy neighbor as thyself. Thou shalt not steal; neither commit adultery, nor kill, *nor do anything like unto it.*" (D&C 59:6; emphasis added.) What things could be "like unto" murder that the Lord would want us to avoid?

The Savior taught that avoiding murder or injurious acts of violence is not enough to be a true disciple, but that a higher righteousness was required in reference to this law.

> Ye have heard that it hath been said by them of old time, and it is also written before you, that thou shalt not kill, and whosoever shall kill shall be in danger of the judgment of God;
>
> But I say unto you, that whosoever is angry with his brother shall be in danger of his judgment. And whosoever shall say to his brother, Raca, shall be in danger of the council, and whosoever shall say, Thou fool, shall be in danger of hell fire.
>
> Therefore, if ye shall come unto me, or shall desire to come unto me, and rememberest that thy brother hath aught against thee—
>
> Go thy way unto thy brother, and first be reconciled to thy brother, and then come unto me with full purpose of heart, and I will receive you.
>
> Agree with thine adversary quickly while thou art in the way with him. (3 Nephi 12:21–25.)

As we look at the ancient command "Thou shalt not kill," we must couple it with Christ's later amplification, "Thou shalt not get angry." If we could eliminate murder in society, that would be great, but if we could "kill" within our own hearts all anger, contention, and ill will toward others, much more than just murder would be rooted out of society.

There is another unique and important usage of the term *murder* in the scriptures. In the Book of Mormon we read of the havoc that Alma the Younger created during his rebellious and apostate period of life. "I had rebelled against my God, and . . . I had not kept his holy commandments," a repentant Alma later recalled. "Yea, and I had murdered many of his children, or rather led them away unto destruction" (Alma 36:13–14). Alma hadn't physically murdered anyone, but he had indeed done so spiritually by leading people away from God and his ways. Someone who would never think of shooting a person with a gun or slashing him with a knife, but who would purposely pressure him to break the commandments of God, would be, like Alma, committing spiritual murder. We are rightfully appalled by physical murder but are less offended by spiritual, because the damage is not as visible. In reality, leading people away from God unto spiritual destruction inflicts even greater wounds and exacts worse consequences spiritually.

There is another kind of "murder" that I see in our society, both in and out of the Church: emotional murder. The wounds are mostly invisible, but they are often horribly painful, and sometimes the scars never heal in mortality. Relationships are destroyed. Self-esteem, innocence, and security are often killed by destructive abuse, angry words, and demeaning behaviors. As a bishop I encountered far too many people whose lives had been adversely affected by this. My heart went out to them, and as I listened to their stories and wiped their tears away, I came to understand that all around us are "murder victims." Jehovah's command "Thou shalt not kill" can have broader application than to just physical death. Life is sacred, not only physical life but also spiritual and emotional life.

## "Thou Shalt Not Commit Adultery"

Loving our fellowmen means that we "will not have a mind to injure one another, but to live peaceably, and to render to every man according to that which is his due" (Mosiah 4:13). King David learned in a most powerful way the injury that adultery inflicts upon others, both the transgressors and the innocent victims. Before his adulterous affair with Bathsheba was known to anyone other than the transgressors themselves, the Lord sent the Prophet Nathan to David with an important message.

> And the Lord sent Nathan unto David. And he came unto him, and said unto him, There were two men in one city; the one rich, and the other poor.

The rich man had exceeding many flocks and herds:

But the poor man had nothing, save one little ewe lamb, which he had bought and nourished up: and it grew together with him, and with his children; it did eat of his own meat, and drank of his own cup, and lay in his bosom, and was unto him as a daughter.

And there came a traveller unto the rich man, and he spared to take one of his own flock and his own herd, to dress for the wayfaring man that was come unto him; but took the poor man's lamb, and dressed it for the man that was come to him.

And David's anger was greatly kindled against the man; and he said to Nathan, As the Lord liveth, the man that hath done this thing shall surely die:

And he shall restore the lamb fourfold, because he did this thing, and because he had no pity.

And Nathan said to David, Thou art the man. Thus saith the Lord God of Israel, I anointed thee king over Israel, and I delivered thee out of the hand of Saul;

And I gave thee thy master's house, and thy master's wives into thy bosom, and gave thee the house of Israel and of Judah; and if that had been too little, I would moreover have given thee such and such things.

Wherefore has thou despised the commandment of the Lord, to do evil in his sight? thou hast killed Uriah the Hittite with the sword, and hast taken his wife to be thy wife, and hast slain him with the sword of the children of Ammon. (2 Samuel 12:1–9.)

With the parable of the lamb, Nathan rebuked David's abominable sins and showed him that as terrible as it would be to steal a poor man's prized ewe, it was far, far worse to steal another man's wife.

In great detail the ancient law prescribed safeguards of human sexuality and the power of procreation and exacted severe punishments to remind the people of the sanctity of marriage and the family (see Exodus 22:16–19; Leviticus 18:16–29; 20:10; Deuteronomy 22:25–27; 23:17–18; 24:1–4). The Savior declared that one must check not just immoral behavior but immoral thoughts as well: "Ye have heard that it was said by them of old time, Thou shalt not commit adultery: but I say unto you, That whosoever looketh on a woman to lust after her hath committed adultery with her already in his heart" (Matthew 5:27–28). The Lord reminded us in modern times, "Thou shalt not commit adultery, . . . nor anything like unto it." Protecting the sanctity of marriage, the divine procreative powers, and the stability of the family requires us to control our minds as well as our actions. "And verily I say unto you, as I have said before," the Lord commanded the Church, "he that looketh on a woman to lust after her, or if any shall commit adultery in their hearts, they shall not have the Spirit, but shall deny the faith and shall fear" (D&C 63:16). Just as the ancient Israelites had many "fences around the law," or smaller rules and laws that prevented the breaking of the "big" commandments such as adultery, keeping the Lord's command "thou shalt not commit adultery" requires the same of us today.

"When it comes to the law of chastity, it is better to prepare and prevent than it is to repair and repent," President Ezra Taft Benson taught.

> May I give six steps that are steps of preparation and prevention, steps that will insure that you never fall into this transgression: Decide now to be chaste. Control your thoughts. Always pray for the power to resist temptation. If you are married, avoid flirtations of any kind. If you are married, avoid being alone with members of the opposite sex whenever possible. For those who are single and dating members of the opposite sex, carefully plan positive and constructive activities so that you are not left to yourselves with nothing to do but share physical affection. . . .
>
> Do not be misled by Satan's lies. There is no lasting happiness in immorality. There is no joy to be found in breaking the law of chastity. Just the opposite is true. There may be momentary pleasure. For a time it may seem like everything is wonderful. But quickly the relationship will sour. Guilt and shame set in. We become fearful that our sins will be discovered. We must sneak and hide, lie and cheat. Love begins to die. Bitterness, jealousy, anger, and even hate begin to grow. All of these are the natural results of sin and transgression. (*The Teachings of Ezra Taft Benson* [Salt Lake City: Bookcraft, 1988], pp. 284–85.)

While serving as a bishop, I had an interesting discussion with a young wife. She told me that her husband felt that she needed to confess something to me. "I don't understand why," she defensively declared. "I haven't done anything wrong. It's not like I committed adultery or something." As the interview progressed I learned that while her husband was out of town she had invited an old boyfriend to spend the night with her. She assured me that there had been no sexual contact, "just a lot of talking, snuggling, hugging, and a little kissing." I was troubled that she could not seem to understand why her husband felt so upset, hurt, and betrayed. "Nothing happened," she repeated several times.

As I prayed for guidance in my counseling of her, a scripture came into my mind: "Thou shalt love thy wife [or husband] with all thy heart, and shall cleave unto her [or him] *and none else*" (D&C 42:22; emphasis added). Sharing the scriptural passage with her, I taught her a concept that she had never before realized, or at least had feigned ignorance of: emotional infidelity. Adultery, like murder, has spiritual and emotional dimensions along with the physical. Those dimensions must be safeguarded as well. Emotional infidelity may occur whenever one allows anyone or anything else to draw away one's complete love, devotion, interests, and affections. President Spencer W. Kimball warned:

> There are those married people who permit their eyes to wander and their hearts to become vagrant, who think it is not improper to flirt a little, to share their hearts and have desire for someone other than the wife or the husband.
>
> And when the Lord says *all* thy heart, it allows for no sharing nor dividing nor depriving. . . . The words *none else* eliminate everyone and everything. The spouse then becomes preeminent in the life of the husband or wife, and neither social life nor occupational life nor political life nor any other interest nor person nor thing shall ever take precedence over the companion spouse. We sometimes find women who absorb and hover over the children at the expense of the husband, sometimes even estranging them from him. . . .
>
> Marriage presupposes total allegiance and total fidelity. Each spouse takes the partner with the understanding that he or she gives totally to the spouse all the heart, strength, loyalty, honor, and affection, with all dignity. Any divergence is sin; any sharing of the heart is transgression. As we should have "an eye single to the glory of God," so should we have an eye, an ear, a heart single to the marriage and spouse and family. . . .
>
> Husbands, come home—body, spirit, mind, loyalties, interests, and affections—and love your companion in an holy and unbreakable relationship.
>
> Wives, come home with all your interests, fidelity, yearnings, loyalties, and affections—working together to make your home a blessed

heaven. Thus would you greatly please your Lord and Master and guarantee yourselves happiness supreme. (*Faith Precedes the Miracle* [Salt Lake City: Deseret Book Co., 1972], pp. 142, 143, 148.)

## "Thou Shalt Not Steal"

I once saw a news report on television about an armored car that had rolled over and nearly two hundred thousand dollars in bills and coins had been scattered on the street. The report showed hundreds of individuals from the community running to the area and gathering up money as fast as they could. They were not collecting it to assist the bank or to be good citizens. They were filling their own pockets and shopping bags with as much as they could get away with.

Several days later, officials reported that less than fifty dollars had been turned in. When reporters interviewed some of the neighbors who had been pocketing the money, they asked if what was being done would be considered stealing. I found their responses interesting. "Pennies from heaven," one person responded. "This is God's way of blessing me." Another stated, "It isn't stealing, because it doesn't really belong to anybody. It's just the bank's money." I couldn't believe my ears. Did they really believe that the money didn't belong to anyone? Did it all just miraculously fall from heaven, like manna?

"Love thy neighbor as thyself," Jesus declared. In contrast to the Savior's Golden Rule, the maxims of the natural man are "Finders keepers, losers weepers" or "Every man for himself." I was left to wonder how these people would have responded—what they would have done and what they would have said to the others—if the money had been their own life savings.

"Stealing is all too common throughout the world," President James E. Faust observed. "For many their reasoning seems to be, 'What can I get away with?' or 'It's OK to do it as long as I don't get caught!' Stealing takes many forms, including shoplifting; taking cars, stereos, CD players, video games, and other items that belong to someone else; stealing time, money, and merchandise from employers; stealing from the government by misuse of the taxpayers' money or making false claims on our income tax returns; or borrowing without any intention of repayment. No one has ever gained anything of value by theft." ("Honesty—a Moral Compass," *Ensign*, November 1996, p. 43.)

In a similar vein, I watched an episode on *The Oprah Winfrey Show* on the subject of personal honesty. Guests to the show had been invited to clear their consciences by bringing back anything that they had stolen. It was amazing. People brought back irons, ironing boards, towels, bathrobes, blankets, and pillows that they had stolen from hotels. Others returned silverware, china, and crystal goblets that had been taken from restaurants. Huge boxes on the stage were filled with the wide array of things that had been pilfered. Once again, the excuses were "I wasn't stealing from a person; it was just a hotel" or "They wouldn't miss it. They had a lot of these."

Their rationalizations and excuses were ridiculous. While the audience had a good laugh at what had been stolen and at the feeble excuses for the thievery, I was sickened by their cavalier attitude toward this most fundamental command, "Thou shalt not steal." Again, I wondered how these people would have felt if each time guests came to visit their home a lamp disappeared, or a favorite painting, or silverware, or clothes. It may be just "stuff," but we would feel terribly invaded and abused.

When we truly think of others as ourselves and respect their property as we would respect our own and would want it protected, there is no stealing. When we truly love others as we would want to be loved, we do not injure them by stealing from them. "Thou shalt not steal" is not just a commandment about property, it is a commandment about consideration, concern, and compassion for others. "Do unto others as you would have others do unto you."

## "Thou Shalt Not Bear False Witness"

Under the law of Moses, the prohibition against bearing false witness was designed primarily to ensure honesty in legal proceedings on the part of all involved—witnesses, judges, and the accused. So important was honesty in such proceedings that the law prescribed that a perjurer must suffer the penalty for the crime of which he had falsely accused someone (see Deuteronomy 19:16–21). In our society, criminal law also forbids bearing false witness. Unfortunately, lying and gossiping often go unpunished yet leave damage and destruction in their wake. "Television recently carried the story of a woman imprisoned for twenty-seven years," Elder Gordon B. Hinckley recounted, "she having been convicted on the testimony of witnesses who have now come forth to confess they had lied. I know that this is an extreme case, but are you not acquainted with instances of reputations damaged, of hearts broken, of careers destroyed by the lying tongues of those who have borne false witness?" ("'An Honest Man—God's Noblest Work,'" *Ensign,* May 1976, p. 61.)

The whole world watched in horror the news footage of a bomb that exploded in Centennial Olympic Park during the 1996 Atlanta Summer Olympic Games. But what occurred in the weeks and months after the bombing was also horrible, inflicting damage and destruction of a different kind. Almost every day news reports focused on one man as the possible bomber. Soon he was hounded by the media and the FBI. It was not until months later that it was clearly demonstrated that this young man had had nothing to do with the terrorist act. The bearing of false witness in its many disguises had ruined his life, and although the FBI apologized for their mistake, a simple apology could never undo what innuendo, false stories, and even lying had done. In the play *Othello,* William Shakespeare has one of his main characters, Iago, teach this important truth:

> Who steals my purse, steals trash; 'tis something, nothing;
> 'Twas mine, 'tis his, and has been slave to thousands:
> But he that fliches from me my good name
> Robs me of that which not enriches him
> And makes me poor indeed.
> (*Othello,* act 3, scene 3, lines 158–62.)

Perhaps each of us can remember a time when we were unjustly accused of something or lied about in some way. The pain can be tremendous, especially when some are so eager to believe and spread lies rather than always seek the truth. When we remember how we felt when someone has deceived us or borne false witness against us, we will not desire to inflict that kind of unfair treatment and unwarranted pain upon someone else. My heart goes out to people whose lives have been severely damaged and sometimes almost totally destroyed by false accusations, whether levied in a court of law or by tongue-wagging gossips in wards and neighborhoods. The Golden Rule would have us speak the truth in love and kindness to all, just as we would want others to speak to or about us. "Let the truth be taught by exam-

ple and precept," President Gordon B. Hinckley has admonished, "that
to steal is evil, that to cheat is wrong, that to lie is a reproach to anyone who indulges in it." ("Four Simple Things to Help Our Families
and Our Nations," *Ensign*, September, 1996, p. 7.)

## "THOU SHALT NOT COVET"

"Thou shalt not covet thy neighbour's house, thou shalt not covet
thy neighbour's wife, nor his manservant, nor his maidservant, nor his
ox, nor his ass, nor any thing that is thy neighbour's" (Exodus 20:17).
This commandment was clearly placed by the Lord in the category of
commandments dealing with our relationships with our fellowmen.
The previous commandments in this category deal with guarding one's
actions, whereas this important commandment is specifically intended
to safeguard one's desires. It may be that this commandment has even
greater relevance in today's materialistic world than it did in Moses'
day. In our modern society that seems to urge people to satisfy their
every desire, obedience to the tenth commandment affords us spiritual
and temporal protection from the effects of a host of other evils. For
example, when we faithfully abstain from covetousness, we will not
break the commandments "Thou shalt not commit adultery" and
"Thou shalt not steal," for we will be free of the unrighteous desires
that precede those sins. Thus, the commandment "Thou shalt not
covet" is intrinsically related to all of the other commandments.

The tenth commandment, in fact, brings us full circle. Not only
does it deal with our relationships and desires regarding others, but it
brings us back to the first commandment, "Thou shalt have no other
gods before me." It teaches us that anything we permit to come between us and the Lord—possessions, power, pleasure, or people—is a
spiritual stumbling block. Covetousness is a form of idolatry, as the
Apostle Paul declared (see Colossians 3:5). It may not involve the worship of graven images in a religious sense, but it certainly includes
having our "hearts . . . set so much upon the things of this world" and
"the honors of men" (D&C 131:35) that we are in danger of forgetting
about eternal, celestial objectives. Covetousness creates divided loyalties, which prevent complete consecration and total devotion to God
and his kingdom.

As with all of God's commandments, the tenth commandment is

evidence of the Lord's love and mercy and his desire to protect us from the painful consequences of sin. Even though it may seem comparatively innocent at first and free from the obvious dangers associated with breaking the other nine commandments, coveting can become a monumental problem and can even be the detonator in breaking all the other commandments.

In addition to protecting us from sin, obedience to the tenth commandment can offer us the blessings that come from increasing our charity, making our service more productive, and developing greater compassion. The Lord commanded in this dispensation: "See that ye love one another; cease to be covetous; learn to impart one to another as the gospel requires" (D&C 88:123). This command to lay aside our desires for the things of the world directs us onto the path of true discipleship. A heart filled with covetous desires has no room for the all-consuming love of God that is required for exaltation.

"Who is on the Lord's side? let him come unto me," Moses declared (Exodus 32:26). Keeping the timeless Ten Commandments today also determines if we are on the Lord's side. Not only does our modern acceptance of these ancient laws determine whose side we are really on, but our obedience or disobedience reflects our love for God, family, and fellowman. "We cannot break the Ten Commandments," Cecil B. DeMille insightfully observed. "We can only break ourselves against them—or else, by keeping them, rise through them to the fulness of freedom under God." (Commencement address, p. 6.)

*If a man vow a vow unto the Lord, or swear an oath to bind his soul with a bond;*
*he shall not break his word, he shall do according to all*
*that proceedeth out of his mouth.*
*—Numbers 30:2*

CHAPTER FOUR

# Consecrated unto the Lord:
# Modern-Day Nazarites

In the Old Testament the Lord gives an interesting law that on the surface seems strange and totally irrelevant to today's world. It is the vow of the Nazarite (sometimes spelled *Nazirite*). Not to be confused with *Nazarene*, meaning someone from Nazareth, the term *Nazarite* comes from the Hebrew word *nazir*, which means to "be separated from" or "set apart unto." One who took the Nazarite vow became "separated from" the world and the normal expectations of being of the house of Israel by being "set apart" unto higher expectations of personal worthiness and greater responsibilities of service. Sometimes the word *nazir* is also translated to mean "consecrated unto the Lord."

> And the Lord spake unto Moses, saying,
>
> Speak unto the children of Israel, and say unto them, When either man or woman shall separate themselves to vow a vow of a Nazarite, to separate themselves unto the Lord:
>
> He shall separate himself from wine and strong drink, and shall drink no vinegar of wine, or vinegar of strong drink, neither shall he drink any liquor of grapes, nor eat moist grapes, or dried.
>
> All of the days of his separation shall he eat nothing that is made of the vine tree, from the kernels even to the husk.

All the days of the vow of his separation there shall no razor come upon his head: until the days be fulfilled, in the which he separateth himself unto the Lord, he shall be holy, and shall let the locks of the hair of his head grow.

All the days that he separateth himself unto the Lord he shall come at no dead body.

He shall not make himself unclean for his father, or for his mother, for his brother, or for his sister, when they die: because the consecration of his God is upon his head.

All the days of his separation he is holy unto the Lord. (Numbers 6:1–8.)

There were three main conditions associated with the Nazarite vow: one must refrain from all wine and grape products, not cut one's hair, and not go near a dead body. There could be other individualized conditions associated with the vow as well. In addition, the vow and its attendant restrictions could range anywhere from short-term—as short as thirty days—to long-term, which could be an entire lifetime. It is also interesting to note that the Nazarite vow could be taken by an individual himself or by a parent, as in the case of Hannah consecrating her son Samuel, even before he was born, to the service of the Lord (see 1 Samuel 1:11). While there is very little in the scriptures about what might be characterized as official Nazarite practice, there is much evidence of the principle in practice among many who made private vows of faithfulness, devotion, and service. Becoming consecrated unto the Lord could be done by taking the official vow of a Nazarite or could be done in principle by being "separated from" the world "set apart unto" a greater life of righteousness.

Samson is probably the most famous (or infamous) Nazarite mentioned in the Old Testament. Like Samuel, Samson was consecrated unto the Lord by his parents before he was born for the mission of helping to rescue the Israelites from their bondage to the Philistines (see Judges 13:1–7). In fact, he is the only person specifically called a Nazarite in the scriptures, yet there were undoubtedly many others in ancient Israel.

Others were dedicated unto the Lord's service or took important vows of worthiness, but were not specifically Nazarites as described in Numbers chapter 6. Joseph the son of Jacob, who was sold by his brothers into Egypt, may be called a *nazir* in that he had been preserved or "separated" to fulfill a great mission of salvation for his family (see Genesis 49:26; Deuteronomy 33:16). In a symbolic way the prophet Jeremiah was a Nazarite, not because he took the explicit vows described in Numbers chapter 6 but because he was "sanctified" (consecrated) and "ordained . . . a prophet unto the nations" before he was "formed in the belly" (Jeremiah 1:5). Most scholars believe that John the Baptist was a literal Nazarite because of his abstinence from wine and his consecrated mission as "forerunner" for the Messiah (see Matthew 3:1–4; 11:18–19; D&C 84:27–28). Some even suggest that Jesus may be characterized as a symbolic type of Nazarite because even before he was born in Bethlehem he was "consecrated" and "set apart" unto his redemptive mission—a "Lamb . . . slain from the foundation of the world" (Moses 7:47).

While there may not be much written in the Old Testament about Nazarites, and to some it may seem archaic and only a cultural curiosity, the concept of Nazarites as "consecrated ones" is relevant and significant to us today. As members of the Church we are modern-day Nazarites who are "separated out of the world" and "set apart unto" special responsibilities and missions of redemption. We can see this principle fulfilled not only in short-term consecrated missions but also in lifetimes of consecrated service unto God.

## Short-Term Consecration

When I ask my students to think of modern-day parallels to the short-term vows of a Nazarite, their most obvious and immediate answer is full-time missionary service. Today full-time missionaries are "separated out of" the normal day-to-day life of young adult men and women, which might involve college life, careers, social life, families, and so on. Older, retired full-time missionary couples are "separated out of" the cherished role of doting grandparents and the relaxed lifestyle of retirement. Both kinds of missionaries are consecrated for a period of time or "set apart unto" full-time service to the Lord. With that consecration comes the giving up of some things that the rest of the Church doesn't have to go without.

I have often imagined that when Moses explained the law of the Nazarites to the Israelites, some of the people might have said, "I understand why no wine, but why can't I eat raisins?" In a similar way, when I had gotten a little tired of white shirts while serving as a missionary, I wondered, *Why only white shirts? Wouldn't a light blue or a nice pin-stripe sometimes be okay?* The message I get from the ancient law of the Nazarites is that the issue is not about grapes or raisins or white shirts or pinstripes. It is not about why other nineteen-year-old Latter-day Saints can go to movies and listen to their favorite top-40 radio stations and why missionaries listen to Mormon Tabernacle Choir tapes. It is not about swimming or dating or any of the myriad other things that some can do and missionaries can't. It is about a vow—a voluntary vow of consecration that sets one apart from the normal things of everyday living in order to do something of great spiritual significance. It's not about what can't be done, it's about what remarkable things can be done when a missionary is consecrated unto the Lord. What is gained from such consecration is far greater than that which is temporarily (and sometimes permanently thereafter) given up.

Another modern-day Nazarite vow of a temporary nature I wanted my students to understand and appreciate was related to their attendance at a Church-sponsored university. "I can be just as good a person with long hair and a beard as I can without one" is a comment that I have heard often from students "kicking against the pricks" of the honor code and dress and grooming standards that are required at Brigham Young University and other Church schools. The students might even point smugly to the beards on the statues of Brigham Young or Karl G. Maeser on campus. Sometimes they might ask, "Why can't I wear shorts, yet other LDS kids can at their schools?" I have heard all kinds of comments such as "Why can't LDS men wear earrings here but can elsewhere? I think they are cool. It doesn't mean you are a bad person." "I know someone who has long hair and a beard and he can go to the temple, but not to BYU. That doesn't seem fair." I have heard it all. The more I hear murmuring and muttering about the "restrictions" of attending Church schools, the more I am convinced that the principle of the Nazarite vow has special relevance today.

One purpose of the ancient law of the Nazarites was that they were to be visibly distinct from everyone else. Anyone entering an Israelite village could immediately recognize the Nazarites. In a broader sense, all of the house of Israel, as God's "peculiar treasure," were to be visibly distinctive from all of the other peoples of the region. This was manifest in their manner of dress, their hairstyles, and their diet. Like Mormon elders, who are readily recognizable by their white shirts, short hair, and name tags, modern-day Nazarites might be students who have been "separated" from the world by enrolling at Church schools and "set apart" by a "style of their own," as President Spencer W. Kimball has described it (see *Faith Precedes the Miracle* [Salt Lake City: Deseret Book Co., 1972], pp. 161–68). The issue surrounding such modern-day Nazarite vows is not one of style. Neither is it about the rightness or wrongness of beards, earrings, shorts, or miniskirts. It is about a vow, voluntarily taken, like that of an ancient Nazarite, to be temporarily different from others in order to do things and receive things in a unique and wonderful setting. Wearing a beard doesn't make one evil, but blatantly repudiating a vow that one has knowingly and wilfully taken upon him- or herself does. It is not merely a matter of dress or grooming standards; it is a matter of personal honor—of consecration to something higher. Just as people anciently could choose whether to take the Nazarite vow, we too make those choices ourselves. When we take a similar vow, no one is restricting us or dictating what we can or can't do, because we made that choice. We chose to "separate ourselves" and become "set apart" with our choice of schools and our personal signing of the vow. When the duration of the vow is over, one can choose to be like everyone else, if that is what one wants. But while enrolled at BYU or any other Church-sponsored school one is duty-bound—no, covenant bound—to live by this contemporary Nazarite vow that he or she has made.

Whether it be for two years as a missionary or four or five years at a Church university, a vow is not about just obeying rules or enduring temporary restrictions; it is about personal honor and individual integrity. It is the turning over of our desires to the will of the Lord. Consecration is not compelled or coerced. It is freely given. It is the willing demonstration outwardly of the vow or covenantal consecration that we espouse inwardly.

## A Life Consecrated unto the Lord

In chapter 23 of Deuteronomy we read: "When thou shalt vow a vow unto the Lord thy God, thou shalt not slack to pay it: for the Lord thy God shall surely require it of thee; and it would be sin in thee. . . . That which is gone out of thy lips thou shalt keep and perform; even a freewill offering, according as thou has vowed unto the Lord thy God, which thou hast promised with thy mouth." (Vv. 21, 23.) By virtue of our membership in the Church we have taken "vows unto the Lord" and are as Nazarites, consecrated unto the Lord for the rest of our days. Our coming forth out of the waters of baptism is symbolic of our coming forth "out of the world" and covenanting that we would "stand as witnesses of God at all times and in all things, and in all places" (Mosiah 18:9). With each new phase of our spiritual development we take upon us Nazarite-like vows such as the oath and the covenant of the priesthood and temple covenants, including covenants of obedience, moral purity, sacrifice, and consecration. We have agreed to become "separate from" the world and "set apart" to serve and bless others. It doesn't matter what the rest of the world does or doesn't do. Our vows require us to be *nazir*, or "sacredly aloof from all uncleanness." We chose to be different from the world, even depriving ourselves of much of what the world and the worldly believe is rightfully theirs. Being a modern-day Nazarite is not about what one can't do or can't have. It is about what one gets to *be*. As Elder Neal A. Maxwell said, becoming covenantally consecrated unto the Lord is not "resignation or mindless caving in. Rather, it is a deliberate expanding outward. . . . Consecration, likewise, is not shoulder-shrugging acceptance, but, instead, shoulder-squaring to better bear the yoke." ("'Swallowed Up in the Will of the Father,'" *Ensign*, November 1995, p. 24.)

The ancient law of Moses prescribed a higher standard of righteousness for the priests and Levites than that required of other members of the house of Israel (see Leviticus 21). A modern comparison could be made to those who are called and set apart to important positions of leadership and responsibility. They are expected to be even more worthy and faithful and are judged as more accountable. In the broader sense, however, we as members of the Church have made Nazarite-like vows of sacrifice and consecration, promising to be "sacredly aloof from all unrighteousness" and "set apart" as the "saviors of men" (see D&C 103:9–10).

Modern-day Nazarites, like those anciently, can be recognized by their outward appearance. But more important than just modest dress and clean and comely grooming, being "sacredly aloof" means "having the image of God engraven upon [our] countenances" (Alma 5:19). It is the spiritual reflection of Christ that our lives must emanate. "An 'image' is not just an outward visual impression but also a vivid representation, a graphic display, or a total likeness of something," one Latter-day Saint scholar explained.

> It is a person or thing very much like another, a copy or counterpart. Likewise, *countenance* does not simply mean a facial expression or visual appearance. The word comes from an old French term originally denoting "behavior," "demeanor," or "conduct." In earlier times the word *countenance* was used with these meanings in mind.
>
> Therefore, to receive Christ's image in one's countenance means to acquire the Savior's likeness in behavior, to be a copy or reflection of the Master's life. This is not possible without a mighty change in one's pattern of living. It requires, too, a change in feelings, attitudes, desires, and spiritual commitment. (Andrew C. Skinner, "Alma's Pure Testimony," in Kent P. Jackson, ed., *1 Nephi to Alma 29*, vol. 7 of *Studies in Scripture* [Salt Lake City: Deseret Book, Co., 1987], p. 301.)

Reflecting the image of God in our countenances requires us to follow the admonition given to all who had consecrated themselves by covenant to serve the Lord: "Come ye out from the wicked, and be ye separate, and touch not their unclean things" (Alma 5:57).

By being consecrated unto the Lord, and by faithfully living our vows and covenants, we can become a "kingdom of priests, and an holy nation" (Exodus 19:6). With such a reward, we give up very little to be modern-day Nazarites in comparison to what we gain.

> *And now, my beloved brethren, I would that ye should come unto Christ, who is the Holy One of Israel, and partake of his salvation, and the power of his redemption. Yea, come unto him, and offer your whole souls as an offering unto him, and continue in fasting and praying, and endure to the end; and as the Lord liveth ye will be saved*
>
> —Omni 1:26

# סְגֻלָּה

## CHAPTER FIVE

# In the Strength of the Lord

From the time I was a child one of my favorite Bible stories has been the account of David slaying Goliath, the Philistine giant. The great adventure story captured my attention as a boy and caused me to fantasize about being a young hero like David. In fact, I even practiced with a sling-shot just in case I ever came across a modern-day Goliath.

It was a dream come true when, many years after first hearing of David's courageous act, I was able to actually walk in the valley where the historical event occurred. When my family lived in Israel one of our favorite places to visit was the valley of Elah. It doesn't look much different from the many other hill-lined valleys of the Holy Land, but my imagination would run wild as we would walk down into the streambed and, like David, each select five smooth stones. With hand-made Palestinian slings we would try our own skill at "slaying" our imaginary Goliaths.

It was always fun to take a class of BYU Jerusalem Center students into the valley and have a sling-off. Sometimes the class would prepare their own cardboard Goliath target; other times the target might be an old abandoned car. Most would just try to keep their rocks some-where in the valley. Few of the students had ever used an old-world type sling, and it was humorous to watch their feeble efforts. In fact, I don't think there was any safe area when they were slinging the stones, because ofttimes as many stones were slung backward as forward. When a student hit the designated target we dubbed him or her "David," while each of us who couldn't hit the broad side of a barn was just another "Dave." Goliath would have lived a long and productive life had any of my students been placed in David's shoes.

Many times as I have heard the story of David and Goliath recounted, there has been great emphasis placed on David's skill as a slingsman and how as a young shepherd he had courageously killed both a lion and a bear that had attacked his father's flocks. I always viewed David as some sort of young Davy Crocket or Daniel Boone. That, however, is not the real image of David that the scriptures emphasize. No doubt brave young David was skilled with a sling, but I wanted my family and my students to know the real source of his skill and courage.

When all of the Israelite army, including David's older brothers, cowered in fear of the Philistine giant, David was seen rallying the troops, encouraging his own brothers to find courage to face the challenge. "Is there not a cause?" David queried.

> And David spake to the men that stood by him, saying, What shall be done to the man that killeth this Philistine, and taketh away the reproach from Israel? for who is this uncircumcised Philistine, that he should defy the armies of the living God?
>
> And David said to Saul, Let no man's heart fail because of him; thy servant will go and fight with this Philistine.
>
> And Saul said unto David, Thou art not able to go against this Philistine to fight with him: for thou art but a youth, and he a man of war from his youth.
>
> And David said unto Saul, Thy servant kept his father's sheep, and there came a lion, and a bear, and took a lamb out of the flock:
>
> And I went out after him, and smote him, and delivered it out of his mouth: and when he arose against me, I caught him by his beard, and smote him, and slew him.
>
> Thy servant slew both the lion and the bear: and this uncircumcised Philistine shall be as one of them, seeing he hath defied the armies of the living God.

David said moreover, The Lord that delivered me out of the paw of the lion, and out of the paw of the bear, he will deliver me out of the hand of this Philistine. And Saul said unto David, Go, and the Lord be with thee. (1 Samuel 17;26, 32–37.)

Perhaps to ease his conscience over his own cowardice, King Saul placed his armor, including his coat of mail and his brass helmet, upon David. He placed in David's hand his own sword. So heavy was all this gear and so awkward was movement in it that David shed the King's armor and walked alone to the brook bed and put five smooth stones into his shepherd's bag. David knew that he had a protective shield greater than the king's armor, and weaponry more powerful than the king's sword or all of his armies.

And when the Philistine looked about, and saw David, he disdained him: for he was but a youth, and ruddy, and of a fair countenance.

And the Philistine said unto David, Am I a dog, that thou comest to me with staves [sticks]? And the Philistine cursed David by his gods.

And the Philistine said to David, Come to me, and I will give thy flesh unto the fowls of the air, and to the beasts of the field.

Then said David to the Philistine, Thou comest to me with a sword, and with a spear, and with a shield: but I come to thee in the name of the Lord of hosts, the God of the armies of Israel, whom thou hast defied.

This day will the Lord deliver thee into mine hand; and I will smite thee, and take thine head from thee; and I will give the carcases of the host of the Philistines this day unto the fowls of the air, and to the wild beasts of the earth; that all the earth may know that there is a God in Israel.

And all this assembly shall know that the Lord saveth not with sword and spear: for the battle is the Lord's, and he will give you into our hands. (1 Samuel 17:42–47.)

## THE PROTECTIVE POWER OF RIGHTEOUSNESS

David was protected from Goliath, not because he was a better soldier but because he was clothed in the armor of God. It may have been a stone cast from a shepherd boy's sling that killed Goliath, but it was the Lord who really won the battle. David's protection was found in his personal righteousness, and his courage was due to his unwavering faith in the God of Israel. Not only did David know that the Lord Jehovah was a protective "shield" unto the righteous (see Genesis 15:1; Psalm 3:3), but he also knew, as Joshua had declared, that "the Lord your God, he it is that fighteth for you" (Joshua 23:10; see also Exodus 14:14). David, like Moses, Joshua, and many others, knew that this promise was conditional, predicated upon faith and righteousness.

"Take good heed . . . unto yourselves," Joshua taught his people, "that ye love the Lord your God" (Joshua 23:11). Time and time again the Lord demonstrated this principle to ancient Israel. When the Israelites were obedient unto the Lord and trusting in his strength, they were preserved from their enemies, ofttimes in miraculous ways. Yet when they rejected the Lord's prophets and turned to wickedness, they were defeated, their cities destroyed, and their families taken into bondage.

This pattern is specifically seen in the scriptural account of the life and ministry of the prophet Joshua. "Be strong and of a good courage; be not afraid, neither be thou dismayed," the Lord promised him, "for the Lord thy God is with thee whithersoever thou goest" (Joshua 1:9). The miraculous capture of Jericho after its walls came tumbling down was not due merely to the marching of the soldiers and the blasts of the rams' horns, but the Lord had given them the victory (see Joshua 6). Similarly, the Israelites miraculously defeated the mighty Amorites. "Fear them not," the Lord told Joshua, "for I have delivered them into thine hand" (Joshua 10:8). The scriptural account records that not only did God cause the sun and moon to stand still so that the Israelites could chase after the fleeing Amorites and slay them, but also, almost as an exclamation point, the "Lord cast down great stones from heaven upon them unto Azekah, and they died: they were more which died with hailstones than they whom the children of Israel slew with the sword" (Joshua 10:11). In contrast to these great victories, the Israelites had been soundly defeated at Ai when they had disobeyed the counsel of the Lord's anointed (see Joshua 7).

What do these stories mean to us today? We are not conquering a promised land, as were Joshua's people, and we are not being invaded by armed marauders of foreign powers, as were the ancient Israelites.

We are, however, fighting our own battles, most often against an unseen enemy. It is not a war with bullets and bombs, but is nonetheless just as real and just as potentially destructive. All around us are the "fiery darts of the adversary" (1 Nephi 15:24). We need to be clothed in the armor of God just as much today, if not more so, as David did as he stood in the valley of Elah facing down Goliath, for we too face many "giants"—our own unique challenges and temptations.

The Lord has declared:

> Wherefore, lift up your hearts and rejoice, and gird up your loins, and take upon you my whole armor, that ye may be able to withstand the evil day, having done all, that ye may be able to stand.
>
> Stand, therefore, having your loins girt about with truth, having on the breastplate of righteousness, and your feet shod with the preparation of the gospel of peace, which I have sent mine angels to commit unto you;
>
> Taking the shield of faith wherewith ye shall be able to quench all the fiery darts of the wicked;
>
> And take the helmet of salvation, and the sword of my Spirit, which I will pour out upon you, and my word which I reveal unto you, and be agreed as touching all things whatsoever ye ask of me, and be faithful until I come, and ye shall be caught up, that where I am ye shall be also. Amen. (D&C 27:15–18; see also Ephesians 6:11–18.)

> And their arm shall be my arm, and I will be their shield and their buckler; and I will gird up their loins, and they shall fight manfully for me; and their enemies shall be under their feet; and I will let fall the sword in their behalf, and by the fire of my indignation will I preserve them. (D&C 35:14; see also 2 Samuel 22:2–3.)

Perhaps the greatest example of the protective power of personal righteousness is found in the experiences of the Prophet Daniel. As a young man Daniel had been taken captive to Babylon. He had won great favor with Nebuchadnezzar because of his faith and righteousness. When Daniel refused to eat the "king's meat" out of his obedience to the Jewish dietary law, the Lord blessed him with health and wisdom (see Daniel 1:6–17). Years later, when some of Daniel's enemies encouraged King Darius to outlaw prayer for thirty days, they hoped to trap Daniel, who faithfully prayed to the God of Israel. As Daniel prayed in the privacy of his room, these enemies waited to have him arrested for defying the king's decree. Even though Daniel was beloved of King Darius and was one of the foremost leaders in Darius' court, the king was pressured against his will by the plotters to put Daniel to death for breaking the royal edict.

> Then the king commanded, and they brought Daniel, and cast him into the den of lions. Now the king spake and said unto Daniel, Thy God whom thou servest continually, he will deliver thee.
>
> And a stone was brought, and laid upon the mouth of the den; and the king sealed it with his own signet, and with the signet of his lords; that the purpose might not be changed concerning Daniel.
>
> Then the king went to his palace, and passed the night fasting: neither were instruments of musick brought before him: and his sleep went from him.
>
> Then the king arose very early in the morning, and went in haste unto the den of lions.
>
> And when he came to the den, he cried with a lamentable voice unto Daniel: and the king spake and said to Daniel, O Daniel, servant of the living God, is thy God, whom thou servest continually, able to deliver thee from the lions?
>
> Then said Daniel unto the king, O king, live for ever.
>
> My God hath sent his angel, and hath shut the lions' mouths, that they have not hurt me: forasmuch as before him innocency was found in me; and also before thee, O king, have I done no hurt.
>
> Then was the king exceeding glad for him, and commanded that they should take Daniel up out of the den. So Daniel was taken up out of the den, and no manner of hurt was found upon him, because he believed in his God. (Daniel 6:16–23.)

Daniel suffered no harm in the lion's den, not because the lions were vegetarians, but because he was miraculously protected by the Lord due to his faith and obedience and his life of righteousness and service. Like his friends Shadrach, Meshach, and Abednego, who refused to worship a false god and were similarly preserved in a fiery furnace (see Daniel 3), Daniel was preserved because he wore the "armor of God" and the "shield of faith."

Today the Lord preserves and protects his righteous people just as he did anciently. The protection afforded the faithful comes in two ways: as the natural protective consequences of living the gospel, and as miraculous spiritual preservations.

## *The Natural Protection That Comes from Living the Gospel*

A very real shield protects us from the "fiery darts of the adversary." It is found in the commandments and covenants of God. There is both physical and spiritual protection when we live the law of chastity and the Word of Wisdom. Many of the serious problems afflicting society will pass us by like the destroying angel if we put on the armor of God by obeying his commandments. Faithfully paying our tithes and offerings is not only protective in that we will be preserved at the Second Coming (see D&C 63:23–24), but it is also a blessing right here and now both temporally and spiritually. Honesty protects us from the ill effects of deceit and preserves a clear conscience. The garment of the holy priesthood can be a protection literally and symbolically. It is an outward symbol of the covenants we make in the temple and reminds us who we are and what the Lord has promised us if we will be obedient to those covenants. When we are continually reminded of those covenants, we can be protected from the temptations that surround us and our own worst impulses as "natural men."

Keeping the commandments protects us in other ways as well. The more obedient we are, the more worthy we are to receive the guidance and companionship of the Holy Spirit. The Holy Spirit can protect us by leading us away from places, people, and circumstances that may cause us to be subjected to danger, both physical and spiritual. In my own life I have felt that guidance almost compelling me, like Joseph of old, to leave my cloak and run away (see Genesis 39:2).

"Pray always," the Lord has admonished us, "that you may come off conqueror; yea, that you may conquer Satan, and that you may escape the hands of the servants of Satan that do uphold his work" (D&C 10:5). Prayer protects as well as strengthens. If we are faithfully remembering to pray unto the Lord and seek his guidance we will be more likely to "watch [ourselves], and [our] thoughts, and [our] words, and [our] deeds, and observe the commandments of God, and continue in the faith" (Mosiah 4:30). Praying and watching continually can shield us from temptations and strengthen our obedience. "If you will earnestly seek guidance from your Heavenly Father, morning and evening," President Ezra Taft Benson promised, "you will be given the strength to shun any temptation" (*The Teachings of Ezra Taft Benson* [Salt Lake City: Bookcraft, 1988], p. 435).

A natural protection comes from living the gospel. By being where we should be and by doing what we should do, we are protected from "fiery darts" because we are out of the devil's range; we are on the Lord's side of the line. President George Albert Smith taught:

> There are two influences in the world today, and have been from the beginning. One is an influence that is constructive, that radiates happiness and builds character. The other influence is one that destroys, turns men into demons, tears down and discourages. We are all susceptible to both. The one comes from our Heavenly Father, and the other comes from the source of evil that has been in the world from the beginning, seeking to bring about the destruction of the human family. . . .
>
> My grandfather used to say to his family, "There is a line of demarcation, well defined, between the Lord's territory and the devil's. If you will stay on the Lord's side of the line you will be under his influence and will have no desire to do wrong; but if you cross to the devil's side of the line one inch, you are in the tempter's power, and if he is successful, you will not be able to think or even reason properly, because you will have lost the spirit of the Lord."
>
> When I have been tempted sometimes to do a certain thing, I have asked myself, "Which side of the line am I on?" If I [am] determined to be on the safe side, the Lord's side, I would do the right thing every time. So when temptation comes, think prayerfully about your problem, and the influence of the spirit of the Lord will enable you to decide wisely. There is safety for us only on the Lord's side of the line.
>
> If you want to be happy, remember, that all happiness worthy of the name is on the Lord's side of the line and all sorrow and disappointment is on the devil's side of the line. (*Sharing the Gospel with Others*, comp. Preston Nibley [Salt Lake City: Deseret Book Co., 1948], pp. 42–43.)

## Miraculous Protection and Preservation

"God has not ceased to be a God of miracles" (Mormon 9:15). Just as the Lord Jehovah went before the children of Israel as a "cloud by day and pillar of fire by night," so does he continue today to miraculously preserve and protect the righteous. Many times in my life I have experienced the miraculous shield of protection provided by the Lord.

As a missionary my life was preserved on many occasions in ways reminiscent of his dealing with the ancients. As I think of my own son serving as a missionary in Korea and numerous others like him serving around the world, I am grateful that the Lord watches over them, especially in light of the strange things they must eat, the difficult conditions they live in, the foreign diseases they are exposed to, and the evils they encounter. "Our missionaries also seem weak and defenseless, powerless against the armaments of the adversary and those who serve him," Elder Dallin H. Oaks stated. "But the Lord has promised them that he 'will be their shield' (D&C 35:14), and that promise is fulfilled every day in many places around the world." (In Conference Report, October 1992, p. 53.)

President Wilford Woodruff described the miraculous manner in which the Lord protected him while he was serving as a missionary:

> On the sixteenth of November, I preached at Brother Camp's, and baptized three. On the day following, it being Sunday, I preached again at Brother Clapp's, and baptized five. At the close of the meeting I mounted my horse to ride to Clark's River, in company with Seth Utley, four other brethren, and two sisters. The distance was twenty miles.
>
> We came to a stream which was so swollen by rains that we could not cross without swimming our horses. To swim would not be safe for the females, so we went up the stream to find a ford. In the attempt we were overtaken by a severe storm of wind and rain, and lost our way in the darkness and wandered through creeks and mud. But the Lord does not forsake his Saints in any of their troubles. While we were in the woods suffering under the blast of the storm, groping like the blind for the wall, a bright light suddenly shone around us, and revealed to us our dangerous situation of the edge of the gulf. The light continued with us until we found the road. We then went on our way rejoicing, though the darkness returned and the rain continued. ("Autobiography of Wilford Woodruff," *Tullidge's Quarterly Magazine* 3 [October 1883]: 9; as quoted in Leon R. Hartshorn, comp., *Classic Stories from the Lives of Our Prophets* [Salt Lake City: Deseret Book Co., 1971], p. 112.)

Perhaps this is a literal manifestation of the Lord's promise that he will "disperse the powers of darkness from before you" (D&C 21:6). We may never know in mortality the many ways that the promised blessing is realized in our daily lives. Darkness can be dispersed literally as in the case of Jehovah's leading the Israelites by night and the light that guided President Woodruff, but it is also dispersed through the directions of the Holy Spirit. Ofttimes the Lord is protecting us, even preserving our very lives, when we are warned by the still, small voice.

President Harold B. Lee often referred to an experience he had as a young boy:

> I think maybe I was around ten or eleven years of age. I was with my father out on a farm away from our home, trying to spend the day busying myself until my father was ready to go home. Over the fence from our place were some tumbledown sheds that would attract a curious boy, and I was adventurous. I started to climb through the fence, and I heard a voice as clearly as you are hearing mine, calling me by name and saying, "Don't go over there!" I turned to look at my father to see if he were talking to me, but he was way up at the other end of the field. There was no person in sight. I realized then, as a child, that there were persons beyond my sight, for I had definitely heard a voice. (*Stand Ye in Holy Places* [Salt Lake City: Deseret Book, Co., 1974], p. 139.)

I heard President Lee later recount that whenever he told this story to a group of youth they would invariably ask him what dangers lurked over the fence in the old sheds. His response to them was, "I don't know. I didn't go!" We are protected when we obediently respond to the promptings of the Spirit.

As I read the remarkable stories in the Old Testament of how the Lord preserved the Israelites and protected the righteous by parting the Red Sea, providing manna from heaven, defeating their enemies, and shutting the mouths of the lions, I am in awe of his love for us. His love for us is as great as it was for those of ancient times, and his protective care continues today. If we will pause and ponder the many ways the Lord's hand has protected us from harm and guided us to safety, we will "stand all amazed" at the miraculous divine preservation that is manifest in our lives. Today our hearts can join with those of the ancients in singing: "O love the Lord, all ye his saints: for the Lord preserveth the faithful. . . . Be of good courage, and he shall strengthen your heart, all ye that hope in the Lord" (Psalm 31:23–24.) I add my own testimony to that of Elder Dallin H. Oaks: "I am grateful for the [scriptural] promise to us of the last days that 'the righteous need not fear,' for the Lord 'will preserve the righteous by his power' (1 Nephi 22:17). I am grateful for the protection promised to those who have kept their covenants and qualified for the blessings promised in sacred places. These and all promises to the faithful children of God are made by the voice and power of the Lord God of Israel." (In Conference Report, October 1992, p. 56.)

## "THEY THAT BE WITH US ARE MORE THAN THEY THAT BE WITH THEM"

One of my favorite stories in the Old Testament that illustrates another way in which the Lord protects and preserves the righteous is the account of the Prophet Elisha and the Syrian armies. The kingdom of Israel had been invaded from the north by the Syrians. Under the inspiration of God, Elisha warned the Israelite king of the invasion and counseled him on how to wage the war against the Syrians. When the Syrian king became aware that Elisha was counseling the king of Israel regarding the positions and strategies of the Syrian army, he sent horses and chariots and numerous soldiers to surround the city and capture Elisha. "And when the servant of the man of God was risen early, and gone forth, behold, an host compassed the city both with horses and chariots. And his servant said unto him, Alas, my master! how shall we do?" (2 Kings 6:15.) In modern vernacular, the servant is really asking Elisha, "How are we going to get out of this mess? We are totally surrounded!"

I am sure that Elisha's unexpected response led this young servant boy to think that either the prophet was totally crazy or hadn't quite awakened and "shaken out the cobwebs." "Fear not," Elisha comforted the servant, "for they that be with us are more than they that be with them" (2 Kings 6:16). How could that be? As the young servant looked around them all he could see was hundreds of Syrian soldiers and their horses and chariots. How could anybody in their right mind say, "They that be with us are more than they that be with them"? The situation likely appeared completely hopeless to this young man as he surveyed the odds. One young boy and an aged man against an entire army! It didn't look good.

Elisha must have seen the fear and confusion in the boy's eyes. "And Elisha prayed, and said, Lord, I pray thee, open his eyes, that he may see. And the Lord opened the eyes of the young man; and he saw: and, behold, the mountain was full of horses and chariots of fire round about Elisha." (2 Kings 6:17.)

If our spiritual eyes could be opened like the eyes of the servant of Elisha, we too would discover that we are never alone or forsaken, for we walk in the presence of angels. "I will go before your face," the Lord has promised. "I will be on your right hand and on your left, and my Spirit shall be in your hearts, and mine angels round about you, to bear you up" (D&C 84:88). Probably more than we realize, we receive guidance, protection, comfort, and support from beyond the veil. Once in a while the veil thins and we can perceive that "they that be with us are more than they that be with them." Just because loved ones may leave us behind as they enter the spirit world, or because premortal friends are separated when they come to earth, it certainly doesn't mean that their love, interest, and concern for us, as well as their efforts in our behalf, are lessened. President Ezra Taft Benson testified: "God loves us. He's watching us, he wants us to succeed, and we'll know someday that he has not left one thing undone for the eternal welfare of each of us. If we only knew it, there are heavenly hosts pulling for us—friends in heaven that we can't remember now, who yearn for our victory." ("Insights: We Seek That Which Is Praiseworthy," *Ensign*, July 1975, p. 63.)

Perhaps the Lord's promise that he will "cause the heavens to shake for [our] good" (D&C 21:6) is more literal than we often suspect. "He shall send his angel before thee" was the promise given to Abraham's servant (Genesis 24:7), which applies just as much to the faithful today (see Psalm 91:11; D&C 103:19; 109:22).

The ancient Israelites were often watched over and guided by unseen angels, but so too were the early Latter-day Saint pioneers, as well as the generations that followed them. The annals of Church history and numerous personal journals and family histories are replete with accounts of divine intervention from beyond the veil. A member of the beleaguered Martin handcart company remembered: "I have pulled my handcart when I was so weak and weary from illness and lack of food that I could hardly put one foot ahead of the other. I have looked ahead and seen a patch of sand or a hill slope and I have said, I can go only that far and there I must give up, for I cannot pull the load through it. . . . I have gone on to that sand and when I reached it, the cart began pushing me. I have looked back many times to see who was pushing my cart, but my eyes saw no one. I knew then that the angels of God were there." (Quoted in President David O. McKay, "Pioneer Women," *Relief Society Magazine*, January 1948, p. 8.)

In our own time there are similar examples, not often spoken of yet just as real, which testify that God is mindful of each of us and our unique needs. There are truly angels among us—rarely seen, sometimes felt, and often unnoticed—who touch our lives in a variety of ways. President Harold B. Lee in a general conference shortly before his death testified of the unseen yet divine powers of protection promised the righteous:

> May I impose upon you for a moment to express appreciation for something that happened to me some time ago, years ago. I was suffering from an ulcer condition that was becoming worse and worse. We had been touring a mission; but my wife, Joan, and I were impressed the next morning that we should return home as quickly as possible, although we had planned to stay for some other meetings.
>
> On the way across the country, we were sitting in the forward section of the airplane. Some of our Church members were in the next section. As we approached a certain point en route, someone laid his hand upon my head. I looked up; I could see no one. That happened again before we arrived home, again with the same experience. Who it was, by what means or what medium, I may never know, except I knew that I was receiving a blessing that I came a few hours later to know I needed most desperately.
>
> As soon as we arrived home, my wife very anxiously called the doctor. It was now about 11 o'clock at night. He called me to come to the telephone, and he asked me how I was. I said, "Well, I am very tired. I think I will be all right." But shortly thereafter, there came massive hemorrhages which, had they occurred while we were in flight, I wouldn't be here today talking about it.
>
> I know that there are powers divine that reach out when all other help is not available. ("'Stand Ye in Holy Places,'" *Ensign*, July 1973, p. 123.)

As I shared President Lee's experience with my family, one of my daughters quietly said, "I've had an experience like that." I was a little taken aback by her straightforward statement and asked her to explain what she meant. She then proceeded to share with us a tender and sacred experience that she had had many years earlier, which she had never before shared with anyone. It occurred shortly after we had experienced a death in the family, and she had been having a very difficult time coming to grips with our loss. One night as she was alone in her room crying from her grief, she felt a presence enter. "I didn't see anyone," she explained, "but I just knew that someone was in my room." She told us that she was not afraid at all, but totally at peace with the presence of the unseen visitor. "He gave me a blessing," she said. "Then I felt better and knew everything would be okay. Then I felt him leave just as surely as I felt him enter." She had come to know in a very special way that God is mindful of each of his children, young and old, and that we can indeed receive help, protection, and comfort from beyond the veil.

There have been other experiences in our lives that powerfully testify to us of the reality of Elisha's declaration: "Fear not, for they that be with us are more than they that be with them." President Joseph F. Smith has further testified of this great blessing:

> I believe we move and have our being in the presence of heavenly messengers and of heavenly beings. We are not separated from them. We begin to realize more and more fully, as we become acquainted with the principles of the gospel, as they have been revealed anew in this dispensation, that we are closely related to our kindred, to our ancestors, to our friends and associates and co-laborers who have preceded us into the spirit world. . . . And therefore, I claim that we live in their presence, they see us, they are solicitous for our welfare, they love us now more than ever. For now they see the dangers that beset us; they can comprehend better than ever before, the weaknesses that are liable to mislead us into dark and forbidden paths. They see the temptations and the evils that beset us in life, and the proneness of mortal beings to yield to temptation and to wrong doing; hence their solicitude for us and their love for us and their desire for our well being must be greater than that which we feel for ourselves. . . .
>
> . . . When messengers are sent to minister to the inhabitants of this earth, they are not strangers, but from the ranks of our kindred, friends, and fellow-beings and fellow-servants. The ancient prophets who died were those who came to visit their fellow creatures upon the

earth. They came to Abraham, to Isaac, and to Jacob; it was such beings—holy beings if you please—who waited upon the Savior and administered to him on the Mount. . . . In like manner our fathers and mothers, brothers, sisters and friends who have passed away from this earth, having been faithful, and worthy to enjoy these rights and privileges, may have a mission given them to visit their relatives and friends upon the earth again, bringing from the divine Presence messages of love, of warning, or reproof and instruction, to those whom they had learned to love in the flesh. (*Gospel Doctrine* [Salt Lake City: Deseret Book Co., 1939], pp. 430–31, 435–36.)

## "THE LORD IS MY STRENGTH"

In stark contrast to the account of the providential protection and spiritual strength afforded David and Daniel is the sad story of Samson. Dedicated unto the Lord as a Nazarite from before his birth, Samson had been consecrated to the mission of helping to deliver the Israelites from Philistine bondage (see Judges 13:5). He was blessed of the Lord, moved upon by the Spirit, and given great physical strength as a gift of God. As he grew to manhood it was apparent that the Lord had indeed greatly blessed him and the hopes of all of Israel were upon him. Yet despite his great gifts and physical strength, Samson was unable to fulfill his foreordained mission. Marrying out of the covenant, breaking his Nazarite vows, and becoming immorally involved with Delilah were all factors in bringing about his terrible demise.

The traditional view of Samson leads us to believe that the secret of his great strength was to be found in his never cutting his hair (see Judges 16:15–20). In truth, however, Samson's strength had begun to wane even before his long locks were cut off from his head. Samson's strength came from the Lord and was to be maintained not by pumping iron daily in the weight room but by keeping his covenants. As he broke his vows and was unfaithful to his God, he became impotent to deliver Israel from bondage, for "his strength went from him" because "the Lord was departed from him" (Judges 16:19–20).

Samson became weak, "like any other man" (Judges 16:17), in the same way that the Nephites "had become weak, like unto their brethren, the Lamanites" (Helaman 4:24). In contrast to the stripling warriors of Helaman's army who were miraculously preserved and endowed with great power because they did "keep the commandments of God and . . . walk uprightly before him" (Alma 53:21), the wicked Nephites lost the protection and strength promised to the faithful. "The Spirit of the Lord did no more preserve them; yea, it had withdrawn from them because the Spirit of the Lord doth not dwell in unholy temples," Mormon recorded. "Thus had they become weak, because of their transgression." (Helaman 4:24, 26.)

"The way of the Lord is strength to the upright," King Solomon wrote, "but destruction shall be to the workers of iniquity" (Proverbs 10:29). The Lord does indeed strengthen those who, in contrast to Samson, keep their sacred covenants and put their trust in God (see Psalm 27:14; 29:11; Habakkuk 3:19). Even in difficult times of adversity or suffering we can be strengthened beyond our natural abilities, like the Nephites of Alma's day whom "the Lord did strengthen . . . that they could bear up their burdens with ease" (Mosiah 24:15; see also Alma 2:28). With the Lord's strength there is nothing we cannot do and no burden too great to bear.

Despite his foreordained mission and God-given gifts, Samson failed to deliver at "crunch time" because he was not pure. In contrast, even in chains and amid abuse and painful persecution, the Prophet Joseph Smith had power over his armed captors because of his righteousness. Elder Parley P. Pratt was with the Prophet in this hour of darkness in a jailhouse in Richmond, Missouri. He later recalled:

> In one of those tedious nights we had lain as if in sleep till the hour of midnight had passed, and our ears and hearts had been pained, while we had listened for hours to the obscene jests, the horrid oaths, the dreadful blasphemies and filthy language of our guards, Colonel Price at their head, as they recounted to each other their deeds of rapine, murder, robbery, etc., which they had committed among the "Mormons" while at Far West and vicinity. They even boasted of defiling by force wives, daughters and virgins, and of shooting or dashing out the brains of men, women and children.
>
> I had listened till I became so disgusted, shocked, horrified, and so filled with the spirit of indignant justice that I could scarcely refrain from rising upon my feet and rebuking the guards; but had said nothing to Joseph, or any one else, although I lay next to him and knew he was awake. On a sudden he arose to his feet, and spoke in a voice of thunder, or as the roaring lion, uttering, as near as I can recollect, the following words.

"SILENCE, ye fiends of the infernal pit. In the name of Jesus Christ I rebuke you, and command you to be still; I will not live another minute and bear such language. Cease such talk, or you or I die THIS INSTANT!"

He ceased to speak. He stood erect in terrible majesty. Chained, and without a weapon; calm, unruffled and dignified as an angel, he looked upon the quailing guards, whose weapons were lowered or dropped to the ground; whose knees smote together, and who, shrinking into a corner, or crouching at his feet, begged his pardon, and remained quiet till a change of guards. (*Autobiography of Parley P. Pratt* [Salt Lake City, Deseret Book, Co., 1985], pp. 179–80.)

We can have that kind of power today—that same divine power of protection and spiritual strength that the ancient patriarchs, pioneers, and prophets have possessed. We can be, and are, preserved by miraculous means as much now as they were then. We may not be cast into fiery furnaces or lions' dens or surrounded by foreign armies, but we can be protected by the armor of God and the shield of faith in our own unique circumstances and challenges. "For the Lord will not forsake his people," the prophet Samuel promised (1 Samuel 12:22). Wherever we stand today, facing whatever modern-day Goliaths that threaten us, we need not fear or tremble. Clothed with faith and righteousness, "in strength of the Lord [we] canst do all things" (Alma 20:4). As Ammon declared:

*I do not boast in my own strength, nor in my own wisdom; but behold my joy is full, yea, my heart is brim with joy, and I will rejoice in my God. Yea, I know that I am nothing; as to my strength I am weak; therefore I will not boast of myself, but I will boast of my God, for in his strength I can do all things.*

*—Alma 26:11–12*

*Behold, I set before you this day a blessing and a curse; a blessing, if ye obey
the commandments of the Lord your God, which I command you this day:
and a curse, if ye will not obey the commandments of the Lord your God,
but turn aside out of the way which I command you this day.*
—Deuteronomy 11:26–28

## CHAPTER SIX

# Blessings and Curses

About halfway between Jerusalem and the Sea of Galilee, in the region of Samaria, lie two prominent mountains—Mount Gerizim and Mount Ebal. They flank the ancient city of Shechem (modern-day Nablus), wherein several important scriptural events occurred from the time of Abraham to Jesus' day (see Genesis 12:6; John 4). Despite the many events that occurred in Shechem, the mountains themselves are significant in Old Testament history and also stand today as visual symbols of Israel's covenant with their God.

The Lord told Moses that he would see the land "that floweth with milk and honey" (Deuteronomy 11:9) but that he would not be going with his people as they crossed the Jordan River and entered the land. As he delivered to the Israelites his exhortation unto righteousness, he gave an inspired and intriguing commandment concerning something they should do when they arrived at those two mountains in the Promised Land.

Behold, I set before you this day a blessing and a curse;
A blessing, if ye obey the commandments of the Lord your God, which I command you this day:

And a curse, if ye will not obey the commandments of the Lord your God, but turn aside out of the way which I command you this day, to go after other gods, which ye have not known.

And it shall come to pass, when the Lord thy God hath brought thee in unto the land whither thou goest to possess it, that thou shalt put the blessing upon mount Gerizim, and the curse upon mount Ebal. . . .

For ye shall pass over Jordan to go in to possess the land which the Lord your God giveth you, and ye shall possess it, and dwell therein.

And ye shall observe to do all the statutes and judgments which I set before you this day. (Deuteronomy 11:26, 29, 31–32.)

Joshua was commanded to bring the children of Israel to those two mountains and there have the law reread to them. The multitude was to be divided into two groups—half on Mount Ebal and the other half on Mount Gerizim. There Joshua and the Levites would recite unto the people "all the words of the law, the blessings and cursings" that would result from their obedience or disobedience (see Joshua 8:33–35). Additionally, there on those mountains the children of Israel would vocally reaffirm their covenant to obey the Lord (see Deuteronomy 27).

What a remarkable spectacle that must have been! I would have loved to see perhaps over a million people sitting and standing on both mountainsides. Can you imagine what it must have sounded like to have Joshua and the Levites shout out the curses for disobedience (and perhaps the people shouting back "Amen" in unison—see Deuteronomy 27:15–26) and the blessings for obedience (and the people again shouting "Amen")? What an unusual yet impressive teaching technique—an audiovisual extravaganza of monumental proportions! Undoubtedly those who participated would never forget this event and surely shared with their children and grandchildren their remarkable experiences on Mount Ebal or Mount Gerizim.

It was not just this event that served to remind the Israelites of their covenant, but the mountains themselves also stood as permanent reminders. Throughout the centuries every succeeding generation of Israelites could look upon Mount Ebal and Mount Gerizim and immediately remember them as the "Mount of Cursings" and the "Mount of Blessings." Deuteronomy chapters 27 and 28, and Leviticus 26, specify in great detail who would be blessed or cursed and what those blessings and curses would be.

| Mount Ebal<br>Cursings | Mount Gerizim<br>Blessings |
|---|---|
| **Those to be cursed:** | **Those to be blessed:** |
| "He that confirmeth not all the words of this law to do them" (Deuteronomy 27:26). | He that shall "hearken diligently unto the voice of the Lord thy God, to observe and to do all his commandments" (Deuteronomy 28:1). |

*Curses for Disobedience*

*Blessings of Obedience*

- Food and flocks diminished
- Soil won't produce
- Frustrations and difficulties
- Sickness
- Exploited and plundered by invaders
- Wives and homes given to others
- No harvest of orchards and vineyards
- Pestilences, drought, famine
- Bondage and destruction

- Productive fields and flocks
- Fertility of soil and fields
- Prosperity and posterity
- General well-being
- Enemies defeated and confounded
- Power over all nations
- Blessed in all endeavors
- Rain in season
- Windows of heaven opened

The entire history of the Israelites as recorded in the Old Testament can be seen in the lists of blessings and curses. Over and over again we see them blessed when they were righteous and faithful and cursed with these very specific curses when they rejected the Lord, disobeyed the law, and broke their covenants.

Ancient Israel's covenant, with its blessings and curses, did not simply require Israel to be obedient to the law of Moses and to avoid worshipping gods other than Jehovah. Implicit in the Israelites' vow to obey the Lord was their promise to follow his chosen prophets— something so important that it is one of the major recurring themes of the Old Testament. A real test of this promise came after Moses was taken from their midst and they had to follow a new prophet. To this prophet, Joshua, the Israelites said: "All that thou commandest us we will do, and whithersoever thou sendest us, we will go. According as we hearkened unto Moses in all things, so will we hearken unto thee." (Joshua 1:16–17.)

One of the most important themes woven throughout all of the books of the Old Testament is the importance of following the Lord's anointed prophets. Mount Ebal and Mount Gerizim stand even today as visual symbols of the blessings of obedience and the curses for rejection of the ancient prophets' teachings of the Lord's words. In graphic detail the Old Testament chronicles the consequences that befell the children of Israel when they rejected the prophets and turned their backs on the prophets' teachings.

Like the Israelites who covenanted on Ebal and Gerizim to obey the Lord, we too as Latter-day Saints have entered into a solemn covenant to "live by every word that proceedeth forth from the mouth of God" (D&C 84:44; see also Deuteronomy 8:3). Living by the word of God requires us also to willingly hear and heed the words of God given by the prophets, for as the Lord himself declared, "Whether by mine own voice or by the voice of my servants, it is the same" (D&C 1:38). And just as there were curses prescribed anciently for rejection of the Lord's law and prophets, in our dispensation the Lord has likewise declared: "And the arm of the Lord shall be revealed; and the day cometh that they who will not hear the voice of the Lord, neither the voice of his servants, neither give heed to the words of the prophets and apostles, shall be cut off from among the people" (D&C 1:14).

There are significant parallels between the Old Testament account of how the ancient Israelites responded to their prophets and the covenantal obligation of our day to sustain the Lord's anointed. We can learn from the examples of the ancients and apply those lessons to our own lives. Whether in ancient times or in our day, very real blessings attend the heeding of the words of the prophets, and very real curses attend the rejection of them.

## How the Lord's Prophets
## Were (and Are) Rejected

There are numerous examples of how the ancient Israelites rejected the prophets whom God had sent among them. Although the historical context and culture of their day may seem dramatically different from our own, the core causes for that rejection remain the same. As we look at these Old Testament examples, a relevant question should be asked: How are we today, specifically as members of the Church, doing these same things? It may be that these episodes in ancient Israelite history were recorded by inspired scribes and prophets not just to chronicle their history but to serve as instructional warnings to those of the last days. Like the Book of Mormon, these words speak to us "out of the dust," and were in reality written for our day. Perhaps the ancient Old Testament prophets, like Mormon and Moroni, saw our day and wrote these things we need to meet the challenges of our modern world.

## Discounting or Discrediting a Prophet's Divine Calling

An interesting account recorded in the book of Numbers illustrates how the Lord feels about those who would discount or discredit the prophets for any number of trivial reasons. Miriam and Aaron were grumbling about Moses' earlier marriage to an Ethiopian woman, and apparently were calling into question his role as a prophet because of that marriage (see Numbers 12:1–2; Josephus, *The Antiquities of the Jews*, 2.10.2). Perhaps they felt that, as his older siblings, they could rightfully criticize and correct him. Jehovah taught them in a dramatic manner that although Moses was their brother, he was the Lord's anointed prophet, and they had no right to find fault with him. To emphasize this important concept to them, the Lord caused a unique "curse" to befall Miriam.

> And the Lord came down in the pillar of the cloud, and stood in the door of the tabernacle, and called Aaron and Miriam: and they both came forth.
> And he said, Hear now my words: If there be a prophet among you, I the Lord will make myself known unto him in a vision, and I will speak unto him in a dream.
> My servant Moses is not so, who is faithful in all mine house.
> With him will I speak mouth to mouth, even apparently, and not in dark speeches; and the similitude of the Lord shall he behold: wherefore then were ye not afraid to speak against my servant Moses?
> And the anger of the Lord was kindled against them; and he departed.
> And the cloud departed from off the tabernacle; and, behold, Miriam became leprous, white as snow: and Aaron looked upon Miriam, and, behold, she was leprous.

And Aaron said unto Moses, Alas, my lord, I beseech thee, lay not the sin upon us, wherein we have done foolishly, and wherein we have sinned. (Numbers 12:5–11.)

It may seem to some that Jehovah treated Miriam rather harshly by using a temporary case of leprosy to make his point. Miriam and Aaron were not being blatantly wicked or rebellious. They felt justified in their rebuke of Moses and their attempted correction of him. From this interesting episode we see that discounting or discrediting the prophets of God, whatever the issue, is no light matter to the Lord, even if one feels justified.

Today some reject the prophets by virtue of some similarly misconceived justification—the obscurity of a prophet's background, his lack of academic credentials or professional training, his personal failings, or any other supposed deficiency. "Various excuses have been used over the centuries to dismiss these divine messengers," President Spencer W. Kimball stated.

There has been denial because the prophet comes from an obscure place. "Can there any good thing come out of Nazareth?" (John 1:46.) Jesus was also met with the question, "Is not this the carpenter's son?" (Matthew 13:55.) By one means or another, the swiftest method of rejection of the holy prophets has been to find a pretext, however false or absurd, to dismiss the man so that his message could also be dismissed. Prophets who were not glib, but slow of speech, were esteemed as naught. . . .

But while there are various excuses for rejection, there's a certain cause for this sad record. It must not be passed over: the cares of the world, the honors of the world, and looking beyond the mark are all determined by a persuasive few who presume to speak for all. . . .

These excuses for rejection of the prophets are poor excuses. The trouble with using obscurity as a test of validity is that God has so often chosen to bring forth his work out of obscurity. He has even said it would be so. (See D&C 1:30.) . . .

The trouble with rejection because of personal familiarity with the prophets is that the prophets are always somebody's son or somebody's neighbor. They are chosen from among the people, not transported from another planet, dramatic as that would be! . . .

. . . The trouble with rejecting the prophets because they lack prestige is that Paul, who knew something of rejection, forewarned

us when he said, speaking of the work of God, "For ye see your calling, brethren, how that not many wise men after the flesh, not many
mighty, not many noble, are called" (1 Corinthians 1:26).

In multiple scriptures the Lord has indicated that he will perform
his work through those whom the world regards as weak and despised. (In Conference Report, April 1978, pp. 115, 116.)

The lesson to be learned from the example of Miriam and Aaron is
that it is the Lord who calls his servants, and so it is he who has the
right to correct them. No matter what some may feel the prophets'
shortcomings are, the Lord upholds them. Those who call the
prophets into question will ultimately be brought to account for their
attitudes and behavior. They may not be stricken with leprosy as was
Miriam, but nonetheless there are spiritual effects that, if left untreated
by repentance, can bring about their spiritual demise.

## Murmuring, Criticism, Rebellion, and Apostasy

As Moses led the children of Israel through the desert wilderness,
it was not uncommon for some to grumble and murmur about various
conditions and difficult circumstances. Some would wonder, both pri-
vately and aloud, whether Moses had lost his way. Among others the
seeds of doubt sown by murmuring against the Lord's anointed grew
into dissension and ultimate rebellion. A group of murmurers and
critics led by Korah, Dathan, Abiram, and about two hundred and
fifty other leaders of the Camp of Israel rebelled against the prophetic
authority of Moses and Aaron. They claimed that they—and, for that
matter, all of the congregation   were every bit as holy as Moses and
therefore were entitled to lead the congregation. This challenge to
their priesthood leaders' authority surely started with secret doubts
about the inspiration and authority of Moses and later developed into
open defiance. Their criticism and contempt of the Lord's anointed,
which began as something internal, soon became an external leaven-
ing influence that adversely affected all of the Camp of Israel. Their attitude became one of "we are right and Moses is wrong"; they pre-
tended to know what was best for themselves because Moses was lost
and "out of touch."

The scriptures recount how this mutiny was put down in a dramatic and terrible way:

And the glory of the Lord appeared unto all the congregation.

And the Lord spake unto Moses and unto Aaron, saying,

Separate yourselves from among this congregation, that I may consume them in a moment.

And they fell upon their faces, and said, O God, the God of the spirits of all flesh, shall one man sin, and wilt thou be wroth with all the congregation?

And the Lord spake unto Moses, saying,

Speak unto the congregation, saying, Get you up from about the tabernacle of Korah, Dathan, and Abiram.

And Moses rose up and went unto Dathan and Abiram; and the elders of Israel followed him.

And he spake unto the congregation, saying, Depart, I pray you, from the tents of these wicked men, and touch nothing of theirs, lest ye be consumed in all their sins.

So they gat up from the tabernacle of Korah, Dathan, and Abiram, on every side: and Dathan and Abiram came out, and stood in the door of their tents, and their wives, and their sons, and their little children.

And Moses said, Hereby ye shall know that the Lord hath sent me to do all these works; for I have not done them of mine own mind.

If these men die the common death of all men, or if they be visited after the visitation of all men; then the Lord hath not sent me.

But if the Lord make a new thing, and the earth open her mouth, and swallow them up, with all that appertain unto them, and they go down quick into the pit; then ye shall understand that these men have provoked the Lord.

And it came to pass, as he had made an end of speaking all these words, that the ground clave asunder that was under them:

And the earth opened her mouth, and swallowed them up, and their houses, and all the men that appertained unto Korah, and all their goods.

They, and all that appertained to them, went down alive into the pit, and the earth closed upon them: and they perished from among the congregation.

And all Israel that were round about them fled at the cry of them: for they said, Lest the earth swallow us up also.

And there came out a fire from the Lord, and consumed the two hundred and fifty men that offered incense. (Numbers 16:20–35.)

Could any object lesson more dramatically impress upon the minds of the children of Israel the gravity of rebelling against the anointed servants of God? Although they had witnessed numerous miraculous manifestations of Moses' power and authority, these rebels chose to rely on the arm of flesh instead, thinking they knew better than did the prophet of God.

This story serves as a relevant warning to us today. Among us are those, who like Korah, Dathan, and Abiram, rebel against the Lord's anointed through criticism and backbiting, and often they ultimately end up in open rebellion against the established authority of the Church. The account demonstrates how deeply the Lord feels about our covenant to uphold, sustain, and not speak evil of the Lord's anointed. "I will give you one of the Keys of the mysteries of the Kingdom," the Prophet Joseph Smith declared. "It is an eternal principle, that has existed with God from all eternity: That man who rises up to condemn others, finding fault with the Church, saying that they are out of the way, while he himself is righteous, then know assuredly, that that man is in the high road to apostasy; and if he does not repent, will apostatize, as God lives." (*Teachings of the Prophet Joseph Smith* [Salt Lake City: Deseret Book Co., 1976], pp., 156–57.)

Another Old Testament account that teaches this same principle is the story of Elisha and the young men from the city of Bethel. Some Bible scholars doubt the historicity of the event because they feel that God would not deal so harshly with his children. But I believe that the account is indeed genuine and purposeful. It once again teaches in dramatic fashion the curses for rejecting the prophets, which is a major message of the Old Testament that the Lord does not want us to overlook.

> And [Elisha] went up from thence unto Bethel: and as he was going up by the way, there came forty [youths] from the city, and mocked him, and said unto him, Go up, thou bald head; go up, thou bald head.
>
> And he turned back, and looked on them, and cursed them in the name of the Lord. And there came forth two she bears out of the wood, and tare forty and two [youths] of them. (2 Kings 2:23–24.)

The young men from Bethel were the children of parents who were notorious for rejecting the prophets of God. As they demeaned and derided Elisha they were not merely participating in immature name-calling but were mocking a prophet of God, thereby questioning his divine mantle. It might seem that Elisha could have simply turned to these youth and said, "Sticks and stones may break my bones, but words will never hurt me." He could have ignored them, but instead he was inspired of God to do something not only as a curse upon the people of Bethel, but also as a vital lesson for us today. With the she-bears as an exclamation point, the Lord was declaring that one cannot demean, criticize, or mock the Lord's anointed with impunity.

Surely members of the Church who demean or criticize the living prophets and the Lord's anointed priesthood leaders have no overt desire to destroy the Church. They may think that they are being true and faithful and that their well-intentioned criticism will actually help the Church in some way. But thinking that one can be faithful in the kingdom while taking it upon oneself to murmur, criticize, attempt to correct, or demean in any manner the Lord's anointed is totally illogical. Such behavior and attitudes would be totally incongruous with the covenants we have taken upon ourselves to sustain, heed, and be loyal to the prophets of God.

Why does the Lord command us not to criticize his servants, recognizing that even they are human and fallible? Why does he condemn the evil speaking of the Lord's anointed in such harsh terms? Why are the curses or consequences for such behavior so severe? Perhaps the Lord's commandment is designed not so much to insulate or protect Church leaders from criticism, but rather to protect us from the deadly spiritual toxins that poison our own souls when we engage in such behavior. The Lord, in his mercy and love, seeks to insulate us from the soul-damaging consequences that will inevitably result from murmuring, criticizing, and fault-finding.

"No man, however strong he may be in the faith, however high in the Priesthood," President George Q. Cannon observed, "can speak evil of the Lord's anointed and find fault with God's authority on earth without incurring His displeasure. The Holy Spirit will withdraw itself from such a man, and he will go into darkness. This being the case, do you not see how important it is that we should be careful? However difficult it may be for us to understand the reason for any action of the authorities of the Church, we should not too hastily call their acts in question and pronounce them wrong." (*Gospel Truth*, comp. Jerreld L. Newquist, 2 vols. [Salt Lake City: Deseret Book Co., 1957–74], 1:278.)

## Indifference and Disobedience

There are many Old Testament examples of prophets being rejected through blatant, overt ways such as criticism and rebellion, but the more common way that ancient Israel rejected the Lord's servants was through indifference and disobedience. They may not have openly cursed or criticized the prophets, but rather, they just ignored them. The prophet Ezekiel, recording the Lord's words unto him, perhaps describes this best:

> Also, thou son of man, the children of thy people still are talking against thee by the walls and in the doors of the houses, and speak one to another, every one to his brother, saying, Come, I pray you, and hear what is the word that cometh forth form the Lord.
>
> And they come unto thee as the people cometh, and they sit before thee as my people, and they hear thy words, but they will not do them: for with their mouth they shew much love, but their heart goeth after their covetousness.
>
> And lo, thou art unto them as a very lovely song of one that hath a pleasant voice, and can play well on an instrument: for they hear thy words, but they do them not.
>
> And when this cometh to pass, (lo, it will come,) then shall they know that a prophet hath been among them. (Ezekiel 33:30–33.)

Ezekiel's words are as much a relevant warning to us today as a reflection of his own people's rejection of his divine role. Unfortunately there are those who profess to be faithful followers of God—members of the Church who have raised their hands to sustain the Lord's anointed, who pray for the prophets every day, who anxiously await the messages of general conference—and yet they "hear [his] words, but they do them not." The most common yet most insidious form of rejection of the prophets may be to listen to their words, acknowledge them, and perhaps even think their messages were inspiring, yet then go one's own way and do what one wants not what the Lord wants. Elder James E. Talmage declared:

> Do you ever think of the inconsistency of raising your right hand in solemn witness before God that you will sustain certain men who have been called and ordained, in the manner appointed of God, as your leaders, as prophets unto the people, verily as revelators, and

then, though perchance you come together and hear their words, going away and pay no attention to them? . . .

You cannot, we cannot, pass by lightly the words that come by way of counsel and instruction from the ordained servants of God, and escape the inevitable penalty of that neglect. Nevertheless, we have our agency; we may choose to disobey, but we must take the consequences of that neglect. (In Conference Report, October 1921, pp. 187, 188.)

## Modern-Day Curses for Rejection of the Prophets

The curses that were shouted out to the ancient Israelites from Ebal were mostly of a physical or temporal nature. Similarly, the curses that befell the ancients who rejected and repudiated the prophets were also physical and violently visible. Today, however, the curses are less visible, yet just as real. One can criticize or make fun of the leaders of the kingdom, rebel against their words, or totally disregard their counsel without fear of being cursed with leprosy, sucked into giant sinkholes, or mauled by she-bears, but inevitably other curses will follow. Though not as visible, these curses may be more spiritually frightening and eternally deadly.

"If they will not hearken to my voice, nor unto the voice of these men whom I have appointed, they shall not be blest," declared the Lord in this dispensation. "Instead of blessings, ye, by your own works, bring cursings, wrath, indignation, and judgments upon your own heads, by your follies." (D&C 124:46, 48.) What are these cursings of God that are promised to befall those who reject the living prophets? They may not seem as sensational as some of the Old Testament penalties, but they make she-bears and leprosy pale in comparison. Concerning those who criticized and persecuted the Prophet Joseph Smith—and, by extension, those who speak evil of any of the Lord's anointed in the last days—the Lord declared:

Cursed are all those that shall lift up the heel against mine anointed, saith the Lord, and cry they have sinned when they have not sinned before me, saith the Lord, but have done that which was meet in mine eyes, and which I commanded them.

But those who cry transgression do it because they are the servants of sin, and are the children of disobedience themselves.

And those who swear falsely against my servants, that they might bring them into bondage and death—

Wo unto them; because they have offended my little ones they shall be severed from the ordinances of mine house.

Their basket shall not be full, their houses and their barns shall perish, and they themselves shall be despised by those that flattered them.

They shall not have right to the priesthood, nor their posterity after them from generation to generation. (D&C 121:16–21.)

Being cut off from the blessings of the temple and the priesthood, losing the comfort and guidance of the Holy Spirit, suffering feelings of insecurity and disappointment, and forfeiting the prosperity of the Lord are among those curses that befall those who murmur against, criticize, rebel against, and lightly regard the prophets of God. Who among us would not choose to have the physical malady of leprosy or the wounds inflicted by wild animals that heal in time, rather than experience those irreversible spiritual consequences described in the scriptures?

Elder Harold B. Lee declared:

I want to bear you my testimony that the experience I have had has taught me that those who criticize the leaders of this Church are showing signs of a spiritual sickness which, unless curbed, will bring about eventually spiritual death. I want to bear my testimony as well that those who in public seek by their criticism, to belittle our leaders or bring them into disrepute, will bring upon themselves more hurt than upon those whom they seek thus to malign. I have watched over the years, and I have read of the history of many of those who fell away from this Church, and I want to bear testimony that no apostate who ever left this Church ever prospered as an influence in his community thereafter. (In Conference Report, October 1947, p. 67.)

In its many disguises, criticism of the Lord's chosen servants sows the seeds of doubt, which may spring forth into disbelief. This in turn causes one to disregard the prophets' teachings, which nearly always leads to spiritual defiance and eventual destruction. The curses of Mount Ebal are just as real and relevant today as in the days of Moses and Joshua.

## How the Lord's Prophets Were
## (and Are) Accepted

The Old Testament also gives many numerous inspiring accounts of faithful men and women who received the prophets of God and were blessed thereby. The peoples of the Old Testament manifested various levels of obedience and acceptance, but the two ends of the continuum have specific application to us today. From Mount Gerizim the blessings of obeying God's laws and the words of his prophets were read out to the Israelites. Mount Gerizim still stands today as a reminder to us that there are very real blessings for obeying the prophets, just as there were (and are) very real curses for disobedience.

### Accepting and Abiding the Simple, Quiet, Unspectacular Counsel of Living Prophets

Not all of the prophets' counsel and teachings require unusual sacrifice or extraordinary effort to obey. Sometimes the prophets ask us to do simple, even seemingly small things, but obeying even the small things yields great blessings. There are several examples of this in the Old Testament, but two specific accounts powerfully illustrate this concept.

As the children of Israel journeyed in the desert they became afflicted by poisonous serpents, "and they bit the people; and much people of Israel died" (Numbers 21:6). The Lord Jehovah inspired Moses to make a serpent of brass and place it on a pole for all the people to see. The prophetic prescription was given to the Israelites: look upon the brazen serpent and you will live. As simple as that! Look and live—that's all. Now, I can imagine some of the people thinking such counsel was too simplistic or superficial, that they wanted "meat instead milk." So while they muttered, "Where is my snake-bite kit?" or "Send me a doctor!" and while they made all kinds of mortal attempts to escape the snakes, people were being bitten and dying around them. It could have been otherwise if they had heeded Moses' counsel to look and live, but to them it seemed too simple. And so, rather than obeying simple counsel, some died instead. (See Alma 33:19–20; 37:46–47.)

Another interesting example of following the simple counsel and teachings of the prophets involves the prophet Elisha and a Syrian military leader. While the Syrians were occupying much of Israel an army captain named Naaman became afflicted with leprosy. He may have thought of returning to his own physician in Damascus to be treated, but his wife's Israelite servant said that he could be healed through the prophet Elisha.

The prophet's prescription for Naaman's leprosy was "Go and wash in Jordan seven times, and thy flesh shall come again to thee, and thou shalt be clean" (2 Kings 5:10). Naaman couldn't believe his ears. Bathing in the muddy Jordan River as a cure for leprosy? He must have thought the Israelites were crazy to believe that Elisha was a prophet of God when he gave such "dumb counsel." Nothing scientific or intellectual or even logical, just simple prophetic counsel: bathe in the Jordan River seven times and you will be clean! And to make matters worse in Naaman's mind, Elisha didn't even come to him in person but sent a messenger to speak to Naaman.

> But Naaman was wroth, and went away, and said, Behold, I thought, He will surely come out to me, and stand, and call on the name of the Lord his God, and strike his hand over the place, and recover the leper.
>
> Are not Abana and Pharpar, rivers of Damascus, better than all the waters of Israel? may I not wash in them, and be clean? So he turned and went away in a rage.
>
> And his servants came near, and spake unto him, and said, My father, if the prophet had bid thee do some great thing, wouldest thou not have done it? how much rather then, when he saith to thee, Wash, and be clean?
>
> Then went he down, and dipped himself seven times in Jordan, according to the saying of the man of God: and his flesh came again like unto the flesh of a little child, and he was clean. (2 Kings 5:11–14.)

Sometimes we are like Naaman in that we would gladly do the "big things" the prophet might ask of us, like pack up our bags and move to Jackson County to build the New Jerusalem. But when the counsel is simple, not sensational, we may not be as enthused, such as when we are urged to hold family home evenings, say our prayers, read our scriptures, or do home or visiting teaching. If we are willing to "do some great thing" when commanded by the prophet, why not also obey the simple things and be blessed?

*Obeying the Prophets Even When It Requires*
*Significant Sacrifice or Inconvenience*

At the other end of the acceptance-of-prophets continuum are Old Testament examples of those who willingly obeyed the Lord's anointed even when it may have seemed impossible to do so. One of my all-time favorite stories in the Old Testament that illustrates this kind of faith is the account of the prophet Elijah's encounter with the widow of Zarephath (see 1 Kings 17). Because wicked King Ahab "did more to provoke the Lord God of Israel to anger than all the kings of Israel that were before him" (1 Kings 16:33), Elijah had sealed the heavens so that it would not rain, nor would even dew be formed. As a result, all of Israel suffered from a great drought and famine.

At the height of the suffering and privations, a widow in the village of Zarephath, recognizing that she had come to the end of all of her foodstuffs, prepared a simple meal of bread for her son and herself. She knew that when this meal was consumed there would be no more flour or oil and they would surely starve to death. At that point Elijah showed up on her doorstep and asked her to feed him what she had prepared. She could have said, "This is all that my son and I have left. We can't share. Go down the street to the Joneses' house—they have a year's supply." The prophet's command may have seemed too inconvenient or difficult, even impossible to obey, yet the widow obeyed his words and gave her last morsel of food to him.

Instead of dying of starvation, the widow of Zarephath—an example of faith in the Lord and obedience to his anointed servants—was blessed in a most miraculous manner.

> And Elijah said unto her, Fear not; go and do as thou has said: but make me thereof a little cake first, and bring it unto me, and after make for thee and for thy son.
>
> For thus saith the Lord God of Israel, The barrel of meal shall not waste, neither shall the cruse of oil fail, until the day that the Lord sendeth rain upon the earth.
>
> And she went and did according to the saying of Elijah: and she, and he, and her house, did eat many days.
>
> And the barrel of meal wasted not, neither did the cruse of oil fail, according to the word of the Lord, which he spoke by Elijah. (1 Kings 17:13–16.)

Not only did her willingness to obey the prophet even when his commandment seemed unrealistic produce a miracle of the continuation of her food storage, but she received an even more remarkable blessing for her obedience. Shortly after this test her only son became ill and died. In despair, she turned to Elijah.

> And he said unto her, Give me thy son. And he took him out of her bosom, and carried him up into a loft, where he abode, and laid him upon his own bed. . . .
> And he stretched himself upon the child three times, and cried unto the Lord, and said, O Lord my God, I pray thee, let this child's soul come into him again.
> And the Lord heard the voice of Elijah; and the soul of the child came into him again, and he revived.
> And Elijah took the child, and brought him down out of the chamber into the house, and delivered him unto his mother: and Elijah said, See, thy son liveth.
> And the woman said to Elijah, Now by this I know that thou art a man of God, and that the word of the Lord in thy mouth is truth. (1 Kings 17:19, 21–24.)

## MODERN-DAY BLESSINGS FOR
## OBEYING THE PROPHETS

Many today, when faced with counsel and commandments from the prophets of God that may interfere with their own desires, reject those counsels because they feel they are "exceptions." On the other hand, those who replace their fears with faith, as President Hugh B. Brown admonished, will follow the prophets even when it seems too difficult to do so (see *The Abundant Life* [Salt Lake City: Bookcraft, 1965], p. 353). "Is any thing too hard for the Lord?" (Genesis 18:14.) To those who will faithfully obey the words of the prophets of God, the Lord has promised rich blessings. They may not be in the form of a never-diminishing storeroom of food or the miraculous raising of a loved one from death, but the promise of blessings for hearkening to the words of the prophets is as rock-solid-sure as Mount Gerizim.

In a revelation given in 1830 the Lord commanded the Saints to "give heed" to the Prophet Joseph Smith. Undoubtedly the same words apply to the Saints and prophets of succeeding generations: "Wherefore, meaning the church, thou shalt give heed unto all his words and commandments which he shall give unto you as he receiveth them, walking in all holiness before me; For his word ye shall receive, as if from mine own mouth, in all patience and faith. For by doing these things the gates of hell shall not prevail against you; yea, and the Lord God will disperse the powers of darkness from before you, and cause the heavens to shake for your good, and his name's glory." (D&C 21:4–6.)

The gates of hell are closed, the powers of darkness are dispersed, and the heavens shake for our good only as we are illuminated and led by the power of the Spirit. The guidance of the Holy Spirit is one of those profound blessings promised to those who will heed the teachings and warnings of the Lord's chosen servants. Elder Neal A. Maxwell wrote: "A lack of obedience to the leaders will, therefore, mean that we will not have the precious promptings of the Spirit, which we need personally—so much and so often. This potential loss would be reason enough for us to be obedient to the prophets, for apparently we cannot have one without the other. Vital as the words of the prophets are, these come to us only periodically. We need the directions of the Spirit daily, even hourly." (All These Things Shall Give Thee Experience [Salt Lake City: Deseret Book Co., 1979], p. 104.)

Closely aligned with the blessing of the constant companionship of the Holy Ghost is the spiritual and sometimes even physical, financial, and emotional safety promised to those who will faithfully "treasure up" the protective words of the living prophets. President Spencer W. Kimball promised that "if we will live the gospel and follow the counsel of the leaders of the Church, we will be blessed to avoid many of the problems that plague the world" ("A Deep Commitment to the Principles of Welfare Service," Ensign, May 1980, p. 92). The path to safety in the last days, as in the time of the ancient Israelites, is found in being loyal to the prophets of God and obedient to their counsel.

Just as the curses for rejecting the prophets have both immediate and long-term consequences, the blessings for hearkening to them benefit us both here and hereafter. Exaltation, with its accompanying "thrones, kingdoms, principalities, and powers" (D&C 132:19), is reserved for those who have accepted and followed the Lord, which also encompasses following his authorized servants. "For he that receiveth my servants receiveth me," the Lord declared; "and he that receiveth me receiveth my Father; and he that receiveth my Father receiveth my Father's kingdom; therefore all that my Father hath shall be given unto him" (D&C 84:36–38). In this promise our eternal safety is secured.

Each time I raise my hand in a vote of common consent to sustain the leaders of the Church (see D&C 20:65; 26:2), I am reminded of Mount Ebal and Mount Gerizim. For I am doing today what the ancient Israelites did on the slopes of those mountains—I am covenanting to be obedient to God and hearken unto the counsel of the Lord's anointed. With that act I pledge my loyalty, love, and obedience, and, in turn, the Lord has promised me blessings untold both here and hereafter. But if I reject the Lord's servants not only will I forfeit rich blessings but will reap instead a harvest of "cursings, wrath, indignation, and judgments" worse than she-bears or sinkholes (see D&C 124:48).

May we earnestly strive for the blessings promised those who hearken to all the words of God. President Lorenzo Snow promised:

> No man can be more happy than by obeying the living prophet's counsel. You may go from east to west, from north to south, and tread this footstool of the Lord all over, and you cannot find a man that can make himself happy in this Church, only by applying the counsel of the living prophet in this life; it is a matter of impossibility for a man to receive a fulness who is not susceptible of receiving and carrying out the living prophet's counsel. An individual that applies the counsel of this Church is bound to increase in all that is good, for there is a fountain of counsel which the Lord has established. He has made it, has deposited that counsel, that wisdom and those riches, and it will circumscribe all that pertains unto good, unto salvation; all that pertains unto peace and unto happiness; all things that pertain to glory and to the exaltation of the Saints in this world and in the world to come. (*The Teachings of Lorenzo Snow*, comp. Clyde J. Williams [Salt Lake City: Bookcraft, 1984], pp. 86–87.)

*Hath the Lord as great delight in burnt offerings and sacrifices,
as in obeying the voice of the Lord? Behold, to obey is better
than sacrifice, and to hearken than the fat of rams.*
*—1 Samuel 15:22*

## CHAPTER SEVEN

# *Obedience Is Better Than Sacrifice*

Perhaps every parent of teenagers has had experiences similar to mine. My teenage daughter came home long after her curfew one night. When I told her that she would be punished, she protested my decision, saying, "But, Dad, there was a good reason for my being late. My friend needed my advice on something very important and it just took longer than I expected."

On another occasion, my wife and I had to leave town for a few days. As we left we told the kids that they were not to have any parties in our house while we were gone. When we returned my neighbor asked me what had been going on at our house a few nights earlier. He then informed me that he couldn't drive his car into his own driveway because there had been so many cars parked in our cul-de-sac. "There must have been fifty cars parked around here," he stated. "There were a zillion kids coming in and out of your house all night. Tiffany must have been having a party." When I asked my daughter about what the neighbor said, she defensively stated, "It wasn't a party! I just had some friends over." (I guess in a teenager's mind there is a fine line between a party and having fifty to sixty friends over for a friendly visit.) "Besides," Tiffany added, "we cleaned the house really well. Doesn't it look good?" (The house not only was still standing but was in really good shape. I became somewhat suspicious of the cleaning job, since Tiffany isn't always keen on cleaning things. My wife's reaction, however, was, "She can have friends over more often if she cleans the house like this!")

In each of these cases—and I could describe hundreds of others like them—my children justified their disobedience of family rules and specific parental instructions on the grounds of doing some good deed. There is also the "technicality defense," such as my daughter's claim that she wasn't *technically* disobeying us because "it wasn't a party; I just had some friends over." Many times I have tried to teach my children that when they disobey, it doesn't matter what they call it, they have still disobeyed. If they only "kind of" disobey, they may not be blatantly rebellious, but they are still disobedient. The scriptures seem to teach that being obedient is pretty much black and white. It's like being pregnant—you either are or you aren't!

One of the great messages of the Old Testament that has relevance for us today is the concept of strict obedience to the commandments of God. No account better illustrates this important theme than that of Saul's disobedience of the prophet Samuel's commandment. Saul was the king of Israel, but Samuel was the Lord's anointed prophet. Inspired of the Lord, Samuel commanded Saul to take the Israelite armies against the Amalekites "and utterly destroy all that they have, and spare them not; but slay both man and woman, infant and suckling, ox and sheep, camel and ass" (1 Samuel 15:3). There had been precedent for this kind of "divine annihilation." Joshua had been similarly commanded not to spare any remnant of the Canaanites, lest the Israelites be led away to pagan gods.

Saul went forth in battle, as commanded by the prophet, and "utterly destroyed all the people with the edge of the sword" (1 Samuel 15:8). He was *almost* totally obedient. He did kill *almost* all of the Amalekites—all except their king. Saul thought it would be a good idea to bring the king back as a prisoner of war, like a trophy that could be displayed to the people. And he *almost* totally destroyed all of the flocks and possessions of the Amalekites as he had been commanded, for "every thing that was vile and refuse, that they destroyed utterly."

But then Saul had another one of his "good ideas"—to keep the best of the spoils of the Amalekite flocks, "the best of the sheep, and of the oxen, and of the fatlings, and the lambs, and all that was good, and [he] would not utterly destroy them" (1 Samuel 15:9). Perhaps he thought it would be such a waste to destroy all the "good stuff"—the spoils of war that could be used to reward his men for their efforts. And then there was Saul's "good idea" to save the best of the Amalekite flocks so that they could be used as sacrifices to Jehovah.

Jubilant in their victory, and with King Saul riding proudly at their head, the Israelite soldiers returned home with the spoils of their destruction of the Amalekites. When Samuel met Saul, the Prophet didn't look happy. "Blessed be thou of the Lord," Saul triumphantly declared unto Samuel; "I have performed the commandment of the Lord" (1 Samuel 15:13). Mission accomplished—or so he thought.

Samuel asked him, "What meaneth then this bleating of the sheep in mine ears, and the lowing of the oxen which I hear?" (1 Samuel 15:14.) The king expected praises and compliments for his extraordinary accomplishment, but instead he received a terrible rebuke. "And Samuel said, When thou wast little in thine own sight, wast thou not made the head of the tribes of Israel, and the Lord anointed thee king over Israel? And the Lord sent thee on a journey, and said, Go and utterly destroy the sinners the Amalekites, and fight against them until they be consumed. Wherefore then didst thou not obey the voice of the Lord, but didst fly upon the spoil, and didst evil in the sight of the Lord?" (1 Samuel 15:17–19.)

Unwilling to admit his grave disobedience, Saul tried the "technicality defense." "I have obeyed the voice of the Lord, and have gone the way which the Lord sent me," he said, ". . . But the people took of the spoil." (1 Samuel 15:20, 21.) He was technically obedient, or so he thought, because he didn't personally take of the spoils (even though he personally took Agag, the Amalekite king—Saul must have conveniently forgotten that fact).

When he saw that the "passing the buck" explanation didn't have much impact on Samuel, he then tried the "greater good" justification, which children give their parents all the time: "I know that I did wrong, but the good that I was doing was more important than the wrong I did." Saul tried to justify his disobedience by explaining that he and his men thought it a good idea not to kill the best of the Amalekite flocks because they could then be sacrificed to the God of

Israel. I am sure that Saul thought this rationalization was his "trump card" and that he could appeal to the spiritual side of the prophet with an emphasis on his good deeds that demonstrated his devotion to God. What could be a nobler cause, he undoubtedly thought, than sacrifices unto Jehovah?

Saul soon found out what was indeed the "greater good" in the eyes of the Lord. "And Samuel said, Hath the Lord as great delight in burnt offerings and sacrifices, as in obeying the voice of the Lord? Behold, to obey is better than sacrifice, and to hearken than the fat of rams.

For rebellion is as the sin of witchcraft, and stubbornness is as iniquity and idolatry. Because thou hast rejected the word of the Lord, he hath also rejected thee from being king." (1 Samuel 15:22–23.)

What a sad ending to the reign of a king who had earlier been described as "a choice young man, and a goodly: and there was not among the children of Israel a goodlier person than he" (1 Samuel 9:2). It must have pained Samuel terribly to tell Saul—the very king he had presented before the people as their king—that he had been rejected by the Lord. Samuel was so grieved that he even "cried unto the Lord all night" (1 Samuel 15:11), hoping to dissuade the Lord from punishing Saul so severely; yet to no avail. Saul was rejected by the Lord not because of any lack of potential, competence, or accomplishments, but because he had failed to obey. How could the Lord fully trust someone who wouldn't obey him or who obeyed him only sometimes? Obedience to the Lord's commandments was more important than any other trait Saul could have possessed as king. Saul's failure to obey with exactness and honor was counted more heavily *against* him than all of his successes, talents, and kingly achievements counted *for* him. The disobedience of King Saul was an inexcusable that overwhelmed all of his commendables.

I learned this principle in a rather painful way as a missionary. While studying Danish in the Language Training Mission at Ricks College, in the days before the Missionary Training Center was located in Provo, I had been called to be the leader of the missionaries who were going to Denmark. As the district leader I was responsible for periodically conducting sacrament meeting for the missionaries in the LTM. When it became our group's turn for the sacrament meeting, I diligently made all of the assignments—speakers, music, administration of the sacrament. I tried very hard to be responsible and made sure that everything was properly taken care of, even following up on the assignments to make sure that the meeting would run smoothly.

When it came time for the meeting, everything was in place. I was conducting and was pleased with how well things were going. The talks were excellent, the musical number superb. I was sure it was the very best program that had been presented in the LTM. I was proud of the Danes—we knew we were the best!

There was only one problem: there were still ten minutes left before the sacrament meeting was to close. The LTM mission president, who was sitting beside me on the stand, leaned over and whispered in my ear, "Why don't you consider calling up from the audience one of the elders to bear his testimony?" I considered it and then dismissed it. I thought the meeting had been just fine, and so, as the district leader, I took the initiative to go ahead and close the meeting. I thought initiative was a virtue. You know the scripture: "Men should . . . do many things of their own free will, and bring to pass much righteousness" (D&C 58:27). Nobody would be upset about getting out a few minutes early, I reasoned. It all appeared to me to be a "good idea."

After the closing prayer, as we were heading to the cafeteria for our Sunday meal, the mission president asked if he could speak with me for a few minutes. I was expecting compliments for the fine program that my district had provided and expressions of praise and appreciation for all of my hard work in organizing the sacrament meeting, or maybe some positive comments about my leadership and how well I had conducted the meeting. None of those expectations was what I received. Instead, I received a profound yet painful chastening.

"When your file leader asks you to do something, you are wise to obey his counsel," the mission president stated.

"But I just thought it was a suggestion," I lamely responded. "Anyway, I didn't think anyone would mind getting out early." I could tell that my explanations weren't very convincing. "I just thought I would take the initiative and close the meeting while the Spirit was so strong." Oh, I was quite impressed with that explanation. Spiritual initiative—wow, that was powerful, I thought. The rebuke that came in return I will never forget.

"Obedience is even more important than initiative," the president said. "There is nothing more important for a missionary than learning to be perfectly obedient. If you are not obedient," he continued, "it will not matter what other skills or attributes you may have. Obedience is more important than initiative, teaching skills, personality, hard work, or anything else. Obedience is the vital key to success as a missionary."

His words still ring in my ears these many years later. At first I was hurt, feeling that he hadn't considered my good explanations and justification for the action I had taken. I wanted to remind him that, in fact, it had been given merely as a "suggestion." My closing the meeting early was not a big deal, I thought over and over again. It certainly had not detracted from the overall spirit of the meeting. But that was not the point. I was like King Saul—I had good motives for what I did, and even thought my ideas were pretty good, yet I had still disobeyed. Nothing can take the place of obedience.

In striking contrast to Saul's disobedience is the faithful obedience of Abraham. If anyone ever had reason to question a commandment or wonder if there was an alternative way, it would have been Father Abraham. He had previously been rescued by an angel of God when he was about to be sacrificed to pagan gods—an action in which his own father was complicit (see Abraham 1). What a terrible irony that many years later Abraham was commanded by God to take his own beloved son the son that he and Sarah had waited so long to have and who had truly been a "miracle baby"—and offer that cherished son as a burnt sacrifice unto Jehovah (see Genesis 22:1–2).

I have often tried to imagine what was going on in Abraham's mind and heart after he received that commandment. I am sure that he must have been tempted to ask the Lord to repeat the commandment because he wasn't sure he had heard God correctly. Or perhaps there were a million other questions that entered Abraham's mind regarding this command. He probably did some of his own thinking and arrived at possible justifications for not doing exactly what the Lord required. Perhaps he came up with his own "good ideas" he wanted to suggest to God as possible other ways of doing things.

No matter what commingling of thoughts and emotions buzzed through Father Abraham's mind, the scriptures clearly state that he obeyed, with no questions asked, no excuses given, no delaying. The very next verse after the scripture relating the Lord's commandment to Abraham states, "And Abraham rose up early in the morning, and saddled his ass, and took two of his young men with him, and Isaac his son, and clave the wood for the burnt offering, and rose up, and went unto the place of which God had told him" (Genesis 22:3). The phrase "rose up early in the morning" gives us insight into Abraham's faith and willingness to obey. Despite his own fears and questions, he obeyed *immediately*. The blessings that came to Father Abraham, and to his seed as well, came not because of any other accomplishment or remarkable achievements or earthly credentials; they came to him because of his complete obedience.

"For now I know that thou fearest God," the angel declared to Abraham as he spared Isaac's life, "seeing thou has not withheld thy son, thine only son from me" (Genesis 22:12). Nothing was more important to Abraham—not his own feelings or aspirations, nor even the tender feelings of his brokenhearted wife or the very life of his only son—than obeying the word of the Lord. Like the two thousand Lamanite stripling warriors in Helaman's army, Abraham "did obey and observe to perform every word of command with exactness" (Alma 57:21). This is also what the Lord expects of us today if we are to be righteous and prove ourselves faithful at all times and in all circumstances and at all costs.

My father taught me a valuable principle when I was young that I have tried to pass on to my own children. It is a further illumination of the doctrine of obedience as taught in the scriptures and as seen in the contrasting examples of Saul and Abraham. As a typical youth, whenever I was "commanded" by my parents to do something or not do something, I usually responded with, "Why?" or "Give me a good reason" (or preferably thirteen good reasons). I have since learned from being a parent myself that such questions are merely rhetorical; there is no answer, however sound or reasonable, that adequately satisfies. It is usually just a child's immature response to counsel that he or she doesn't want to obey. My father wouldn't get dragged into arguments or lengthy discussions about all the possible reasons for the counsel. A man of few words, he always told me the same story. As a young boy, fighting my own natural urges to disobey and do what I wanted to do, I learned about Adam's obedience to God's commandment to offer sacrifices. Dad would tell me that even Adam didn't always understand (or, as in my case, agree with) the commandments, but he obeyed for a higher reason.

I heard my father quote a particular scriptural passage many times in my youth. Today I use it to teach my own children that obeying God simply as an act of faith and submission to the Lord is a good enough reason in and of itself. "And he gave unto them commandments, that they should worship the Lord their God, and should offer the firstlings of their flocks, for an offering unto the Lord. And Adam was obedient unto the commandments of the Lord.

And after many days an angel of the Lord appeared unto Adam, saying: Why dost thou offer sacrifices unto the Lord? And Adam said unto him: I know not, save the Lord commanded me." (Moses 4:5–6.)

## OBEDIENCE BRINGS FORTH
## THE BLESSINGS OF HEAVEN

Even if we don't fully understand the reasons behind the Lord's commandments, as was the case with Adam, or if we think the commandment defies all logic, such as may have been the case for Abraham, we can still rest assured that the commandments of God are always given to bless and protect us and to ensure our ultimate happiness. "Whatever God commands is right," the Prophet Joseph declared (*Teachings of the Prophet Joseph Smith* [Salt Lake City: Deseret Book Co., 1976], p. 256). On another occasion he wrote, "Therefore let your heart be comforted; live in strict obedience to the commandments of God, and walk humbly before Him, and He will exalt thee in His own due time" (*History of the Church* 1:408). The early Saints were chastened by the Lord for their disobedience of his previous command to build a temple (see D&C 95:1–6). They could have given many excuses or justifications, such as their poverty, the need to establish their own farms and homes, the severe persecution by their enemies, and so on, but they were only hurting themselves by delaying their obedience. God didn't demand a temple and their obedience for his sake, but rather for theirs. He had promised to "endow them with power" if they would obey (see D&C 43:16; 95:8). No benefit or advantage that could have been gained by disregarding or delaying obedience of this commandment could in any way compare with the blessings of heaven that were forfeited through their disobedience.

One warm spring day when I was in junior high school, I learned a valuable lesson about obedience. Unfortunately it was one of those difficult learning experiences we sometimes must have. My friends had invited me to go swimming with them in an irrigation canal near our home. It was dangerous, but that just added all the more to the enticement and excitement. When I asked my mother for permission to go with my friends, she told me I couldn't go.

"Give me a good reason," I demanded.

"Because I just don't feel right about it," she responded.

That was the worst possible reason that could be given to a teenager who didn't want to have to stay home. Besides, I was an Eagle Scout, a good swimmer with the lifesaving merit badge to my credit. What could possibly happen?

After a spirited discussion, and when I saw that my mother was not budging from her decision, I disobeyed her and it nearly cost me my life. While having a great time floating the canal, I noticed that a younger swimmer, a boy of perhaps eight or nine, had been separated from the tube he was floating on. He had scrambled to the shore, but his tube floated downstream into another canal and was caught up against the irrigation headgate that controlled the flow of water into the farmers' fields. Being an Eagle Scout and an all-around nice kid, I decided to do a good turn, as prescribed by the Boy Scout motto, and swim down the canal and retrieve the young boy's float tube. It all seemed so noble until I was sucked under the headgate. The jagged metal of the bottom of the headgate tore the skin off my chest and held me under water for what seemed like an eternity. I could have easily been trapped under the headgate and drowned, but miraculously I slipped through, and my friends dragged me out of the canal to the shore. I was lucky to be alive.

That night my mother saw the deep scratches on my chest and asked what had happened. Sheepishly I told her how I had disobeyed her. She didn't need to scold me; I felt bad enough just having to face her disappointment. It would have seemed silly for me to then justify my disobedience, like King Saul, by explaining how I, as a good Boy Scout, had done a "good turn" in helping the little boy get his float tube back. I could almost hear her response to such a notion: "Well, that's all good and dandy, but obedience is better than even doing good turns."

## RIGHTEOUSNESS IS MORE IMPORTANT THAN RITUAL

Just as obedience is more desired of the Lord than sacrifice, real righteousness is better than ritual. The prophet Isaiah criticized the ancient Israelites' hollow involvement in the ordinances and rituals of their faith because they failed in the "weightier matters." They might have responded to his rebuke with comments like, "Why condemn us? We are active in the Church and regularly say our prayers and offer the prescribed sacrifices." Isaiah reminded them that all of these good deeds were vain unless accompanied by obedience and faithful keeping of the Lord's commandments.

> Hear the word of the Lord, ye rulers of Sodom; give ear unto the law of our God, ye people of Gomorrah.
>
> To what purpose is the multitude of your sacrifices unto me? saith the Lord: I am full of the burnt offerings of rams, and the fat of fed beasts; and I delight not in the blood of bullocks, or of lambs, or of he goats.
>
> When ye come to appear before me, who hath required this at your hand, to tread my courts?
>
> Bring no more vain oblations; incense is an abomination unto me; the new moons and sabbaths, the calling of assemblies, I cannot away with; it is iniquity, even the solemn meeting.
>
> Your new moons and your appointed feasts my soul hateth: they are a trouble unto me; I am weary to bear them.
>
> And when ye spread forth your hands, I will hide mine eyes from you: yea, when ye make many prayers, I will not hear: your hands are full of blood.
>
> Wash you, make you clean; put away the evil of your doings from before mine eyes; cease to do evil;
>
> Learn to do well. (Isaiah 1:10–17.)

More important to the Lord than observing all of the holy days and sacrifices prescribed under the law of Moses, and more important than even prayer, is simple obedience, personal righteousness, and keeping the commandments of God.

The message to us today is that it doesn't matter what good turns we are doing as members of the Church—what callings we hold, what meetings we attend, how often we go to the temple, how many minutes a day we read our scriptures, or how many acts of charitable service and compassion we render—if we are not obedient to the commandments of God. Just being active is not the same as being righteous. As the Lord himself declared, only two things offend God and one of those is disobedience (see D&C 59:21).

The Prophet Joseph Smith learned firsthand that no amount of good works or spiritual experiences can compensate for failure to obey the Lord. After he had repeatedly questioned the Lord's commands—which questioning led to Martin Harris's loss of the 116 pages of Book of Mormon manuscript—the Lord declared: "For although a man may have many revelations, and have power to do many mighty works, yet if he boasts in his own strength, and sets at naught the counsels of God, and follows after the dictates of his own will and carnal desires, he must fall and incur the vengeance of a just God upon him" (D&C 3:4). Similarly, during his earthly ministry Jesus taught, "Many will say to me in that day, Lord, Lord, have we not prophesied in thy name? and in thy name have cast out devils? and in thy name done many wonderful works? And then will I profess unto them, I never knew you: depart from me, ye that work iniquity." (Matthew 7:22–23.) Why will people who have done all these wonderful good turns still not be allowed into the kingdom of heaven? The Savior emphatically stated that just saying "Lord, Lord" and doing good deeds would not be enough; one must do "the will of my Father which is in heaven" (Matthew 7:21).

King Saul sadly learned that disobedience exacts a terrible toll. For him it cost him his kingdom. The Lord has promised us a crown of eternal life and a kingdom far greater than Saul's; indeed, he has promised us "thrones, kingdoms, principalities, and powers, dominions, all heights and depths" if we will be obedient (see D&C 132:19). Through Joseph Smith he has stated, "I, the Lord, am bound when ye do what I say; but when ye do not what I say, ye have no promise" (D&C 82:10). Obedience yields blessings. "If ye be willing and obedient," Isaiah taught, "ye shall eat the good of the land" (Isaiah 1:19). Blessings predicated upon obedience transcend even the goodness of the earth, for they also include the riches of heaven. Elder Joseph F. Smith testified: "Every good and perfect gift comes from the Father of Light, who is no respecter of persons and in whom there is no variableness, nor shadow of turning. To please him we must not only worship him with thanksgiving and praise, but render willing obedience to his commandments. By so doing he is bound to bestow his blessings; for it is upon this principle (obedience to law) that all blessings are predicated." (*Gospel Doctrine* [Salt Lake City: Deseret Book Co., 1939], p. 217.)

*How long halt ye between two opinions?*
*If the Lord be God, follow him:*
*but if Baal, then follow him.*
*—1 Kings 18:21*

CHAPTER EIGHT

# "Choose You This Day
# Whom Ye Will Serve"

On the desk in my office is a beautifully carved olive-wood statue of the prophet Elijah. It is a treasured gift from my Old Testament students whom I taught at the BYU Jerusalem Center for Near-Eastern Studies. It is a very special gift, not only because it represents their appreciation but also because they knew how much I love Elijah.

While living in Israel I gained a greater insight into the mission of this ancient prophet and his importance to both Jews and Christians. The Jews consider him one of the greatest of the prophets, perhaps even next to Moses in his importance and power and in the many mighty miracles he performed during his mortal ministry. To us as Latter-day Saints, Elijah takes on additional importance as a forerunner of the Savior in both his earthly mission and his Second Coming, and as a restorer of vital keys of the priesthood (see Malachi 4:5–6; Matthew 17:1–3; D&C 110:13–16). Because of his latter-day importance I wanted my students to come to know this great prophet in a personal way. So I emphasized a great deal in class the scriptural accounts of his miracles and prophecies. It helped bring the scriptures to life when we would visit certain locations in the Holy Land that had significance to the ministry of Elijah. At those places we would read the scriptural accounts and try to imagine Elijah performing great miracles, calling the wicked to repentance, and declaring the ways of righteousness.

One of my favorite sites in the Holy Land is Mount Carmel. At the summit of the mountain is an impressive statue of the prophet Elijah with drawn sword in hand. There on that mountain my students and I would read of one of the most important events in the life of Elijah—an event that miraculously testified to ancient Israel of Jehovah's saving power. It was not just a watershed event in the history of the ancient kingdom of Israel, but it also has an important message for all today who are serious about serving God and striving to be found as faithful disciples. The olive-wood statue of Elijah on my desk is not only a cherished gift from my students but also a reminder of that singular event and its personal meaning to me. It is a continual reminder that, as Elijah taught the Israelites, no one can serve God and Satan too.

Ancient Israel, under the kingship of Ahab and the wicked influences of the pagan-worshipping Phoenician princess he married, Jezebel, had turned to the pernicious practice of idolatrous worship of the false gods Baal and Ashtoreth. Involved in this false worship of the fertility gods were cultic practices that often involved prostitution and other repugnant immoral behaviors. From even before the children of Israel crossed over the Jordan River into the promised land, Jehovah had warned against being drawn to the false gods. Throughout the Old Testament the Lord through his prophets warned the Israelites of such idolatry, called them to repentance when they became involved, and prophesied destruction if they did not turn from their pagan worship and worship him faithfully and exclusively (see Deuteronomy 16:21–22; Judges 2:11–23; Jeremiah 11:13; Hosea 9:10; Micah 5:13).

Much of the ministry of Elijah was spent in spiritually fighting against the worship of Baal that had become the quasi-official religion of the kingdom of Israel. When his teachings and prophecies went unheeded, almost as a last-ditch effort Elijah confronted the state-sponsored and subsidized priests and prophets from the cult of Baal, dramatically demonstrating the power of Jehovah and the futility of idolatry. On Mount Carmel Elijah called for the "ultimate challenge of the gods"—the test of tests of which religion truly possessed saving power. In remarkable fashion, he threw down the gauntlet to the priests of Baal. To use a common phrase from our modern vernacular, Elijah was essentially saying to these wicked priests and to all who worshipped Baal, "Put up or shut up!" This object lesson was not only a testimony against the wickedness of the ancient Israelites but an important and relevant warning to us as Latter-day Saints striving to live the gospel in a modern world.

> And it came to pass, when Ahab saw Elijah, that Ahab said unto him, Art thou he that troubleth Israel?
>
> And he answered, I have not troubled Israel; but thou, and thy father's house, in that ye have forsaken the commandments of the Lord, and thou hast followed Baalim.
>
> Now therefore send, and gather to me all Israel unto mount Carmel, and the prophets of Baal four hundred and fifty, and the prophets of the groves four hundred, which eat at Jezebel's table.
>
> So Ahab sent unto all the children of Israel, and gathered the prophets together unto mount Carmel.
>
> And Elijah came unto all the people, and said, How long halt ye between two opinions? If the Lord be God, follow him: but if Baal, then follow him. And the people answered him not a word.
>
> Then said Elijah unto the people, I, even I only, remain a prophet of the Lord; but Baal's prophets are four hundred and fifty men.
>
> Let them therefore give us two bullocks; and let them choose one bullock for themselves, and cut it in pieces, and lay it on wood, and put no fire under: and I will dress the other bullock, and lay it on wood, and put no fire under:
>
> And call ye on the name of your gods, and I will call on the name of the Lord: and the God that answereth by fire, let him be God. And all the people answered and said, It is well spoken. (1 Kings 18:17–24.)

What an impressive sight it must have been, with 450 priests of Baal busily building their sacrificial altar, preparing the firewood, slaughtering the young bull, and making everything ready for the contest. On the other side was one lone, aged prophet doing the same work that was being done by hundreds of others—which was not accidental but was an important part of the symbolic lesson to be taught. Since Elijah, at least in the minds of the Israelites, was the "underdog," he had the Baal prophets go first in seeking to call down fire from heaven to consume their prepared sacrifice. The next part of the story is my favorite part. When Baal had failed to show his power after many hours and much prayerful petitioning by the 450 priests, Elijah did something that may seem antithetical to his role as a prophet of

God; yet it is purposeful in the lesson he wanted to teach Israel. He mocked, teased, and even humiliated the priests of Baal, all to show the impotence of their false god.

> And [the priests of Baal] took the bullock which was given them, and they dressed it, and called on the name of Baal from morning even until noon, saying, O Baal, hear us. But there was no voice, nor any that answered. And they leaped upon the altar which was made.
>
> And it came to pass at noon, that Elijah mocked them, and said, Cry aloud: for he is a god; either he is talking, or he is pursuing [or distracted], or he is in a journey, or peradventure he sleepeth, and must be awaked.
>
> And they cried aloud, and cut themselves after their manner with knives and lancets, till the blood gushed out upon them.
>
> And it came to pass, when midday was past, and they prophesied until the time of the offering of the evening sacrifice, that there was neither voice, nor any to answer, nor any that regarded. (1 Kings 18:26–29.)

How ridiculous to think of a god that is so easily distracted, or caught up in himself, or off on a vacation somewhere in the cosmos, or taking an extended nap, that he does not nor will not respond to the petitions of his children. That is the very point that Elijah wanted to make. His demonstration was not so much for the benefit of the priests of Baal and the devout Baal worshippers but for the Israelites whose faith had been wavering.

When it became his turn, Elijah, as the "underdog," did something even more dramatic and brash (even more bold than the cocky young quarterback Joe Namath of the prohibitive underdog New York Jets "guaranteeing" a victory in the Super Bowl against the mighty Baltimore Colts led by Hall of Fame quarterback Johnny Unitas). After he prepared the sacrifice he had a trench dug around the altar and barrels of water prepared to be poured over the sacrificial bullock and the altar—not once, not twice, but three times. The sacrifice was saturated with water, the firewood fully waterlogged, the altar drenched and dripping, and the trench filled to the brim with water. It was a bold demonstration to emphatically declare that no mortal efforts could ignite a fire on this altar; it could be done only through the true power of God. I can imagine that many of the onlookers thought Elijah was totally crazy, with his humiliating mockery of the priests of Baal now coupled with this outlandish soaking of the sacrificial altar. Could any sane person really believe that a fire could be ignited under such circumstances?

With all eyes now focused on Elijah, he was ready to demonstrate whose God had real power. He didn't need several hours of petitioning, ritualistic dancing, or bleeding to get the attention of his God; indeed, it was time for the evening sacrifice as prescribed by the law of Moses.

> And it came to pass at the time of the offering of the evening sacrifice, that Elijah the prophet came near, and said, Lord God of Abraham, Isaac, and of Israel, let it be known this day that thou art God in Israel, and that I am thy servant, and that I have done all these things at thy word.
>
> Hear me, O Lord, hear me, that this people may know that thou art the Lord God, and that thou has turned their heart back again.
>
> Then the fire of the Lord fell, and consumed the burnt sacrifice, and the wood, and the stones, and the dust, and licked up the water that was in the trench.
>
> And when all the people saw it, they fell on their faces: and they said, The Lord, he is the God; the Lord, he is the God. (1 Kings 18:36–39.)

With nothing left of the altar—no sacrifice, wood, or stones, and even the three barrels of water in the trench consumed in an instant by the "fire of the Lord"—the people were quick to acknowledge that Elijah had "won" the contest and Jehovah was indeed the real God. As an additional evidence of God's power and Elijah's prophetic mantle, the prophet unsealed the heavens so that there would be rain, ending the long drought and famine (see 1 Kings 18:41–46). Despite the remarkable spectacle on Mount Carmel and the opening of the heavens with God-given and prophet-promised rain, Ahab and the Israelites didn't repent and turn their hearts to God. Almost before the smoke had cleared from the mountain, Ahab and Jezebel sought to kill the prophet Elijah, forcing him into hiding (see 1 Kings 19:1–3).

What is the meaning of this significant scriptural episode for us today? Is it nothing more than just one of many faith-promoting stories contained in the Old Testament? Are we that much different—so much more righteous and sophisticated than those ancient Israelites that there is no parallel or application to us today? No, on the contrary. This episode should be viewed as one of those Old Testament messages that Elder Neal A. Maxwell characterized as "relevancy within antiquity." Elijah was demonstrating the saving power of Jehovah not so much for the sakes of Ahab, Jezebel, or the hundreds of priests of Baal, or the blatantly wicked who would not hear the word of the Lord, but rather for those who had been seduced by Baal worship and yet still claimed to be faithful followers of the God of Israel.

Many among us today have also been seduced by the world and are guilty of transgressions and justifications similar to those of the Israelites who also served Baal. Three specific behaviors of the ancients Israelites who sacrificed to Jehovah on the Sabbath and Baal on other days can be seen in the lives of Modern Saints who want to hold on to the iron rod yet dance and dine in the great and spacious building. These behaviors include secular and spiritual compartmentalization, spiritual slothfulness and procrastination, and the attempt to "serve God without offending the devil."

## SECULAR AND SPIRITUAL COMPARTMENTALIZATION: SEEKING TO SEPARATE RELIGION FROM THE REST OF LIFE

We often think that the children of Israel became involved in Baal worship, or other kinds of pagan worship indigenous to the land of Canaan, because they were seduced by the sexuality and carnal nature of its practice. It is true that some Israelites were attracted to the kinky aspects of Canaanite worship and therefore were easily drawn away into immoral behaviors, but many were attracted to another aspect of this worship. Baal and his female consort, Ashtoreth, were deities of fertility, and worship of them was designed to bring about rain in season, increased fertility of fields and flocks, and increased fertility in women of childbearing age. All of these elements were absolutely essential in an agrarian society. The generation of Israelites that crossed into the promised land had been nomads for forty years. They had not been farmers or ranchers and had little experience with preparing and planting fields and harvesting crops. For forty years they had been concerned mostly with simple survival; now as they entered their new homeland they needed to learn agricultural skills.

Being an avid gardener myself, I can almost hear the Israelites asking their Canaanite neighbors, "What kinds of seeds do you plant, and when do you plant?" or "How do you get your sheep to grow so big?" or "Why do your cows produce more milk than mine?" As they would swap ideas and suggestions, the Canaanites surely said, "Baal and Ashtoreth, the god and goddess of fertility, are the answer. Keep them happy and you'll have good flocks and fields forever." Undoubtedly the more the Israelites learned from their neighbors about the "keys to success" as farmers and herdsmen in Palestine, the more they were pointed toward Baal worship. I am quite convinced that they did not think they were abandoning their religion or their identity as God's covenant people. They viewed Baal worship as means to an end, the end being productive flocks and bounteous harvests. To them, at least at first, it was more like deciding between organic gardening or using commercial fertilizer. "To have ignored the Baal rites in those days," observed noted Bible scholar Bernhard W. Anderson, "would have seemed as impractical as for a modern farmer to ignore science in the cultivation of the land" (*Understanding the Old Testament*, 4th ed. [Englewood Cliffs, New Jersey: Prentice-Hall, 1986], p. 189). This created a fragmentation of their religious beliefs —a compartmentalization of spiritual values and secular needs. I'm sure they honestly believed they worshipped Jehovah exclusively, at least in the religious part of their lives. They convinced themselves that they practiced Baal worship not for religious reasons exclusively but, rather, for business reasons. Hence, they employed one set of values and practices in the spiritual part of their lives and another set in their everyday secular lives.

Unfortunately there are some within the Church today who do the same thing. How they act and what they say on Sunday may be different from what they do during the rest of the week. For example, there is the priesthood leader who counsels couples with marital problems but is less than kind, considerate, and affectionate to his own wife and children. And there is the Church member who teaches on Sunday the need for honesty and integrity and then cheats on his or her taxes or cuts corners in business. "That's business," they might respond. "It has nothing to do with my religion." Wrong! We cannot be like the ancient Israelites who served Baal for business and Jehovah for religion. True worship and religion cannot be separated from what we do and who we are. One cannot truly possess deeply held convictions about spiritual things and then ignore or abandon them in the course of secular life. One cannot be a "righteous" person on Sunday and claim to be religious, yet be dishonest, uncaring, abusive, and unkind at home, work, or elsewhere.

True religion cannot be compartmentalized. It must infuse every aspect of our lives every day. In fact, the word *religion* comes from the same Latin root from which the word *ligament* comes—*ligare*, meaning "to bind, fasten, connect, or hold together." True religion binds us to God and holds together all aspects of our lives, and cannot be separated out or compartmentalized. Like the Israelites, we cannot worship God spiritually and then put on a different uniform and worship Baal or any of his modern counterparts secularly, for all things are spiritual unto the Lord (see D&C 29:34). We cannot play by different rules at different times. The laws of God are not a sliding scale to be manipulated or ignored when we want to get ahead in the world.

## SPIRITUAL SLOTHFULNESS AND PROCRASTINATION

Another allurement of Baal worship for some of the Israelites was its striking similarity in many respects to Jehovah worship, but with one huge difference—a difference that would be considered a nice feature to the spiritually lazy and uncommitted. The religion required considerably less effort for one to be considered faithful. There was a conscientious effort on the part of some Israelites to make Baal worship seem totally compatible with Jehovah worship. They began to believe that there really was no difference between the two. This was totally false, but they rationalized it to the point that many believed it so Baal worship would be more palatable than if it had been presented to them as some totally strange, pagan religion. This made it look as if they could believe many of the same things and even do some similar practices, yet with much less effort and sacrifice. It didn't require being righteous as much as it required performing acts of ritual. One of the selling features of Baal worship, as explained by King Rehoboam of the northern kingdom of Israel, was that he could provide a "temple" both in Bethel and Dan so that the Israelites wouldn't have to travel all the way to Jerusalem. *What a deal—a religion that not only requires less of its adherents, but is so convenient too!* Rehoboam probably reasoned. In many respects, Baal worship could be characterized as an ancient "drive-through religion."

Not only was Elijah's contest with the priests of Baal a demonstration to the ancients of the impotence and futility of false worship, but it is also a message to modern Saints who want to be active members of the Church but who don't want to have to expend too much energy, effort, commitment, or sacrifice. Such spiritual slothfulness is manifested by the following:

— Those who think the expectations of worship and discipleship are pretty much confined to the three-hour meeting block;
— Those who have nice leather-bound scriptures with their names embossed on them but with pages still crisp from never being opened;
— Those who have pretty pictures of temples in their homes but "don't have time" to attend and serve in them;
— Those who pay token offerings now and then to the Church but who are not willing to consecrate their all;
— Those who want to serve in Church callings but want theirs to be Sunday-only assignments or, better yet, want to pick and choose which callings would be acceptable;
— Those who profess to love their neighbors but can't minister as home teachers or visiting teachers to a few people just around the block.

These modern-day Baal-worshippers don't want to forsake the Lord, but neither do they want to fully submit to him or completely commit themselves to gospel living, for they feel such commitment and submission may be too costly, inconvenient, or even painful at times.

Sometimes such modern Baal worshippers' desire for "easy religion" comes in the form of spiritual procrastination, a sister sin of spiritual slothfulness. They know in their heads what is involved in following Christ, but in their hearts they say, "I will—but not yet!" This spiritual slothfulness and procrastination, like ancient Baal worship, has no power to lead one to salvation. Elder Neal A. Maxwell taught:

> Indeed, one of the most cruel games anyone can play with self is the 'not yet' game—hoping to sin just a bit more before ceasing; to enjoy the praise of the world a little longer before turning away from the applause; to win just once more in the wearying sweepstakes of materialism; to be chaste, but not yet; to be good neighbors, but not now. One can play upon the harpstrings of hesitations and reservations

just so long, and then one faces that special moment—a moment when what has been sensed, mutely, suddenly finds voice and cries out with tears, "Lord, I believe; help thou mine unbelief" (Mark 9:24).

The truth is that "not yet" usually means "never." Trying to run away from the responsibility to decide about Christ is childish. ("Why Not Now?" *Ensign*, November 1974, p. 13.)

## TRYING TO SERVE GOD WITHOUT OFFENDING THE DEVIL

Elijah's searching question "How long halt ye between two opinions?" was not directed at Ahab or the priests of Baal, for they were not torn between two opinions. They had fully embraced Baal worship, or at least they were loyal to their beliefs. Elijah's question was directed to the Israelites who couldn't seem to decide which way to go and so, to play it safe, didn't fully embrace one religion or the other. Elijah's question is really an indictment of the "double-mindedness" of these Israelites. "Literally, [the phrase means] 'How long hop ye about upon two boughs?'" explained Adam Clarke, one of the world's preeminent Old Testament scholars.

> This is a metaphor taken from birds hopping about from bough to bough, not knowing on which to settle. Perhaps the idea of *limping* through *lameness* should not be overlooked. They were *halt*, they could not walk uprightly; they dreaded Jehovah, and therefore could not totally abandon him; they feared the king and queen, and therefore thought they *must* embrace the religion of the state. Their conscience forbade them to do the former; their fear of man persuaded them to do the latter; but in neither were they heartily engaged; and at this juncture their minds seemed in equipoise, and they were waiting for a favourable opportunity to make their decision. Such an opportunity now, through the mercy of God, presented itself. (*Clarke's Commentary*, 3 vols. [Nashville: Abingdon, n.d.], 1:457.)

That imagery of a lame bird hopping back and forth from branch to branch symbolizes more than those who are unable to decide between religions. It also symbolizes those among us who have not totally let go of the world's ways and enthusiastically embraced the ways of the Lord. Today there are members of the Church who want to toy with evil but still be considered righteous and faithful. It is kind of like the old familiar saying "Having your cake and eating it too." As I heard a teenager once say, "I want to be good but not *too* good, and I want to be bad but not *too* bad." This is the very attitude of the ancient Israelites as they "hopped" between Baal and Jehovah, never giving full allegiance to either, never willing to fully turn their backs on one or the other. The Apostle James characterized this kind of attitude as "double-mindedness," stating that "a double minded man is unstable in all his ways" (James 1:8). A double-minded person has not yet decided to be totally committed, and his or her instability may be likened to Jell-O, which may be okay to eat, but you wouldn't want to build a house on it. The Savior himself condemned this kind of thinking and behaving. "I know thy works, that thou art neither cold nor hot: I would thou wert cold or hot. So then because thou art lukewarm, and neither cold nor hot, I will spue [vomit] thee out of my mouth." (Revelation 3:15–16.)

Speaking to the students of Brigham Young University in 1955, Elder Marion G. Romney expressed concern over this "spiritual schizophrenia," or what he characterized as "trying to serve the Lord without offending the devil" (*The Price of Peace*, Brigham Young University Speeches of the Year [1 March 1955], p. 7). In a general conference address he later said, "The consequences of [man's] choices are of the all-or-nothing sort. There is no way for him to escape the influence of these opposing powers. Inevitably he is led by one or the other. His God given free agency gives him the power and option to choose. But choose he must. Nor can he serve both of them at the same time, for, as Jesus said, 'No man can serve two masters: . . . Ye cannot serve God and mammon '" (In Conference Report, October 1962, p. 94.)

Satan cleverly disguises his evil ways so that they are not always easily discerned as black or white; instead they are often camouflaged or are in the gray area, where bad doesn't look so bad. The danger, however, is that it doesn't take long after wandering off the marked trail into the gray area before we are enveloped in a "mist of darkness" so exceedingly dark, as Lehi described, "that they who had commenced in the path did lose their way, that they wandered off and were lost" (1 Nephi 8:23). It is impossible to partake of the fruit of the tree of life while dancing and dining in the great and spacious building, for they are symbolically miles apart. You must either "press forward," hanging on to the iron rod, or you have to let go; you can't have it both ways. Divided loyalties inevitably lead to diminished righteousness.

As parents my wife and I have tried to teach this concept on many occasions to our own children, with mixed results. Perhaps we have emphasized this lesson (and the example of Elijah's contest with the priests of Baal) most often when we have taken our teenage daughters shopping for clothes. It is not easy trying to get them to have what President Spencer W. Kimball characterized as "a style of our own" (see *Faith Precedes the Miracle* [Salt Lake City: Deseret Book Co., 1972], pp. 161–68). We haven't always agreed among ourselves what that style is, or even what modesty means. Our children mistakenly surmise that we want them to dress like the Amish, and we mistakenly surmise that they want to look like gang members or streetwalkers. Neither is true. "Just because we dress in a certain style," my daughters have said, "doesn't mean we act a certain way or let our standards down." While that is true, I have often responded, "You know that and I know that, but will others know that from looking at you?" I'm not sure they understand when I say to them, "It's not a matter of style, it's a matter of allegiance—it's a matter of what is most important to you."

We encounter many examples like this every day—very real dilemmas that our youth and we as adults have to struggle with. For instance, I once had a student who told me that he was the "designated driver" for all of his drunk friends. He went to all the same parties, spent time with the same people, and engaged in virtually all the same activities that his friends did—just to a lesser degree. He didn't want to miss out on all the fun, and he certainly didn't want to be labeled a "goody-goody," but neither did he want to do all the things his friends were doing. He was like the ancient Israelites who "hopped" from one camp of values to another, or were "frequent flyers" between Zion and Gommorah, not wanting to become leading citizens of either.

I feel that one of Satan's greatest allurements today is a belief held also by the Israelites who worshipped Baal—the belief that we can follow the styles and trends and practices of the world, but to a lesser degree and at a slower pace. Yet we cannot afford to even be going in the same downward direction. "In this difficult environment we will be expected to steer our own course in an upward direction," Elder Dean L. Larsen declared.

. . . It will neither be acceptable nor safe to remain on the plateaus where our present conduct has kept us. Abrupt downward forces, represented by increasing wickedness in the world, can only be offset by forces that move correspondingly upward. Our lives must be better than they have ever been before. This simply means that we will become increasingly different from those around us whose lives follow the world's way. It is not easy to be different. There are intense pressures that work against us. But we must clearly understand that it is not safe to move in the same direction the world is moving, even though we remain slightly behind the pace they set. Such a course will eventually lead us to the same problems and heartaches. It will not permit us to perform the work the Lord has chosen us to do. It would disqualify us from his blessing and his protecting care. (In Conference Report, April 1983, p. 48.)

The challenge of Elijah beckons to us today. His question "How long will you lamely hop back and forth before you choose to totally follow God?" echoes through the generations into our ears. The time has come to make our choice. As Elder Bruce R. McConkie testified:

There neither are nor can be any neutrals in this war. Every member of the Church is on one side or the other. . . .

In this war all who do not stand forth courageously and valiantly are by that fact alone aiding the cause of the enemy. "They who are not for me are against me, saith our God" (2 Nephi 10.16).

We are either for the Church or we are against it. We either take its part or we take the consequences. We cannot survive spiritually with one foot in the Church and the other in the world. We must make the choice. It is either the Church or the world. There is no middle ground. (In Conference Report, October 1974, p. 44.)

Although I'm using it out of its cultural context, a popular song from my teenage years still has an important spiritual message to me, one that reflects Elijah's call to all of us today:

> Did you ever have to make up your mind?
> Say yes to one and leave the other behind.
> It's not always easy and not often kind.
> Did you ever have to make up your mind?

The time has come to make up our minds. Do we truly love the Lord more than Satan? (See Moses 5:13–28.) The decision need not be difficult and need be made only once. Putting it off is the same as deciding not to follow the Lord. We cannot have it both ways. It cannot be delayed any longer, for when we finally make the decision to truly love the Lord with all our heart, mind, and strength, there are far fewer "things of the world" that we must decide upon. The time for our most significant decision has arrived—the time to decide to fully follow the Lord is *now!* Joshua said it best:

> *Now therefore fear the Lord, and serve him in sincerity and in truth: and put away the gods which your fathers served . . . and serve the Lord. And if it seem evil unto you to serve the Lord, choose ye this day whom ye will serve; whether the gods which your fathers served that were on the other side of the flood, or the gods of the Amorites, in whose land ye dwell: but as for me and my house, we will serve the Lord.*
>
> *—Joshua 24:14–15*

*Trust in the Lord with all thine heart; and lean not unto thine own understanding.*
*In all thy ways acknowledge him, and he shall direct thy paths.*
*—Proverbs 3:5–6*

## CHAPTER NINE

# "Though He Slay Me, Yet Will I Trust in Him"

The Old Testament account of Job has become the classic story of how trials and tribulations can make or break a person. People all around the world, Bible believing or not, associate the name Job with adversity and suffering. Phrases such as "the patience of Job" or "Job-like trials" are used every day by people who may not have ever even read the biblical account.

This famous scripture story has enormous relevance for us today because suffering and tribulation are a universal part of life and an integral element of the plan of salvation. Some Bible scholars debate the historicity of the story, but whether Job was a real person and whether the events actually happened, Latter-day Saints have a unique perspective on the value of the book of Job. During the unspeakable suffering and humiliations of the Liberty Jail experience, the Lord compared the Prophet Joseph Smith's predicament to that of Job's during ancient times: "My son, peace be unto thy soul; thine adversity and thine affflictions shall be but a small moment;

And then, if thou endure it well, God shall exalt thee on high; thou shalt triumph over all thy foes.

Thy friends do stand by thee, and they shall hail thee again with warm hearts and friendly hands.

Thou are not yet as Job; thy friends do not contend against thee, neither charge thee with transgression, as they did Job." (D&C 121:7–10.) From this reference we are led to believe that Job was indeed a real person who suffered real trials and tribulations, because it would have been unfair, even cruel, for God to compare Joseph's very real and painful afflictions to those of a merely fictional character.

From the account of Job's personal tragedies and his ultimate triumph we gain insight into the role that suffering and sorrow play in the testing process of the plan of salvation. Job's unfailing faith in the Lord and his purposes is a relevant example for us today as we struggle with our own trials and utter heartfelt pleadings such as "Why me?" "Why this?" and "Why now?" Job teaches us that essential adversity-enduring strength and power come with a personal knowledge of God. Even when all around him were accusing him of transgression and bringing his own sufferings upon himself, and when his own wife urged him to "curse God, and die" (Job 2:9), Job continually looked to God for the strength to endure and for his ultimate salvation. "Though he slay me," declared Job, "yet will I trust in him" (Job 13:15). Perhaps the highlight of the story of Job is the message of divine compensation for sorrows and sufferings faithfully endured, which is found in blessings in this life and an eternal reward in the life to come.

## SUFFERING AND THE PLAN OF SALVATION

The Lord described Job as "a perfect and an upright man, one that feareth God, and escheweth evil" (Job 2:3). He lost his home and financial security, he suffered the deaths of his children, he was cursed and ridiculed by friends and loved ones, and he was afflicted with painful physical maladies. "In all this Job sinned not, nor charged God foolishly" (Job 1:22). He was a model of faith, integrity, endurance, and patience in affliction. Yet this man who looked to God throughout his life also was left at times with more distressing questions than comforting answers. "Why died I not from the womb?" he questioned aloud. "Why did I not give up the ghost when I came out of the belly?" (Job 3:11.) "My soul is weary of my life; I will leave my complaint upon myself; I will speak in the bitterness of my soul.

I will say unto God, Do not condemn me; shew me wherefore thou contendest with me.

Is it good unto thee that thou shouldest oppress, that shouldest despise the work of thine hands, and shine upon the counsel of the wicked?" (Job 10:1–3.)

Job struggled with the age-old questions that haunt us even today: If God loves his children, why does he allow them to experience so much suffering and sorrow? Why must one who is righteous, like Job, and who continually strives to serve the Lord suffer so much tribulation, while many of the wicked and unbelieving seem to "breeze through" life? What is the meaning in the madness of mortality?

Job questioned God, "Wherefore then hast thou brought me forth out of the womb?" (Job 10:18.) Couched in his questioning and pleading with the Lord was his wrestle with the terrible ironies of adversity. The prophet Jeremiah questioned the Lord, "Wherefore doth the way of the wicked prosper? wherefore are all they happy that deal very treacherously?" (Jeremiah 12:1.) While the story of Job as a symbol of universal suffering may leave us at times with more questions than answers, it also shows us that there is indeed a divine purpose in the trials and tribulations of life.

## The Righteous Are Not Immune to Suffering

From the opening chapter of the book of Job, it becomes apparent that God is an "accomplice" in Job's trials—he allows this testing process. While the story of his bargain with Satan may be completely symbolic, the lesson to be learned is that all people will be touched by adversity in some form or another, for it is a universal part of our mortal existence. "[Your Father in Heaven] maketh his sun to rise on the evil and on the good, and sendeth rain on the just and on the unjust" the Savior taught in the Sermon on the Mount (Matthew 5:45). From Job we learn that even the righteous will be exposed to pain and problems, through no fault of their own most of the time but just as a normal part of living.

Speaking of the trials and tribulations associated with the last days and the Second Coming of the Savior, the Prophet Joseph Smith declared:

> I explained concerning the coming of the Son of Man; also that it is a false idea that the Saints will escape all the judgments, whilst the wicked suffer; for all flesh is subject to suffer, and "the righteous shall

hardly escape;" still many of the Saints will escape, for the just shall live by faith; yet many of the righteous shall fall a prey to disease, to pestilence, etc., by reason of the weakness of the flesh, and yet be saved in the Kingdom of God. So that it is an unhallowed principle to say that such and such have transgressed because they have been preyed upon by disease or death, for all flesh is subject to death; and the Savior has said, "Judge not, lest ye be judged." (*Teachings of the Prophet Joseph Smith*, comp. Joseph Fielding Smith [Salt Lake City: Deseret Book Co., 1976], pp. 162–63.)

Job's "friends" and even his wife accused him of wickedness, supposing that he would not be suffering so if he were righteous. But this was not the case. It is not to be thought that all suffering is the result of sin, any more than we should suppose that everything of an adverse nature was directly willed or caused by God. As someone once quipped, "Expecting life to treat you fairly just because you are a good person is like expecting a bull not to charge you because you are a vegetarian." The very laws that are established to provide great blessings and happiness in mortality are also a necessary source of opposition that enables the plan of salvation to fully operate. Blaming ourselves or others for all of the suffering we experience actually stifles our spiritual strength to endure the challenges that beset all of us as a universal condition of mortality.

"We must remember that all suffering is not punishment," Elder Marvin J. Ashton counseled.

> Sometimes we spend so much time trying to determine what we did wrong in the past to deserve the unpleasant happenings of the moment that we fail to resolve the challenges of the present. . . .
>
> . . . It is important that we not look upon our afflictions as a punishment from God. True, our own actions may cause some of our problems, but often there is no evident misconduct that has caused our trials. Just the normal journey through life teaches us that nothing worthwhile comes easy. ("'If Thou Endure it Well,'" *Ensign*, November 1984, pp. 20, 22.)

## Turning Our Hearts to God

One cannot read the book of Job without seeing in almost every chapter how his tribulations helped turn his heart unto the Lord. In

Job we observe not doubt about God or bitterness concerning his ways, but rather an abiding testimony and a strong desire for a deep personal relationship with God. "For I know that my redeemer liveth, and that he shall stand at the latter day upon the earth," Job testified. "And though after my skin worms destory this body, yet in my flesh shall I see God." (Job 19:25.)

Sometimes suffering and sorrow can actually be our greatest bene-factors. They can turn our attention toward God, intensify our devo-tion to him, and strengthen our faith. God's use of adversity to turn the hearts and minds of his children to him not only is found in the account of Job but is also a recurring theme throughout all of the Old Testament (see Leviticus 26; 1 Kings 8:35–36; 2 Chronicles 20:9; Isaiah 30:20; 48:10; Hosea 5:15).

Perhaps the most profound and poignant illustration comes from the poetic pen of the Psalmist. Describing the rebelliousness of the children of Israel after their exodus from Egypt, he wrote:

> And they sinned yet more against [the Lord] by provoking the most High in the wilderness.
>
> And they tempted God in their heart by asking meat for their lust. . . .
>
> And he let it fall in the midst of their camp, round about their habitations.
>
> So they did eat, and were well filled: for he gave them their own desire;
>
> They were not estranged from their lust. But while their meat was yet in their mouths,
>
> The wrath of God came upon them, and slew the fattest of them, and smote down the chosen men of Israel.
>
> For all this they sinned still, and believed not for his wondrous works.
>
> Therefore their days did he consume in vanity, and their years in trouble.
>
> *When he slew them, then they sought him: and they returned and en-quired early after God.*
>
> *And they remembered that God was their rock, and the high God their redeemer.* (Psalm 78:17–18, 28–35; emphasis added.)

An editorial comment of Mormon reflects this same theme of how ad-versity can actually be a tool in God's hand to bring his children back to him and to those values that have saving power. In recounting the Nephite-Lamanite history and their problems with prosperity, pride, affliction, and adversity, Mormon wrote:

> And thus we can behold how false, and also the unsteadiness of the hearts of the children of men; yea, we can see that the Lord in his great infinite goodness doth bless and prosper those who put their trust in him.
>
> Yea, and we may see at the very time when he doth prosper his people, yea, in the increase of their fields, their flocks and their herds, and in gold, and in silver, and in all manner of precious things of every kind and art; . . . yea, and in fine, doing all things for the welfare and happiness of his people; yea, then is the time that they do harden their hearts, and do forget the Lord their God, and do trample under their feet the Holy One—yea, and this because of their ease, and their exceedingly great prosperity.
>
> And thus we see that except the Lord doth chasten his people with many afflictions, yea, except he doth visit them with death and with terror, and with famine and with all manner of pestilence, they will not remember him. (Helaman 12:1–3.)

It may seem rather cruel that the Lord would use apparently harsh means to ensure that we always remember him, but in fact it is a merciful gift from a loving God who desires our ultimate happiness. We can see all around us and in our own lives how what Nephi called "carnal security" (2 Nephi 28:21) actually prevents us from turning our lives totally over to God and loving him with all our heart, might, mind, and strength. During seasons of ease and comfort there may come a quiet, almost unnoticeable tendency to become more secure in ourselves and in the things of the world and less dependent upon the Lord.

C. S. Lewis, in his reflective work *The Problem of Pain*, characterized pain and suffering as God's "megaphone to rouse a deaf world." "Pain insists on being attended to," he wrote. "God whispers to us in our pleasures, speaks in our conscience, but shouts in our pains."

> If the first and lowest operation of pain shatters the illusion that all is well, the second shatters the illusion that what we have, whether good or bad in itself, is our own and enough for us. Everyone has noticed how hard it is to turn our thoughts to God when

everything is going well with us. We "have all we want" is a terrible saying when "all" does not include God. We find God an interruption. As St. Augustine says somewhere, "God wants to give us something, but cannot, because our hands are full—there's nowhere for Him to put it." Or as a friend of mine said, "We regard God as an airman regards his parachute; it's there for emergencies but he hopes he'll never have to use it." Now God, who has made us, knows what we are and that our happines lies in Him. Yet we will not seek it in Him as long as He leaves us any other resort where it can even plausibly be looked for. While what we call "our own life" remains agreeable we will not surrender it to Him. What then can God do in our interests but make "our own life" less agreeable to us, and take away the plausible sources of false happiness? It is just here, where God's providence seems at first to be most cruel, that the Divine humility, the stooping down of the Highest, most deserves praise. (*The Problem of Pain* [New York: Macmillan Publishing Co., 1962], pp. 93, 95–96.)

## The Trial of Faith

Despite the terrible pain he was suffering and the apparent unfairness of his afflictions, Job recognized that a major reason for his predicament was to try his faith. "But [God] knoweth the way that I take," he declared; "when he hath tried me, I shall come forth as gold" (Job 23:10). One of the primary purposes for our mortal sojourn is to be tried and tested "to see if [we] will do all things whatsoever the Lord [our] God shall command [us]" (Abraham 3:25). The example of Job, together with the examples of other prophets both ancient and modern, teaches us that in addition to the natural bumps and bruises we experience as we travel the road of life are individualized troubles and tribulations that are designed to try our faith in God (see D&C 98:11–12; 136:31; see also Joseph Smith, *Teachings of the Prophet Joseph Smith*, comp. Joseph Fielding Smith [Salt Lake City: Deseret Book Co., 1976], p. 150). President John Taylor remembered, "I heard the Prophet Joseph say, in speaking to the Twelve on one occasion: 'You will have all kinds of trials to pass through. And it is quite as necessary for you to be tried as it was for Abraham and other men of God, and (said he) God will feel after you, and He will take hold of you and wrench your very heart strings, and if you cannot stand it you will not be fit for an inheritance in the Celestial Kingdom of God.'" (In *Journal of Discourses* 24:197.)

Faith like that of Job, Father Abraham, and many others requires testing such as they experienced. The test of adversity, the kind of test possibly accompanied by the feeling of forsakenness experienced not only by Job but even by Jesus, powerfully strips away false faith and superficial spirituality. Only when we hang by the thread of our testimony do we find out what we really believe, to whom we are really loyal, and what spiritual substance really fills our souls. The exact nature of such saving tests of faith will not necessarily be the same, or perhaps not even remotely similar, for all. We are assured, however, that the plan of salvation provides for such tests and trials that are adapted to our individual needs, capacities, and circumstances. President George Q. Cannon taught:

> If we will be faithful to our God, He will redeem us, no matter what the circumstances may be through which we may be called to pass. We may wade through sorrow. We may have to endure persecution. We may have to meet with death. We may have to endure imprisonment and many other things that our predecessors had to endure. God may test us in this manner.
>
> Every human being that is connected with this work will have to be tested before he can enter into the Celestial Kingdom of our God. He will try us to the uttermost. If we have any spot more tender than another, He will feel after it. He will test all in some way or other. . . .
>
> We have learned that there are plenty of trials and difficulties for all, if they will live faithful, to have their full share and all that are necessary to test them and their faith and integrity to the fullest extent. Each generation may not have to pass through exactly the same scenes. They are apt to vary as the circumstances which surround each vary; but they will, nevertheless, accomplish the desired end. There is one thing certain, every Latter-day Saint who is faithful to the truth and who lives to the ordinary age of man will have all the opportunities of this kind he or she can desire to gain experience and to have his or her zeal, integrity, courage and devotion to the truth fully exhibited. (*Gospel Truth*, comp. Jerreld L. Newquist, 2 vols. [Salt Lake City: Deseret Book Co., 1957–74], 2:25–26.)

We need to recognize both the importance and the diversity of such tests of faith. God will indeed try us and our faith "to the uttermost," and we can see that life's hardships and heartaches are, at least in part, an important and essential element in that process. We may also discover that some of the "big tests" of faith may actually be much different from what we expect. Sometimes the "little things" can challenge us even more than the "big things" that may be more obvious afflictions. Job-like trials and tribulations may test our faith and integrity, but so also may comfort and ease. Knowing that we must be "chastened and tried, even as Abraham" (D&C 101:4) to fulfill God's purposes for us and to be sanctified helps us understand our suffering. Whether by means of peace and prosperity or pain and problems, life is not only a time of testing but also a time of training.

## The Lord Chastens Those He Loves

"Behold, happy is the man whom God correcteth," the book of Job declares, "therefore despise not thou the chastening of the Almighty" (Job 5:17). Adversity, a redemptive reminder of who God is and how we must totally depend on him, is much like the loud ringing of a school bell. It grabs our attention, startles us out of our comfort zone, awakens us from our daydreaming, and beckons us to commence the important task of learning. It serves as an attention-getting signal which summons us to class, but the real education is obtained not from the school bell but from the schoolmaster. The God-permitted and God-created, purposeful tribulations we experience in life are not only like the school bell but also, in a broader and more significant way, like the schoolmaster who patiently and sometimes even sternly shapes and stretches each student to his or her fullest potential. Of this soul-shaping role of adversity the Lord declared: "Whom I love I also chasten that their sins may be forgiven, for with the chastisement I prepare a way for their deliverance in all things out of temptation, and I have loved you—wherefore, ye must needs be chastened" (D&C 95:1–2).

As was the case with Job, the Lord loves each of us with such a perfect and infinite love that he uses adversity and affliction to chasten and strengthen us. This may seem contradictory if we define the word *chasten* only in terms of punishment. The broader meaning of the word, however, adds such important elements as "to instruct, restrain, or moderate" and the spiritually significant terms "to purify and refine." This divinely designed and desirable chastening process involves a stripping away of undesirable traits and false allegiances. Job spoke of this process as the bringing forth of gold (see Job 23:10), and other scriptures speak of it as a "refiner's fire" (Malachi 3:2). "In the pain, the agony, and the heroic endeavors of life, we pass through a refiner's fire," Elder James E. Faust explained, "and the insignificant and unimportant in our lives can melt away like dross and make our faith bright, intact, and strong."

> In this way the divine image can be mirrored from the soul. It is part of the purging toll exacted of some to become acquainted with God. In the agonies of life, we seem to listen better to the faint, godly whisperings of the Divine Shepherd.
>
> Into every life there come the painful, despairing days of adversity and buffeting. There seems to be a full measure of anguish, sorrow, and often heartbreak for everyone, including those who earnestly seek to do right and be faithful. The thorns that prick, that stick in the flesh, that hurt, often change lives which seem robbed of significance and hope. This change comes about through a refining process which often seems cruel and hard. In this way the soul can become like soft clay in the hands of the Master in building lives of faith, usefulness, beauty, and strength. For some, the refiner's fire causes a loss of belief and faith in God, but those with eternal perspective understand that such refining is part of the perfection process. (In Conference Report, April 1979, p. 77.)

Refining implies a melting away or an elimination of things undesirable or unnecessary. After the refining there must also be a reshaping or reconstruction. Just as undesirable qualities need to be eliminated, those traits that are essential to our happiness and spiritual progress need to be added to and reinforced in our lives. Adversity and affliction can be important tools whereby this spiritual remodeling may be accomplished.

Every remodeling job has its accompanying cost and inconvenience. The remodeling and reshaping of souls is no different; it has its own cost in pain and sorrow, yet yields a palatial enlargement of our souls, an enhancement of our spirituality, and a remaking of our very beings in the image of him who "hath descended below" all suffering and pain (see D&C 122:8).

Because of the very nature of the plan of salvation and the purposes of our existence, each of us is like Job in that we are all enrolled in the "school of hard knocks." Adversity, regardless of the cause, provides us with a most necessary and unique tutorial. This kind of chastening through adversity is also an education for eternity. All of the different types of experiences of mortality—both the painful and the peaceful, the frustrating and the fulfilling, the happy and the hard—are essential elements of that education. Without tribulations and sorrow, life's core curriculum would be incomplete and totally inadequate. Elder Orson F. Whitney taught:

> No pain that we suffer, no trial that we experience is wasted. It ministers to our education, to the development of such qualities of patience, faith, fortitude and humility. All that we suffer and all that we endure, especially when we endure it patiently, builds up our characters, purifies our hearts, expands our souls, and makes us more tender and charitable, more worthy to be called the children of God . . . and it is through sorrow and suffering, toil and tribulation, that we gain the education that we come here to acquire and which will make us more like our Father and Mother in heaven. (As quoted in Spencer W. Kimball, *Faith Precedes the Miracle* [Salt Lake City: Deseret Book Co., 1972], p. 98.)

## FACING ADVERSITY WITH FAITH AND PATIENCE

Job undergoes an interesting metamorphosis near the end of his book. As he continues to dwell upon the reasons for his suffering and the apparent inequities of his situation, he makes little spiritual progress. But when he no longer petitions the Lord for logical understanding but rather puts his trust totally in God's purposes, praises the Almighty, and pleads for strength to endure, then we see the faithful endurance and patience that have become synonymous with his name.

Amid our own suffering, we, like Job, usually ask the same "why" questions. However, we are not usually seeking for cognitive answers to mortally unanswerable questions. I see this phenomenon quite often with my own children when their desires do not mesh with my parental responsibilities. Their question "Why can't I do this?" is not an invitation for reason or rational explanation but is, rather, a statement of disagreement with my will and an insistence that it be otherwise. Similarly, our "why" questions are usually vocalized desires on our part that our circumstances would be different and that God would change his mind.

Knowing the answers may not necessarily add to our capacity to faithfully and patiently endure anyway. Instead, through our questions we often are in reality summoning spiritual strength and pleading for power to be able to endure our trials. By putting our complete trust in the Lord, or being willing to say "Thy will be done" and really mean it, we gain the strength and fortitude needed to pass the painful tests of life. But, oh, that is hard—much easier said than done!

Elder Richard G. Scott has given us some wise counsel, forged in the trials of his own personal experience, concerning the value of questioning the Lord amid our adversity.

> When you face adversity, you can be led to ask many questions. Some serve a useful purpose; others do not. To ask, Why does this have to happen to me? Why do I have to suffer this now? What have I done to cause this? will lead you into blind alleys. It really does no good to ask questions that reflect opposition to the will of God. Rather ask, What am I to do? What am I to learn from this experience? What am I to change? Whom am I to help? How can I remember my many blessings in times of trial? Willing sacrifice of deeply held personal desires in favor of the will of God is very hard to do. Yet when you pray with real conviction, "Please let me know Thy will" and "May Thy will be done," you are in the strongest position to receive the maximum help from your loving Father. (In Conference Report, October 1995, p. 18.)

We often acknowledge in our heads that God's ways are higher than our ways (see Isaiah 55:8–9), but when faced with Job-like ironies and inequities of adversity, we may sometimes feel in our hearts that God doesn't know what he is doing and that there is no "meaning in the madness." When God's omniscient will and designs painfully collide with our own limited ideas of what is best for us, we often resist and resent his efforts because we do not perceive his purposes. Elder James E. Talmage profoundly taught this principle by using an insightful personal experience:

> Sometimes I find myself under obligations of work requiring quiet and seclusion such as neither my comfortable office nor the cozy study at home insures. My favorite retreat is an upper room in the tower of a large building, well removed from the noise and confu-

sion of the city streets. The room is somewhat difficult of access, and relatively secure against human intrusion. Therein I have spent many peaceful and busy hours with books and pen.

I am not always without visitors, however, especially in summertime; for, when I sit with windows open, flying insects occasionally find entrance and share the place with me. These self-invited guests are not unwelcome. Many a time I have laid down the pen, and, forgetful of my theme, have watched with interest the activities of these winged visitants, with an after-thought that the time so spent had not been wasted, for, is it not true, that even a butterfly, a beetle, or a bee, may be a bearer of lessons to the receptive student?

A wild bee from the neighboring hills once flew into the room; and at intervals during an hour or more I caught the pleasing hum of its flight. The little creature realized that it was a prisoner, yet all its efforts to find the exit through the partly opened casement failed. When ready to close up the room and leave, I threw the window wide, and tried at first to guide and then to drive the bee to liberty and safety, knowing well that if left in the room it would die as other insects there entrapped had perished in the dry atmosphere of the enclosure. The more I tried to drive it out, the more determinedly did it oppose and resist my efforts. Its erstwhile peaceful hum developed into an angry roar; its darting flight became hostile and threatening.

Then it caught me off my guard and stung my hand—the hand that would have guided it to freedom. At last it alighted on a pendant attached to the ceiling, beyond my reach of help or injury. The sharp pain of its unkind sting aroused in me rather pity than anger. I knew the inevitable penalty of its mistaken opposition and defiance; and I had to leave the creature to its fate. Three days later I returned to the room and found the dried, lifeless body of the bee on the writing table. It had paid for its stubbornness with its life.

To the bee's short-sightedness and selfish misunderstanding I was a foe, a persistent persecutor, a mortal enemy bent on its destruction, while in truth I was its friend, offering it ransom of the life it had put in forfeit through its own error, striving to redeem it, in spite of itself, from the prison-house of death and restore it to the outer air of liberty.

Are we so much wiser than the bee that no analogy lies between its unwise course and our lives? We are prone to contend, sometimes with vehemence and anger, against the adversity which after all may be the manifestation of superior wisdom and loving care, directed against our temporary comfort for our permanent blessing. In the tribulations and sufferings of mortality there is a divine ministry which only the godless soul can wholly fail to discern. To many the loss of wealth has been a boon, a providential means of leading or driving them from the confines of selfish indulgence to the sunshine and open, where boundless opportunity waits on effort. Disappointment, sorrow, and affliction may be the expression of an all-wise Father's kindness.

Consider the lesson of the unwise bee!

"Trust in the Lord with all thine heart; and lean not unto thine own understanding. In all thy ways acknowledge him, and he shall direct thy paths." (Proverbs 3:5–6.) ("The Parable of the Unwise Bee," *Improvement Era*, September 1914, pp. 1008.)

In contrast to the unwise bee, Job came to a point in his life when, even though he did not cognitively understand why he was suffering so, and even though those around him offered their unsolicited and uninspired explanations, he turned his gaze toward God. "Though he slay me," he declared, "yet will I trust in him" (Job 13:15). Because of this abiding trust—a trust that may be devoid of all logical explanation and understanding—Job stands as an example of faithful endurance.

The scriptures and modern-day prophets beckon us to walk in the exemplary footsteps of Job. Our willingness to trust when we don't understand and to exercise faith when we feel forsaken is an imperative ingredient in our mortal "survival kit" that enables us to endure life's inexplicable inequities. "God is our refuge and strength, a very present help in trouble," sang the Psalmist in poetic testimony of the power of trusting in the Lord.

> Therefore will not we fear, though the earth be removed, and though the mountains be carried into the midst of the sea;
>
> Though the waters thereof roar and be troubled, though the mountains shake with the swelling thereof. . . .
>
> There is a river, the streams whereof shall make glad the city of God, the holy place of the tabernacles of the most High.
>
> God is in the midst of her; she shall not be moved: God shall help her, and that right early.
>
> The heathen raged, the kingdoms were moved: he uttered his voice, the earth melted.
>
> The Lord of hosts is with us; the God of Jacob is our refuge. . . .

Be still, and know that I am God: I will be exalted among the heathen, I will be exalted in the earth.

The Lord of hosts is with us; the God of Jacob is our refuge. (Psalm 46:2–7, 10–11.)

Enhanced endurance of life's adversities results only from our willingness to trust God even when our hearts may be breaking and understanding may be absent. Without this assurance that God loves us, that he is mindful of our needs, and that he is performing a work that will enlarge us and exalt us, all other efforts to find peace for our troubled souls and strength to endure tribulation will be limited. Trusting in the Lord in times of sorrow and suffering requires us to walk to the edge of the light, and sometimes even into the darkness. Only when we are willing to put our total trust in the "Light of the World" will the darkness be dispelled and the pathway of endurance and spiritual strength be illuminated.

Just as the Lord counseled the ancient Israelites and the early Saints of this dispensation during their dark times of trouble, so he extends to us his beckoning invitation to put our trust in him and receive of his promise of comfort: "Let your hearts be comforted . . . for all flesh is in mine hands; be still and know that I am God" (D&C 101:16).

Closely associated with our willingness to trust in the Lord is our patience amid adversity. It is difficult to "wait upon the Lord" (Isaiah 40:31), yet numerous scriptural passages admonish us to be patient in tribulation (see D&C 31:9; 54:10; 66:9; 122:5–7; Alma 26:27). It is a natural inclination to be impatient and to think that no matter how long our "small moments" of adversity may last, they are too long (see D&C 122:4). This natural tendency can be characterized by a saying I first saw on a plaque on the kitchen wall of my parents' home: "God grant me patience—RIGHT NOW!"

Impatience and a lack of trust in God are twin traits found in the natural man. Just as the natural man is an "enemy to God" (Mosiah 3:19), impatience and an unwillingness to trust in God's designs for us can become enemies to our spiritual development and faithful endurance. "When we are unduly impatient," Elder Neal A. Maxwell observed, "we are suggesting that we know what is best—better than does God. Or, at least, we are asserting that our timetable is better than His. Either way we are questioning the reality of God's omniscience as if, as some seem to believe, God were on some sort of post-doctoral fellowship and were not quite in charge of everything." ("Patience," In *1979 Devotional Speeches of the Year* [Provo, Utah: Brigham Young University Press, 1980], p. 215.)

Patient endurance requires waiting—not passive waiting, foolish fretting, or idle twiddling of our thumbs, but waiting upon the Lord. "Wait on the Lord: be of good courage, and he shall strengthen thine heart: wait, I say, on the Lord" (Psalm 27:14). Waiting on the Lord implies not only trust but also active submissiveness to his ultimate purposes for our lives. This kind of faithful submission to the Lord's will means humbly accepting not only the "what" but also the "when" and the "how long." Tribulations and trials bring us to our knees until we, like Job, stop resisting and surrender our lives to the Lord. Only through such liberating surrender can we find, amid our our own suffering, the peace and comfort that Job ultimately found.

## DIVINE COMPENSATION

Part of the story of Job is often overlooked yet may be the most transcendent contribution of the entire account: the happy ending and its symbolic meaning. As we read of the results of Job's patient endurance, we see, as it were, the windows of heaven opened and the promised blessings being showered upon Job. All of his losses—his health, wealth, family, and friends—were recompensed unto him.

> And the Lord turned the captivity [affliction or suffering] of Job, when he prayed for his friends: also the Lord gave Job twice as much as he had before.
>
> Then came there unto him all his brethren, and all his sisters, and all they that had been of his acquaintance before, and did eat bread with him in his house: and they bemoaned him, and comforted him over all the evil that the Lord had brought upon him: every man also gave him a piece of money, and every one an earring of gold.
>
> So the Lord blessed the latter end of Job more than his beginning: for he had fourteen thousand sheep, and six thousand camels, and a thousand yoke of oxen, and a thousand she asses.
>
> He had also seven sons and three daughters. . . .

> And in all the land were no women found so fair as the daughters of Job: and their father gave them inheritance among their brethren.
>
> After this lived Job an hundred and forty years, and saw his sons, and his sons' sons, even four generations.
>
> So Job died, being old and full of days. (Job 42:10–17.)

Happy endings in classic novels or good movies sometimes enable us to escape our own suffering temporarily and make us feel good for the moment. Yet these fictional endings do not impact our own circumstances or permanently relieve our heartaches. The scriptural account of Job, however, serves as a divine type or foreshadowing of things to come, whether the happy ending is literal or simply symbolic. It is a powerful witness of the Lord's promise that blessings will follow faithful endurance of adversity. In our own day the Lord has promised that tribulations can be turned into triumphs and blessings can flow from the "water of affliction" (Isaiah 30:20):

> For verily I say unto you, blessed is he that keepeth my commandments, whether in life or in death; and he that is faithful in tribulation, the reward of the same is greater in the kingdom of heaven.
>
> Ye cannot behold with your natural eyes, for the present time, the design of your God concerning those things which shall come hereafter, and the glory which shall follow after much tribulation.
>
> For after much tribulation come the blessings. . . .
>
> Remember this, which I tell you before, that you may lay it to heart, and receive that which is to follow. (D&C 58:2–4, 5.)

Like Job, we are promised that adversity and affliction faithfully endured in righteousness will yield glory and blessings. Thus we can come to understand more fully the familiar saying "The darkest hour is just before dawn." Suffering and sorrow can produce deferred blessings and glory, but also may be blessings of themselves in disguise. "[The Saints] may be afflicted and pass through numerous trials of a severe character," President Lorenzo Snow taught, "but these will prove blessings in disguise and bring them out brighter and better than they were before. The people of God are precious in His sight; His love for them will always endure, and in His might and strength and affection, they will triumph and be brought off more than conqueror." (*The Teachings of Lorenzo Snow*, comp. Clyde J. Williams [Salt Lake City: Bookcraft, 1984], p. 121.)

Faithful endurance of adversity brings riches in mortality: our souls are enlarged, our character is refined, our service is sanctified, and our enjoyment and appreciation of life are enriched. In addition to all of these adversity-induced blessings there await even greater rewards, even the "riches of eternity" that surpass all hopeful expectation. It is as the Lord has promised: "After much tribulation come the blessings," both here and hereafter.

In the story of Job, his losses were recompensed while he yet lived. For us, however, the losses sustained in the course of life's adversities cannot always be restored in mortality, nor can all of our anguish and affliction be completely eliminated. We are promised, however, that if we are faithful we will be beneficiaries of a divine law of compensation—one that is infinitely more generous and just than any earthly remuneration, including the recompense that came to Job. It is through the Atonement of Jesus Christ that ultimately all losses can be restored, all suffering can cease, and all inequities and injustices can be rectified. Although there is some mortal compensation proffered to those who faithfully endure the sorrows and sufferings of life, complete compensation and perfect peace must wait until the next life. President Spencer W. Kimball taught:

> This life, this narrow sphere we call mortality, does not, within the short space of time we are allowed here, give to all of us perfect justice, perfect health, or perfect opportunities. Perfect justice, however, will come eventually through a divine plan, as will the perfection of all other conditions and blessings—to those who have lived to merit them. . . .
>
> On the earth there are many apparent injustices, when man must judge man and when uncontrollable situations seem to bring undeserved disaster, but in the judgment of God there will be no injustice and no soul will receive any blessing, reward, or glory which he has not earned, and no soul will be punished through deprivation or otherwise for anything of which he was not guilty. (*The Teachings of Spencer W. Kimball*, ed. Edward L. Kimball [Salt Lake City: Bookcraft, 1982], pp. 46–47.)

The relevant message of the book of Job for us today is not found only in the insights we gain into the reasons why people must suffer in mortality, or in Job's example of faith and patience. It is found also in the hope the scriptural account gives us concerning the "glory which shall follow after much tribulation." That hope is anchored in the Atonement of Jesus Christ. It is through him and through taking his yoke upon us that we can find peace (see Matthew 11:28–30). Because he had descended below all human anguish and affliction and has born our infirmities, he can draw us unto him and lift us up. The book of Job is an ancient story with a modern message, a universal message of hope—a message needed as much now, if not more, than ever. If we learn from Job and face our own personal tests and trials with Job-like trust and patience, we will dwell in the celestial kingdom of God with him and all the other valiant Saints who have faithfully endured adversity. As seen in vision by John the Revelator:

> These are they which came out of great tribulation, and have washed their robes, and made them white in the blood of the Lamb.
>
> Therefore are they before the throne of God, and serve him day and night in his temple: and he that sitteth on the throne shall dwell among them.
>
> They shall hunger no more, neither thirst any more; neither shall the sun light on them, nor any heat.
>
> For the Lamb which is in the midst of the throne shall feed them, and shall lead them unto living fountains of waters: and God shall wipe away all tears from their eyes. (Revelation 7:14–17.)

CHAPTER TEN

# The Bride and
# the Bridegroom

One of the most joyous and spiritual occasions of my life was when my oldest daughter was married for time and eternity in the Salt Lake Temple. As hard as I tried I could not hold back the tears—tears of sadness on one hand that I was giving her away and that she would not be living with us anymore, and tears of joy as the years of teaching and praying were culminated in this most significant and sacred ordinance. As I observed the happy couple kiss across the altar, I saw their reflection in the mirrors on the walls of the sealing room, which seemed to provide a glimpse of immortality and eternal life, of an eternal family, and of endless joy.

As we left the temple, I took my new son-in-law by the arm and said, "Well, now you are married to Jessica for all eternity. There is no warranty on her. You took her 'as is.' So you can't give her back." I was mostly teasing, but in the back of my mind I also had thoughts of so many others whose marriages had started in ways just as happy and sacred as what we had experienced that November morning. For them, however, the happiness had been supplanted with contention, abuse, and even infidelity. They had all started with the same covenantal promises and high aspirations for eternal bliss, but had ended in divorce and bitterness.

Many years ago as I taught the Old Testament to a high school seminary class in Arizona, I asked my students to imagine the feelings they would have for their future eternal companion as I showed them slides of temples, sealing rooms, and couples and families, all set to a beautiful love song that played in the background. After we discussed the feelings we were having, I asked them to imagine that after several years of marriage and a few children, their spouse committed adultery and abandoned the family. "Would you still love him or her?" I asked. "Could you forgive? Would you take him or her back?" There was serious discussion among the students. One could feel the dramatic shift in the emotions and spirit of the class.

I was using this hypothetical example and discussion as an object lesson to teach one of the most important themes of the Old Testament: the long-suffering, tender mercies, love, compassion, and forgiveness of the Bridegroom, Jehovah, which is extended to his bride, Israel. In the Old Testament we see this loving Bridegroom who is continually imploring his lambs to return to his flock and watchful care (see Ezekiel 34:11–25). Perhaps in no place in the Old Testament is this image clearer than in the intriguing and important account of the marriage of the prophet Hosea to the harlot Gomer (see Hosea 1–3). The story is intriguing because of the unusual circumstances surrounding the marriage, but it is important because it demonstrates so poignantly and painfully God's perfect love and his unfailing offer of mercy. "By no other of the Old Testament witnesses," wrote one Bible scholar, "is the tender intimacy and the triumphant power of the love of God so deeply comprehended and so fully expressed as by Hosea" (Artur Weiser, quoted in Nolan B. Harmon, ed., *The Interpreter's Bible*, 12 vols. [New York: Abingdon Press, 1956], 6:690).

"Go, take unto thee a wife of whoredoms," the Lord commanded Hosea (Hosea 1:2). Would God actually ask his anointed prophet to marry a promiscuous woman? Would not such a marriage compromise Hosea's prophetic position and pronouncements? These and other similar questions reflect the problematic nature of this command and have caused scripture scholars through the centuries to debate the actuality of this marriage. Some scholars believe that the story is literal—that there was indeed a marriage between the prophet

Hosea and a woman of questionable morality. Others claim that the marriage was nothing more than an allegory used by Hosea in his teachings. The controversy will perhaps not be resolved in this life, but in Hosea's relationship to Gomer we are nonetheless able to see a profound and unmistakable message for Israel, with another deeply personal meaning for us today. The historicity of the marriage may be a peripheral issue, but Jehovah's love and mercy are at the very heart of the scriptural account of the marriage of Hosea and Gomer.

## JEHOVAH'S "STEADFAST LOVE" FOR ISRAEL

There is perhaps as much consensus among scholars concerning the meaning of Hosea's message as there is controversy concerning the nature of the marriage. Hosea chapter 2 alludes to Gomer's adulterous abandonment of Hosea. In that chapter her return to a life of immorality graphically represents the idolatry and wickedness of the ancient Israelites. Just as Gomer had been unfaithful to her marriage covenant with Hosea, so had Israel been unfaithful to her covenants with Jehovah. The graphic imagery of physical adultery is used many times in the scriptures to characterize Israel's spiritual idolatry and unfaithfulness.

When a man and a woman enter into the sacred covenant of marriage, they make certain promises to each other, either explicitly or implicitly, which form the very foundation of their union. Chief among these covenant promises are honesty, unfailing love, and strict faithfulness. Often in the scriptures the covenant which God made with Israel is referred to as a marriage covenant. The same conditions which are at the core of the bond of marriage are also at the core of the bond between Jehovah and Israel—honesty, love, and fidelity. The covenant of marriage and God's covenant with his chosen people are, in fact, very similar. Hosea's message concerning Jehovah and his people is expressed in that kind of language. Yet even more graphically, the violation of that covenant of honesty, love, and fidelity is expressed as adultery—the violation of the sanctity of marriage. The dissolution of that covenant is described as divorce. (Kent P. Jackson, "The Marriage of Hosea and Jehovah's Covenant with Israel," in Monte S. Nyman, ed., *Isaiah and the Prophets* [Provo, Utah: Religious Studies Center, Brigham Young University, 1984], p. 60.)

Hosea was the first Old Testament prophet to testify of Jehovah's covenant with Israel by comparing it to marriage, but others who followed amplified the imagery. "For thy Maker is thine husband; the Lord of hosts is his name," declared Isaiah as he spoke of Israel as Jehovah's "wife of youth" (Isaiah 54:5–6). To Israel the Lord declared through Jeremiah, "I am married unto you" (Jeremiah 3:14).

> They say, If a man put away his wife, and she go from him, and become another man's, shall he return unto her again? shall not that land be greatly polluted? but thou hast played the harlot with many lovers; yet return again to me, saith the Lord. . . .
>
> The Lord said also unto me in the days of Josiah the king, Hast thou seen that which backsliding Israel hath done? she is gone up upon every high mountain and under every green tree, and there hath played the harlot.
>
> And I said after she had done all these things, Turn thou unto me. But she returned not. And her treacherous sister Judah saw it.
>
> And I saw, when for all the causes whereby backsliding Israel committed adultery I had put her away, and given her a bill of divorce; yet her treacherous sister Judah feared not, but went and played the harlot also. (Jeremiah 3:1, 6–8.)

In the book of Ezekiel the Lord used similar symbolism in his testimony against Jerusalem:

> Now when I passed by thee, and looked upon thee, behold, thy time was the time of love; and I spread my skirt over thee, and covered thy nakedness: yea, I sware unto thee, and entered into a covenant with thee, saith the Lord God, and thou becamest mine.
>
> Then washed I thee with water; yea, I thoroughly washed away thy blood from thee, and I anointed thee with oil. . . .
>
> And thy renown went forth among the heathen for thy beauty: for it was perfect through my comeliness, which I had put upon thee, saith the Lord God.
>
> But thou didst trust in thine own beauty, and playedst the harlot because of thy renown, and pouredst out thy fornications on every one that passed by; his it was. . . .
>
> Nevertheless I will remember my covenant with thee in the days of thy youth, and I will establish unto thee an everlasting covenant. . . .
>
> And I will establish my covenant with thee; and thou shalt know that I am the Lord. (Ezekiel 16:8–9, 14–15, 60, 62.)

Just as Gomer represents Israel both in committing wickedness and in suffering its painful consequences, Hosea represents Jehovah in extending love and mercy and in his untiring efforts to reestablish his covenant with Israel. In the Hebrew this type of love that exists within a covenantal relationship is called *chesed*—"loyal love" or "steadfast love." The word is always used in conjunction with or parallel to the word *faithfulness* (see Psalm 36:5). Because the Lord has betrothed Israel to himself in "steadfast love" despite her infidelity, he cannot and will not forsake her. Wicked Israel will be punished by God, but he will always love her.

The reclaiming of scattered Israel and the renewal of Jehovah's covenant with her, as symbolized by Gomer's ultimate reunion with Hosea (see Hosea 3), were also themes of later prophets such as Isaiah, Jeremiah, and Ezekiel (see Isaiah 62; Jeremiah 3; Ezekiel 16, 36). Their prophetic warnings to the kingdoms of Israel and Judah are not just ancient prophecies about ancient peoples with only ancient applications and fulfillments. The message of the covenant between the bride and bridegroom is also timely and timeless, for it beckons covenant Israel in all generations to cease her unfaithfulness and return to the Lord.

This symbolism is not unique to the Old Testament but is also found in the New Testament and modern scriptures. John the Baptist alluded to Christ as the Bridegroom (see John 3:27–30), and the Savior himself spoke of this symbolism in his parable of the ten virgins (see Matthew 25:1–13). John the Revelator referred many times to the Church as the bride who would be made ready through righteousness and repentance to receive the Bridegroom at his glorious Second Coming (see Revelation 19:7–9; 21:9).

To the modern Church, the Savior has reemphasized this redemptive relationship by using marriage symbolism. This message is not only instructional but also invitational.

> Wherefore, be faithful, praying always, having your lamps trimmed and burning, and oil with you, that you may be ready at the coming of the Bridegroom—
>
> For behold, verily, verily, I say unto you, that I come quickly (D&C 33:17–18).

> That [the] church may come forth out of the wilderness of darkness, and shine forth fair as the moon, clear as the sun, and terrible as an army with banners;

And be adorned as a bride for that day when [the Lord] shalt unveil the heavens, and cause the mountains to flow down at [his] presence, and the valleys to be exalted, the rough places made smooth; that [his] glory may fill the earth. (D&C 109:73–74.)

Yea, let the cry go forth among all people: Awake and arise and go forth to meet the Bridegroom; behold and lo, the Bridegroom cometh; go ye out to meet him. Prepare yourselves for the great day of the Lord. (D&C 133:10.)

The symbolism of the bride and the bridegroom as taught in the Old Testament has a collective application to the gathering and redemption of Israel, both anciently and in the latter days. Such an application is doctrinally significant and must not be overlooked or minimized, but there is a further application of this symbolism that can do more than just teach doctrine. It also testifies of the perfect love of Christ and the possibility of personal redemption, which he extends to every person individually through his atoning blood.

## THE DIVINE LOVE OF THE SAVIOR

By likening the scriptures to ourselves, as Nephi admonished (see 1 Nephi 19:23), we can see in the story of Hosea and Gomer and in other examples of marriage symbolism in the Old Testament a personal message of hope amid despair, a message of love for the sinner amid his or her feelings of self-rejection. In fact, one of the most common yet most debilitating by-products of sin is the notion that by virtue of our own disobedience and unfaithfulness we are unlovable and unforgivable. This mistaken impression, spawned by questions such as "How can the Lord still love me after what I have done?" and "How can I ever be forgiven?" can become a major roadblock to repentance.

"There are multitudes of men and women—in and out of the Church—who are struggling vainly against obstacles in their path," observed Elder Jeffrey R. Holland. "Many are fighting the battle of life—and losing. Indeed, there are those among us who consider themselves the vilest of sinners. . . . How many broken hearts remain broken because those people feel they are beyond the pale of God's restorative power? How many bruised and battered spirits are certain that they have sunk to a depth at which the light of redeeming hope and grace will never again shine?" (*However Long and Hard the Road* [Salt Lake City: Deseret Book Co., 1985], p. 77.)

How can we overcome these sometimes overwhelming, ill-inspired feelings that seem to chain us down, especially when we feel unworthy to approach the only Being who can deliver us? We can find relief in the scriptures. Like the other standard works, the Old Testament can provide hope for the hopeless and love for the unlovable. The scriptural account of the profound love of the prophet Hosea for his unfaithful wife, Gomer, offers a motivating message to all whose hearts are or have been heavy with burdens of sin and feelings of unworthiness and spiritual rejection.

Gomer, the "wife of whoredoms," not only symbolizes wayward Israel, who went "whoring" after other gods (see Deuteronomy 31: 16–17; Hosea 9:1), but also represents each of us individually. Just as she was unfaithful to the bridegroom, Hosea, and to the covenants she made with him, each of us to some degree has also been remiss by breaking covenants or being unfaithful in our spiritual duties.

Hosea, on the other hand, stands as a graphic reminder of the steadfast love the Savior has for each of us. We cannot help but marvel at the continued compassion and love Hosea demonstrated for his wicked wife. Of course he abhorred her adultery. He could not and did not minimize the severity of her sins or ignore her infidelity, but he loved her still and yearned for her return. Similarly, Jehovah, our Savior and Bridegroom, loves us with a perfect and divine love. "I have loved thee with an everlasting love," he declared to Israel through the prophet Jeremiah, "therefore with lovingkindness have I drawn thee" (Jeremiah 31:3). While others may withhold love for us because of our sins and unworthy ways, Jesus stands ever ready to encircle us about "in the arms of his love" (2 Nephi 1:15). Despite our moments of weakness and spiritual infidelity, we are loved with his *chesed*, or "steadfast love," which the Apostle Paul said "passeth knowledge" (see Ephesians 3:19). Almost as if echoing from eternity we can hear the prophet Hosea testifying from his own painful personal experience that no matter who we are, no matter how unworthy we may feel, we are not rejected or alone, for the Savior of the world loves us still.

The message of the bride and the bridegroom inspires and invites us to come unto the Savior and partake of the fruit of the tree of life.

"If we could feel or were sensitive even in the slightest to the matchless love of our Savior and his willingness to suffer for our individual sins," Elder David B. Haight testified, "we would cease procrastination and 'clean the slate,' and repent of all our transgressions" ("Our Lord and Savior," *Ensign*, May 1988, p. 23.) When we or those around us feel unloved, rejected, or forgotten by the Lord, the love story of Gomer and Hosea—living symbols of the bride and the bridegroom— can convey a deeply personal message of love and hope. While some may think the God of the Old Testament is cold, cruel, and austere, in this symbolism we catch a spiritual glimpse of Jehovah's "steadfast love," the "pure love of Christ." It is of this love the Bridegroom has for the house of Israel, both collectively and individually, that the prophet Isaiah testified: "But Zion said, The Lord hath forsaken me, and my Lord hath forgotten me.

Can a woman forget her sucking child, that she should not have compassion on the son of her womb? yea, they may forget, yet will I not forget thee.

Behold, I have graven thee upon the palms of my hands; thy walls are continually before me " (Isaiah 49:14–16.)

## THE AVAILABILITY OF PERSONAL FORGIVENESS AND REDEMPTION

There are those among us who feel that they have sinned to such an extent that they cannot have any claim upon the mercy of God. "While wallowing in deep despair, true repentance is impossible," wrote Neal A. Maxwell. "The feeling of futility can render one powerless to further resist the adversary; it can blur the vital difference between understanding the possibility of forgiveness for the sinner, while rejecting the sinful act." ("Hope for the Hopeless," *Instructor*, August 1966, p. 318.) To these dejected souls the Old Testament account of Hosea's marriage, as well as other marriage symbols and prophecies, offers what may be the most hopeful and significant message in the scriptures: that through the Atonement of Jesus Christ we can be clean and pure again.

The story of Hosea and Gomer contains an interesting parallel to Christ. Not only is Hosea willing to take his adulterous wife back, but he actually purchases her back (see Hosea 3:2). That is one of the most important symbols in the story, because it represents the Savior's Atonement whereby, as the Apostle Paul testified, he "bought [us] with a price" (1 Corinthians 6:20).

Although the bridegroom's love for the bride is continual and unconditional, his forgiveness of her wickedness and his reacceptance of her into a covenantal relationship is conditioned upon a probationary period of repentance and rehabilitation. Just as ancient Israel had to abandon her worship of false gods and return to faithful worship of and obedience to Jehovah to be reclaimed as God's chosen people, or his *segullah*, so too must we meet certain conditions to receive redemption from our personal sins. Just as Hosea reached out to reclaim his bride, the Savior also "sendeth an invitation unto all men, for the arms of mercy are extended towards them, and he saith: Repent, and I will receive you. Yea, he saith: Come unto me and ye shall partake of the fruit of the tree of life; yea, ye shall eat and drink of the bread and the waters of life freely." (Alma 5:33–34.) Jesus, as the Bridegroom, will extend his forgiveness to us and accept us into his presence when we exercise faith in him, practice true repentance, and faithfully observe his laws and commandments.

The imagery of the bride and bridegroom, as seen in the Old Testament, is a message of messianic mercy and individual hope, a personal promise of redemption of lost lambs as well as the collective promise of the gathering of the flock of Israel. The words of Elder Spencer W. Kimball serve as a witness along with the words of Hosea, Isaiah, Jeremiah, and Ezekiel, who have all testified so eloquently of the covenantal relationship between the bride and the Bridegroom:

> God will wipe away from their eyes the tears of anguish, and remorse, and consternation, and fear, and guilt. Dry eyes will replace the wet ones, and smiles of satisfaction will replace the worried, anxious look.
>
> What relief! What comfort! What joy! Those laden with transgressions and sorrows and sin may be forgiven and cleansed and purified if they will return to their Lord, learn of him, and keep his commandments. And all of us needing to repent of day-to-day follies and weaknesses can likewise share in this miracle. (*The Miracle of Forgiveness* [Salt Lake City: Bookcraft, 1969], p. 368.)

## Our Responsibility to Love and Forgive Others

The example of the prophet Hosea's love for and forgiveness of his wayward wife, Gomer, not only is a powerful symbol of Christ's perfect love for all mankind and his mercy and forgiveness of those who repent, but also is a reminder of how we should treat our fellowmen. Many who have come to experience Jehovah's perfect love and the miracle of his forgiveness may still face another major obstacle—the need to forgive and lovingly accept others. Hosea's exemplary dealings with his unfaithful wife teach us that we too must be willing to continue to love and show concern for those around us who, much like Gomer, have gone astray, broken covenants, and wounded the hearts of those who love them. As a symbol of Christ's love for the sinner, the imagery of the bridegroom illustrates this "pure love of Christ" that we too must possess. "A new commandment I give unto you," the Savior declared unto his disciples, "That ye love one another. . . . By this shall all men know that ye are my disciples, if ye have love one to another." (John 13:34–35.)

In contrast to the Lord's conditional redemption of Israel and his conditional forgiveness of our sins, our forgiveness of others must be unconditional. The Lord declared:

> I, the Lord, forgive sins unto those who confess their sins before me and ask forgiveness, who have not sinned unto death.
>
> My disciples, in days of old, sought occasion against one another and forgave not one another in their hearts; and for this evil they were afflicted and sorely chastened.
>
> Wherefore, I say unto you, that ye ought to forgive one another; for he that forgiveth not his brother his trespasses standeth condemned before the Lord; for there remaineth in him the greater sin.
>
> I, the Lord, will forgive whom I will forgive, but of you it is required to forgive all men. (D&C 64:7–10.)

As the bridegroom lovingly and mercifully reclaims his beloved bride, we also have a sacred obligation to reach out to those around us who not only desire to return to the Lord and partake of his "steadfast love" and mercy, but who also need to feel *our* love, forgiveness, and acceptation. Our arms of mercy should be extended to "succor the weak, lift up the hands which hang down, and strengthen the feeble knees" (D&C 81:5). Elder Vaughn J. Featherstone spoke of the love and mercy epitomized by the prophet Hosea that should also be an essential part of our own lives. "We invite all those who are not here to come home. We gaze steadily down the road, anxious for your return. We will run with open arms, and hearts filled with compassion. . . . Come home and we will rejoice together." ("'However Faint the Light May Glow,'" *Ensign*, November 1982, p. 73.)

Like the law of Moses and many other Old Testament types and symbols, the scriptural account of Hosea and Gomer and the other prophetic references to the bride and the bridegroom serve as a "schoolmaster" that "[points] our souls to [Christ]" (Galatians 3:24; Jacob 4:5). This imagery can be deeply personal as we liken ourselves to the wayward bride and see in the bridegroom the Savior, who beckons each of us to return to the marriage, or to our covenantal relationship with him. This beautiful Old Testament imagery is a contemporary, relevant reminder that Christ loves us with a "steadfast love," which is stronger than all the sins of the world. He not only wants us back but has in very deed purchased us with his own blood. The imagery bears witness of the divine love, tender intimacy, and triumphant power of the Bridegroom. It points us to Christ. Perhaps there can be no greater message in the Old Testament.

> *I will mention the lovingkindnesses of the Lord, and the praises of the Lord, according to all that the Lord hath bestowed on us, and the great goodness toward the house of Israel, which he hath bestowed on them according to his mercies, and according to the multitude of his lovingkindnesses. For he said, Surely they are my people, children that will not lie: so he was their Saviour.*
> —Isaiah 63:7–8

*A new heart also will I give you, and a new spirit will I put within you:*
*and I will take away the stony heart out of your flesh,*
*and I will give you an heart of flesh. And I will*
*put my spirit within you, and cause you*
*to walk in my statutes, and ye*
*shall keep my judgments,*
*and do them.*
*—Ezekiel 36:26–27*

## CHAPTER ELEVEN

# A New Heart and
# a New Spirit

One day as other BYU Jerusalem Center faculty and I were taking a busload of students to visit important sites in the northern Galilee and Golan regions of Israel, our bus was stopped at a military checkpoint. "You must turn around," the Israeli military officer said to us. When we tried to press him for an explanation, he merely pointed in the direction opposite of where we wanted to go and said again, "Turn around."

There was some grumbling on the bus. We couldn't fully understand why we couldn't go on and visit the sites we had hoped to see, but we knew enough not to disobey the Israeli military. The students were disappointed, and some even expressed their frustration with statements such as, "I paid several thousand dollars to come on this program, and now I can't even visit the places I want to visit." We were not "happy campers" as the bus turned around and headed back to our accommodations at kibbutz Ein Gev. What had started out as a bus full of excited, talkative students anxious to visit new and interesting places became a quiet, glum bus of students murmuring and grumbling about the inconvenience and the inexplicable change of plans.

That evening, however, the griping and grumbling were replaced with grateful hearts when we heard fighter jets screaming by overhead and artillery shells and rockets exploding. A mini-war between the Israeli army and Palestinian-Arab freedom fighters from southern Lebanon had erupted in northern Galilee and near the Golan Heights. As the students learned of the war from our Israeli friends at the kibbutz, they better understood why we could not visit the planned field-trip sites and why the army officer so emphatically declared, "Turn around." While some of the students—the foolish, macho, thrill-seeking kind—wanted to be right in the middle of the action, most of us felt too close to the action as it was and were grateful to be out of harm's way, even though we could clearly see the smoke, hear the bombs and rockets exploding, and feel the earth shake with each explosion.

The order to "turn around" was not designed to ruin our fun or arbitrarily interfere with our studies; rather, it was a stern command intended to keep us from getting into a situation that perhaps could cost us our very lives. The disruption and inconvenience of being "turned around" no longer seemed to be such a bad thing but was seen instead as a prudent, even providential course to pursue.

What a great lesson was learned from this experience! As I have pondered the spiritual significance and application of this episode in the years since, I have come to realize that one of the major messages of the Old Testament—in fact, of the entire gospel—is the message to "turn around" our lives. The word *turn* is used scores of times in the Old Testament. The Hebrew word *shuv* that is often translated as "to repent" literally means "to turn around." From the scriptures we see that "turning around" requires both a *turning from* and a *turning to*—turning from sinfulness and turning to God. These two dimensions that together bring about a 180-degree "turnaround" are clearly taught, both by precept and example, in the Old Testament. Jonah 3:8 states, "Let them turn every one from his evil way." The prophet Joel recorded, "Therefore also now, saith the Lord, turn ye even to me with all your heart, and with fasting, and with weeping, and with mourning . . . and repent, and turn unto the Lord your God; for he is gracious and merciful, slow to anger, and of great kindness, and he will turn away the evil from you" (JST, Joel 2:12–13). Through the prophet Ezekiel the Lord said, "Repent, and turn yourselves from all your transgressions; so iniquity shall not be your ruin. Cast away from you all your transgressions, whereby ye have transgressed; and make you a new heart and a new spirit." (Ezekiel 18:30–31.)

## TURNING FROM EVIL

In this dispensation the Lord revealed to the Prophet Joseph Smith that the indicators of true repentance, or of the "turning around" of one's life, are the confession and forsaking of sin (see D&C 58:43; 64:7). While this doctrine was revealed anew in the latter days, it is not unique to the modern Church but rather is everlasting and is taught in the ancient scriptures as well. The Old Testament clearly teaches the need to turn from evil both in our attitudes as well as our actions and in our desires as well as our deeds: "He that covereth his sins shall not prosper: but whoso confesseth and forsaketh them shall have mercy" (Proverbs 28:13). "I acknowledged my sin unto thee, and mine iniquity have I not hid. I said, I will confess my transgressions unto the Lord; and thou forgavest the iniquity of my sin." (Psalm 32:5.)

In addition to containing prophetic teachings regarding the doctrine of faith and repentance, the Old Testament also records that formal public ritual was utilized to remind the Israelites of the need to forsake evil inwardly as well as outwardly. This was particularly evident in certain sacrifices prescribed under the law of Moses: "And if a soul sin, . . . he shall confess that he hath sinned in that thing: and he shall bring his trespass offering unto the Lord for his sin which he hath sinned, . . , and the priest shall make an atonement for him concerning his sin" (Leviticus 5:1, 5–6).

The trespass offering was the outward acknowledgment of sin, which served to remind the transgressor of other attitudes and behaviors, both internal and external, that are requisite elements of true repentance. Each part of the sacrificial animal was symbolic of a certain aspect of the sinner's personal life. Though it was a public sacrifice, the ritual was to symbolize the inner thoughts, feelings, and affections of the heart of the individual, not just his or her outward demeanor or behavior. This was a symbolic teaching method designed to instruct ancient Israel that turning from evil requires a turning of one's heart as well as a turning of one's behavior.

## A Broken Heart and a Contrite Spirit

The prophet Daniel's earnest prayer unto the Lord on behalf of all of Israel illustrates the contrition of spirit, deep humility, and sincere confession of sin that are essential elements of true repentance:

> And I set my face unto the Lord God, to seek by prayer and supplications, with fasting, and sackcloth, and ashes:
>
> And I prayed unto the Lord my God, and made my confession, and said, O Lord, the great and dreadful God, keeping the covenant and mercy to them that love him, and to them that keep his commandments;
>
> We have sinned, and have committed iniquity, and have done wickedly, and have rebelled, even by departing from thy precepts. . . .
>
> O Lord, hear; O Lord, forgive; O Lord, hearken and do. (Daniel 9:3–5, 19.)

Similarly, in the New Testament the Apostle Paul spoke of the spiritual sorrow that comes from an awakening of our unworthiness before God as a "godly sorrow" which "worketh repentance to salvation" (2 Corinthians 7:9–10). The Book of Mormon prophets spoke of this same inward "turning around" as "a broken heart and a contrite spirit." Both terms can be used interchangeably to teach the concept of a kind of inward remorse and revulsion for sin, or the feeling of sorrow for our sins that God would have us feel in order to bring about repentance and submission to him. "To have a broken heart and a contrite spirit," wrote Elder Bruce R. McConkie, "is to be broken down with deep sorrow for sin, to be humbly and thoroughly penitent, to have attained sincere and purposeful repentance." Godly sorrow for sin, he said, "includes an honest, heartfelt contrition of soul, a contrition born of a broken heart and a contrite spirit. It presupposes a frank, personal acknowledgment that one's acts have been evil in the sight of Him who is holy. There is no mental reservation in godly sorrow, no feeling that perhaps one's sins are not so gross or serious after all. It is certainly more than regret either because the sin has been brought to light or because some preferential reward or status has been lost because of it." (*Mormon Doctrine*, 2d ed., [Salt Lake City: Bookcraft, 1966], pp. 161, 292.)

There is probably no more beautiful expression of true godly sorrow for sin in all of holy writ than in the poignant, almost pitiful pleadings of King David as expressed in his inspired psalms. Although he could not fully repent of his complicity in the murder of Uriah, he desired with all his heart and soul to "turn around" and make his life different from what it had been.

> O Lord, rebuke me not in thy wrath: neither chasten me in thy hot displeasure.
>
> For thine arrows stick fast in me, and thy hand presseth me sore.
>
> There is no soundness in my flesh because of thine anger; neither is there any rest in my bones because of my sin.
>
> For mine iniquities are gone over mine head: as an heavy burden they are too heavy for me.
>
> My wounds stink and are corrupt because of my foolishness.
>
> I am troubled; I am bowed down greatly; I go mourning all the day long.
>
> For my loins are filled with a loathsome disease: and there is no soundness in my flesh.
>
> I am feeble and sore broken: I have roared by reason of the disquietness of my heart.
>
> Lord, all my desire is before thee; and my groaning is not hid from thee.
>
> My heart panteth, my strength faileth me: as for the light of mine eyes, it also is gone from me.
>
> My lovers and my friends stand aloof from my sore; and my kinsmen stand afar off. . . .
>
> For I am ready to halt, and my sorrow is continually before me.
>
> For I will declare mine iniquity; I will be sorry for my sin. (Psalm 38:1–11, 17–18.)

This kind of "sackcloth and ashes" humility and godly sorrow for sin promotes spiritual growth and leads one to a condition described by one writer as a "change of nature befitting heaven" (as quoted in David O. McKay, *Gospel Ideals* [Salt Lake City: Improvement Era, 1953], p. 13). It is more than just regret or remorse; it is a turning of our broken hearts away from sinful desires as well as a contrite confessing of our sins. "Repentance is the turning away from that which is low and the striving for that which is higher," President David O. McKay taught. "As a principle of salvation, it involves not only a desire for that which is better, but also a sorrow—not merely remorse—but true sorrow for having become contaminated in any degree with things sinful." (Ibid., p. 13.)

As painful and difficult as such godly sorrow and confession may be, this is not the conclusion of the repentance process prescribed by the Lord. Godly sorrow—the broken heart and contrite spirit—may open the gate, but we must walk through that gate with "fruits meet for repentance." Repentance, or, as in the Hebrew, "turning around," is not complete without the fulfillment of another element required of the Lord. "By this ye may know if a man repenteth of his sins," the Lord declared in our day; "behold, he will confess them and forsake them" (D&C 58:43). As essential as godly sorrow and confession are, the true test of repentance is in forsaking sin.

## Turning Our Backs on Sin

Numerous passages in the Old Testament and in all of the standard works speak of the necessity of forsaking sin and turning away from it. Too often, however, this concept is misunderstood to mean that one merely stops committing the particular sin of which he is repenting—kind of like "sin du jour" and "forsake du jour." The cessation of one designated sin at a time is necessary and is certainly required to "turn away" from iniquity, but to view the scriptural concept of "turning from sin" by this narrow and compartmentalized definition may rob us of a complete perspective of the true nature of repentance. Isaiah condemned those who think they can give up one sin and yet cling tenaciously to others. "Woe unto them that draw iniquity with cords of vanity, and sin as it were with a cart rope" (Isaiah 5:18). Occasionally we cut the "cords of vanity" and let go of a favorite sin, but all too often we only periodically cast off from our cart a sin here and there rather than just letting go of the cart rope. As Elder Spencer W. Kimball taught, there can be no true "turning around" of our lives if we forsake only some selected sins but continue to embrace sinfulness: "That transgressor is not fully repentant who neglects his tithing, misses his meetings, breaks the Sabbath, fails in his family prayers, does not sustain the authorities of the Church, breaks the Word of Wisdom, does not love the Lord nor his fellowmen. A reforming adulterer who drinks or curses is not repentant. The repenting burglar who has sex play is not ready for forgiveness. God cannot forgive unless the transgressor shows a true repentance which spreads to all areas of his life." (*The Miracle of Forgiveness* [Salt Lake City: Bookcraft, 1969], p. 203.)

"Repent, and turn yourselves from all your transgressions," the Lord admonished through Ezekiel (Ezekiel 18:30). True repentance involves a change of heart and spirit and a comprehensive abandonment of evil desires and deeds. This kind of total "turning around" brings with it a newness of attitude, character, and being.

Many centuries after the Lord commanded ancient Israel to "turn around," the Apostle Paul similarly taught that repentance requires much more than just stopping one particular sin; it requires a total reformation of life. He explained that it implied such a mighty change that a person actually becomes a "new creature" (2 Corinthians 5:17). Through our "faith unto repentance" (Alma 34:15) our old ways of evil become "crucified" with Christ and we begin to "walk in newness of life" (Romans 6:2–6). Both the book of Ezekiel in the Old Testament and Paul's epistle to the Ephesians in the New Testament emphasize that this "turning around"—this metamorphosis from the "old man" of sin to a "new man" which God has "created in righteousness and true holiness" (Ephesians 4:24)—comes as a gift to us through the grace and mercy of Christ (see also Ezekiel 36:25–27). Though a gift of grace, this mighty change is bestowed upon us through the exercise of our own faith in the Lord and as we live in such way that we bring forth "fruits worthy of repentance" (Luke 3:8–14; see also Helaman 15:7).

This blending of man's faith and works with God's grace is reflected in the Greek word *metanoia*, which is the New Testament companion to the Hebrew word *shuv* found in the Old Testament. The definition, however, encompasses much more than turning our backs on a particular sin and changing our behavior. It involves a change of thoughts, attitudes, and desires. *Metanoia* literally means "afterthought" or "change of mind," but it also implies complete conversion. Further implicit in the definitions of both *shuv* and *metanoia* is the fact that a conscientious relinquishing of sin must be combined with a determined shunning of the trappings of sinfulness that may distract us from the required spiritual surrender to God. We must evolve from a lower way of thinking and acting to a higher one in which our thoughts, desires, and attitudes coincide with the mind of Christ.

We often speak of the "Rs of Repentance," but when we more fully understand the scriptural concept of "turning around" we will recognize some important Rs that must not be overlooked: a *reeducation* of our minds, a *reordering* of our priorities, a *redirecting* of our desires, and a *reshaping* of our characters. This kind of repentance is so powerful that it literally changes our very way of life. Through repentance we can become "partakers of the divine nature" by leaving behind the lusts of the world and doing instead those things that reflect the mind of Christ (see 2 Peter 1:4–8).

President Spencer W. Kimball further declared that turning our backs on sin may also of necessity include changing our friends and associations as well as our circumstances and environments. "There must be an abandonment of the transgression," he wrote. "It must be genuine and consistent and continuing. . . . And a temporary, momentary change of life is not sufficient." For people to truly forsake sin and turn their lives around they must "make changes in their lives, transformation in their habits, and . . . add new thoughts to their minds." President Kimball also cautioned: "True repentance incorporates within it a washing, a purging, a changing of attitudes, a reappraising, a strengthening toward self-mastery. It is not a simple matter for one to transform his life overnight, nor to change attitudes in a moment, nor to rid himself in a hurry of unworthy companions." ("What Is True Repentance?" *New Era*, May 1974, pp. 5, 6, 7.)

It is clear from the scriptures, both ancient and modern, that to be truly repentant and to really "turn our backs on sin" we must become different, in a positive and righteous way, from the people of the world—doing different deeds, thinking different thoughts, and practicing principles of righteousness. As Isaiah taught, "Wash you, make you clean; put away the evil of your doings from before mine eyes; cease to do evil" (Isaiah 1:16).

## TURNING TO GOD

The Hebrew concept of repentance, or "turning around," implies not only a turning *from* our sins but also a turning *to* God with greater devotion. "Turn thou to thy God," Hosea declared as he called the Is-raelites to repentance (Hosea 12:6). Similarly Ezekiel highlighted three important elements of repentance: "turn from his sin," "do that which is lawful," and "restore the pledge" (see Ezekiel 33:14–16). As seen in the words of Ezekiel, turning to God requires greater devotion to him and his ways, increased love and service to our fellowmen, and a restitution for transgression.

## Increased Devotion to God

A person hasn't really "turned around" in the true spirit of repen-tance if there isn't increased devotion to God and renewed commit-ment to living righteously. That person may back away from sin, but unless he or she "turns around" and faces God and serves him, true repentance hasn't occurred. "One of the requisites for repentance is the living of the commandments of the Lord," President Kimball de-clared. "Perhaps few people realize that as an important element; though one may have abandoned a particular sin and even confessed it to his bishop, yet he is not repentant if he has not developed a life of action and service and righteousness, which the Lord has indicated to be very necessary: '. . . He that repents and does the commandments of the Lord shall be forgiven.'" ("What Is True Repentance?" p. 7.)

Mormon noted this type of transformed lifestyle among the repen-tant Nephites in the time of Helaman. He described their increased in-volvement in spiritual behaviors such as fasting, prayer, and dedicated study of the scriptures, but he wrote that sanctification came to them "because of their yielding their hearts unto God" (Helaman 3:35). Yielding our hearts to God naturally precipitates an increased love for him and thus increased involvement in his earthly kingdom and more diligent and conscientious efforts to increase our spirituality.

Sometimes, because of our feelings of unworthiness or embarrass-ment that accompany our sins, we may feel to recoil from Church activ-ities and involvement in spiritual development. We may not feel worthy to pray or have the disposition to search the scriptures or fast; yet these are the very things that will "turn us around." President Kimball wrote:

Since all of us sin in greater or lesser degree, we are all in need of constant repentance, of continually raising our sights and our perfor-mance. One can hardly do the commandments of the Lord in a day, a week, a month or a year. This is an effort which must be extended through the remainder of one's years. To accomplish it every soul should develop the same spirit of devotion and dedication to the work of the Lord as the bishop and the Relief Society president enjoy. Most often theirs is near total devotion.

This devotion needs to be applied as much in mental as in spiritual and physical effort. To understand the gospel so that true obedience can be intelligently given to its requirements takes time and application. . . . [This involves] serving and attending and participating in . . . meetings and conferences, and all this in addition to the study of the gospel and many hours on [one's] knees in prayer. . . .

. . . Repentance must involve an all-out, total surrender to the program of the Lord. (*The Miracle of Forgiveness*, pp. 202–3.)

In a garden, it is not enough just to eradicate the weeds. They will inevitably reinvade unless we plant good seeds and continually cultivate and nurture those plants so we can ultimately partake of their fruits. We must likewise fill our lives with righteousness so that there is less room in our hearts and minds for evil.

## Increased Love and Service to Our Fellowmen

There is perhaps no greater earthly evidence of our hearts being turned to God than in the manifestation of our hearts being turned to our fellowmen. "When ye are in the service of your fellow beings," King Benjamin declared, "ye are only in the service of your God" (Mosiah 2:17). In all the standard works there is probably not a more profound example of how true repentance engenders a greater desire to serve others than in the story of the sons of Mosiah. Before their remarkable conversion these young men were, according to the scriptures, "the very vilest of sinners" (Mosiah 28:4). Because of their sincere repentance and their intense gratitude for the Atonement of Christ that had turned them around, we later find them "zealously striving to repair all the injuries which they had done to the church, confessing all their sins, and publishing all the things which they had seen, and explaining the prophecies and the scriptures to all who desired to hear them. And thus they were instruments in the hands of God in bringing many to the knowledge of the truth. . . . Now they were desirous that salvation should be declared to every creature, for they could not bear that any human soul should perish." (Mosiah 27:35–36; 28:3.)

Whether it be through formal or informal missionary service, work for the dead in temples, faithfulness in our Church callings, or the subtle, simple, often unnoticed service of a visiting teacher, home teacher, neighbor, friend, or family member, our devotion to others demonstrates our desire to "turn from all evil" and shows that our hearts are turned to God. After Isaiah called Israel to repentance and pleaded with her to "cease to do evil," he further explained that "turning around" requires not only that one abandon sin but also that one "learn to do well; seek [justice], relieve the oppressed, judge [mercifully] the fatherless, plead for the widow" (Isaiah 1:17).

### Restitution

One of the elements of repentance Ezekiel identified was the "restoring of the pledge," which referred specifically to the principle of restitution that had been taught by earlier prophets and was an integral part of the law of Moses. It required a repayment or restoration of that which was stolen or lost through sin. Often this meant paying back even more than that which was originally lost (see Exodus 22:1–6; Leviticus 6:2–5). In the Church today, we still attempt, when possible, to pay back that which was lost as a result of our sins. Sometimes this is easy, such as paying for or returning an item that was stolen. However, often only partial restitution is feasible, and sometimes it may be impossible to fully restore what was lost. Sometimes all we can do is devote our lives to restitution through righteousness, relying upon the grace of Christ to mercifully rectify that which we could never correct ourselves.

"Restoring the pledge" also refers to a greater restitution than just paying for our sins—it involves an entire lifetime of expressing our love and appreciation for the Savior's Atonement through our actions and service. While it is true that we can in no way, of ourselves, completely repay the Savior for "turning us around," we can, like the sons of Mosiah, spend the rest of our lives "zealously striving to repair all injuries" caused by our sins by loving and serving our fellowmen and leading them unto Christ. Thus, restoring the pledge requires more than mere "trespass offerings" of dollars or transitory deeds. Our very lives—our changed *beings* as well as our changed *behavior*—verify our awe and appreciation for the atoning blood of Christ that bought us with a price and made us "new creatures." Because we will always remain "unprofitable servants," eternally indebted to God for his goodness, we must continually restore the pledge through our deeds, desires, and devotion.

"Turn around!" What a blessing it was those many years ago that an Israeli military officer insisted that we turn back. As a result, we were literally protected and our lives spared. How grateful I am for the message of the Old Testament that safety and protection here and eternal rewards hereafter await those who will "turn around" by turning from evil and turning to God. How grateful I am for the message of the Old Testament that because of Christ, the Holy One of Israel, I can "turn around." This is a message of hope and love, an important message that can be a catalyst for change and a blessing of comfort. By "turning around," or by faithfully and continually repenting of sins, keeping the commandments, and serving God, we will indeed be blessed with a new heart and a new spirit.

> Come now, and let us reason together, saith the Lord: though your sins be as scarlet, they shall be as white as snow; though they be red like crimson, they shall be as wool.
> —Isaiah 1:18

*Surely he hath borne our griefs, and carried our sorrows: yet we did esteem him*
*stricken, smitten of God, and afflicted. But he was wounded for*
*our transgressions, he was bruised for our inquities:*
*the chastisement of our peace was upon him;*
*and with his stripes we are healed.*
*—Isaiah 53:4–5*

## CHAPTER TWELVE

# All Things Point to Christ

I never have liked reading the Old Testament," one of my Old Testament students at the BYU Jerusalem Center earnestly said to me. "I have always loved reading the Book of Mormon because I could understand it and it so clearly testifies of Christ." He continued, "I came to the Holy Land not to study the Old Testament—in fact, I only took this class because I had to—but to study the life and teachings of Jesus as found in the New Testament, and to walk where he had walked. I came to the Holy Land to find Christ. I found him, all right, but I never would have dreamed that it would have been through studying the Old Testament."

This student's comments, which have been echoed by numerous others, demonstrate the real message of the Old Testament both anciently and for our day. The greatest message of that volume of holy writ is not found merely in its faith-promoting stories, nor is it found solely in the great prophecies concerning ancient Israel or the events of the last days. "The message of the Old Testament," President Marion G. Romney declared, "is the message of Christ and his coming and his atonement" ("The Message of the Old Testament," address delivered at the 3rd Annual Church Educational System Religious Educators Symposium—Old Testament, 16–18 August 1979, Brigham Young University, Provo, Utah, typescript, p. 5.) The Old Testament, as its title implies, is indeed a "testament"—a witness, a testimony, an affirmation, a tangible verification—of the divinity of Jesus Christ and the reality of his atoning sacrifice.

The Book of Mormon prophet Jacob taught that the Jews would reject the Messiah for the same reasons that they "despised the words of plainness, and killed the prophets." He explained that this spiritual blindness afflicting the ancient Jews came "by looking beyond the mark." (Jacob 4:14.) The "mark" they were looking beyond was the Messiah, even Jesus Christ, whom they missed because they failed to see in him the fulfillment of the very essence of their scriptures, though every practice, every principle, and every prophecy pointed to his coming.

While it is true that many "plain and precious things" that more clearly testified of Christ have been lost from our scriptures, there is still much that points us to him if we will but see and understand. We often condemn the ancients for "looking beyond the mark" and missing their Messiah, but we may unwittingly do the same thing if we view the Old Testament as merely a collection of faith-promoting stories at best, or, at worst, an incomprehensible, irrelevant ancient record—a strange history of an obscure people. In contrast, Nephi treasured the Old Testament and gloried in its divine contents (see 2 Nephi 4:15–16). It was not just for their genealogy on the brass plates that his father, Lehi, sent his sons back to Jerusalem at the peril of their lives (see 1 Nephi 3–6). It was also because the plates contained a record of prophecies, principles, and practices, all centered in Christ, that were of "great worth" unto them and unto us today.

In confounding the anti-Christ Sherem, Jacob asked him if he believed the scriptures (see Jacob 7:10). The scriptures Jacob was referring to were not our modern-day leather-bound quads, but the Nephite equivalent of the Old Testament. The value of the those scriptures to them anciently is the same as the value of the Old Testament for us today. "They truly testify of Christ," Jacob declared. "Behold, I say unto you that none of the prophets have written, nor prophesied, save they have spoken concerning this Christ." (Jacob 7:11.) All the ancient prophets bore powerful testimony of the coming of Christ and the redemptive power of his atoning sacrifice (see 1 Nephi 10:4–5; Jacob 4:11; Mosiah 13:33–35; 15:11).

Christ is the central figure of the Old Testament, just as he is in all scripture. All other messages are secondary. The faith-promoting stories, the accounts of the blessings and prosperity enjoyed by the Israelites because of their obedience and the destruction they suffered because of their disobedience, and the descriptions of the covenants and prophecies of scattering and gathering have no saving power without the message of Christ. They are like appetizers at a great feast, but Christ—his gospel, his teachings, his Atonement—is the main course. If we only pick at parts of the Old Testament and never feast on the main course, we will walk away having eaten some small, tasty morsels, yet we will still be hungry and our souls unsatisfied. Christ is the reason for studying the Old Testament. There are many things in the Old Testament that are interesting, but the message of Christ and his saving power is the book's imperative. As President Spencer W. Kimball testified: "Old Testament prophets from Adam to Malachi are testifying of the divinity of the Lord Jesus Christ and our Heavenly Father. Jesus Christ was the God of the Old Testament, and it was He who conversed with Abraham and Moses. It was He who inspired Isaiah and Jeremiah; it was He who foretold through those chosen men the happenings of the future, even to the lastest day and hour." (In Conference Report, April 1977, p. 113.)

So important is this central message that God has utilized many different methodologies within the book to keep our attention upon it. There are types and shadows, as well as symbols in sacrifices, to draw our attention to Christ on almost every page. Permeating the entire Old Testament are also Messianic prophecies and doctrinal teachings that remind us that couched within all other secondary messages and events recorded in the book is the primary reason for scripture—to testify of Christ and to point our souls to him. The prophet Abinadi testified: "Behold I say unto you, that whosoever has heard the words of the prophets, yea, all the holy prophets who have prophesied concerning the coming of the Lord—I say unto you, that all those who have hearkened unto their words, and believed that the Lord would redeem his people, and have looked forward to that day for a remission of their sins, I say unto you, that these are his seed, or they are the heirs of the kingdom of God." (Mosiah 15:11.)

## TYPES AND SHADOWS OF CHRIST

All scriptures, but specifically the Old Testament, utilize figurative imagery to teach important doctrinal concepts. Sometimes a very simple symbol, something that is easily recognized by people on different intellectual and cultural levels, can represent a deeply spiritual doctrine or teach a highly complex concept. Explaining the purposes of God in using types and shadows and other forms of symbolic instruction, Elder Bruce R. McConkie wrote: "To crystallize in our minds the eternal verities which we must accept and believe to be saved, to dramatize their true meaning and import with an impact never to be forgotten, to center our attention on these saving truths, again and again and again, the Lord uses similitudes. Abstract principles may easily be forgotten or their deep meaning overlooked, but visual performances and actual experiences are registered on the mind in such a way as never to be lost." (*The Promised Messiah* [Salt Lake City: Deseret Book Co., 1978], p. 377.)

The Savior often used metaphors, parables, and other symbols in his mortal ministry. Sometimes this kind of scriptural imagery was used as much to conceal the deep doctrinal truths from the spiritually immature or critical as it was to reveal important messages that could be understood by all, regardless of their spiritual or intellectual capacities. A *type* is such a symbol; it represents, illustrates, or exemplifies something else. In the scriptures a physical object or type often is used to embody or epitomize a spiritual concept. Similarly, a *shadow* is a symbol or representation that foreshadows something that will occur in the future. (See 2 Nephi 11:4; Mosiah 3:15; 13:31.) Volumes have been written about scriptural symbolism and the numerous types and shadows of Christ found in holy writ, but here are a few from the Old Testament that have special meaning to me and a profound relevance to us as Latter-day Saints.

### Abraham and Isaac

Father Abraham had waited so long to have his "only begotten son" of promise born to him and Sarah (see Hebrews 11:17–19). The command to take Isaac to Mount Moriah and present him as a burnt offering unto God is both a type and a shadow. It typifies the "great and last sacrifice" of the Son of God (see Alma 34:10; Jacob 4:5). It is a shadow in that it portends the supreme sacrifice that would occur in the meridian of time on the very same mountain, later to be called Golgotha. There are several types within this story: the father, the son, the mountain, the sacrifice, and even the ram that was provided to spare Isaac. Jewish legend also adds additional symbolism to this type and shadow. The book of Jasher, in Jewish Midrash, records that Isaac was twenty-five years old and could have easily fought off Abraham and escaped had he wanted to. The legend further states that when Abraham's resolve began to falter—when it became too difficult for him to sacrifice his only son—Isaac encouraged his father and was willing to die of his own accord, knowing his father had been commanded of God.

"I have felt that the Lord wanted us to understand that He loves us," Elder Melvin J. Ballard explained.

He was teaching us this when He gave to Abraham the test of his life, to offer his son, Isaac, whom he loved with all his heart, the child of his promise, to give him as a sacrifice, he was speaking to us of His love through the test of Father Abraham. . . .

Take the case of Abraham: he was to be the example and the pattern or illustration of the love and affection that the Father had for his children. "Take your only begotten son and offer him as a sacrifice." I have thought of the poor man gathering up the fagots, starting up the mountain with his child of promise. Three days they walked until they reached the place where the sacrifice was to take place, and then his only child and son of promise said to his father: "We have forgotten something, father. Where is the sacrifice?" Oh, how it must have torn the father, made his heart to bleed to hear from the innocent lips of his child, whom he loved better than life itself, the reminder that he should take the life of his child! He could not speak, his heart must have swelled almost to bursting. And still he went on day after day, until he reached the spot. The altar was erected, the fagots placed upon it, the child bound, the steel bared, the arm raised that should strike the blow. "It is enough," said the angel who stayed the hand. Here is the sacrifice. It was to make you feel what our Father felt, when He who loved His Son better than it is possible for mortals to love their own flesh and blood, gave His Son to the world, for the world's redemption, for the world's peace, and the world's salvation. Do you not think that while the Father, who had the power to save His Son from the abuse, from the crown of thorns, from the whippings and mistreatment; do you not think it was a trial for Him, who had

the power to save His Son, to stand by and witness the appeal of the
Son, in agony until great drops of blood came from His body. "If it is
possible, save me, O Father!" Think of your own child. If your child
was in distress, is there a man among us entrusted with the power to
save, and would not use it? God knows that we are so human that if
He should give us power to save our own, we would save them every
time. And yet He had the power to save and did not save. What
mother would not fly through fire and water at hearing the appeal of
her child in distress. How it must have tried the Father to hear the
cry and lamentation of the Son: "If it is possible, Father, let it pass
by!" I say the Father was grief-stricken when He heard the taunting of
those who stood by. "He saved others, why don't He save Himself?"
After the hours of grief and agony, there came a moment when Jesus
cried out, "My God, my God, why hast thou forsaken me?" If Jesus
truly said that, it was not that the Father had forsaken, but that the
hour had arrived, which often arrives in our own human experience,
an hour when the mother, for example, who cannot any longer stand
to bear the sight of her dying child, after the farewell is given, is taken
out of the room, not to witness the last dying struggles of her loved
one. And so, the Father, taxed to the utmost, had withdrawn, and
somewhere was weeping for His beloved Son. Even He could not
stand the sight any longer. But as I have thought of it, in my heart I
have thanked God, that when in that last critical moment, He might
have saved His Son, He saw us, perishing in the grave, lost to Him,
and lost to that salvation which is to come, he saw that on the one
hand, and the appeals and the suffering of His Son on the other; and,
thank God, He decided in our favor, and allowed the suffering and
death of His Son. (In Conference Report, October 1914, pp. 68–69.)

## All Prophets Are Types of Christ

The Hebrew concept of a prophet was one of a mediator, or one
who stood between God and man (see Bible Dictionary, s.v.
"prophet"). We see within that role a type for Christ as our mediator.
Through his Atonement, he mediates the spiritual and physical estrangement that came upon all mankind through the fall of Adam and
through our sinfulness. "No man cometh unto the Father, but by me,"
Jesus declared (John 14:6). In a symbolic way, prophets were media-
tors and intercessors between Deity and their wicked peoples. In addition to the mediator role, prophets were types of Christ as advocates

for their people before God. One of the most significant examples in the Old Testament is Moses pleading on behalf of his own people, whom God was going to destroy on account of their wickedness (see Exodus 32:31–34; Numbers 16:44–48). This typifies Jesus' advocacy of us before the Father (see D&C 45:2–3).

Melchizedek is also a type of Christ in that his very name or title points us to the Savior of the world. From the Hebrew language as well as modern revelation, we learn that his name means "king of heaven" or "king of righteousness" (see JST, Genesis 14:36; Hebrews 7:2). The Old Testament recounts that he was the ruler of Salem (see Genesis 14:18; JST, Genesis 14:33). *Salem* comes from the Semitic root that means "peace." Hence, Melchizedek could be referred to as a prince or king of peace (see Alma 13:18). It is also interesting to see how the Lord sometimes addresses his prophets with another title that is clearly ascribed to Christ: "Son of Man." That type and shadow is used scores of times in the book of Ezekiel (see Ezekiel 33:30–33).

Joseph and Moses are also important types of Christ. Joseph, who was sold by his brethren to be a slave—like Christ, who was "sold" for thirty pieces of silver, which was the prescribed price for a slave—became a great deliverer of his brethren. Similarly, Moses, as a deliverer of the Israelites who were under Egyptian bondage, symbolizes Christ as the great deliverer of all mankind from the bondage of death and hell. The Joseph Smith Translation (Genesis 50:24–38) clearly expounds to us the "typifying of Christ" seen in the mortal missions of Joseph and Moses.

The prophets Elijah and Elisha were also types and shadows of Christ. The great miracles they performed among the people of ancient Israel, such as healing the sick and raising the dead, were but a foreshadowing of the miracles Jesus would perform in his earthly ministry—miracles which in and of themselves were types and shadows. They symbolized the ultimate miracles of his Atonement: the resurrection of the dead and the healing of sick souls through redemption from spiritual death.

The prophet Jonah and his encounter with a great fish is also a graphic symbol of Christ. His being swallowed into the belly of a fish for three days and then being delivered up again unto freedom is characterized in the scriptures as the "sign of the prophet Jonas." This type and shadow Jesus himself said symbolized his death, burial, and resurrection (see Matthew 12:39–40).

*"The Sure Mercies of David"*

Next to Moses, there is perhaps no greater type of Christ than King David. Almost every aspect of his life—until his sinful involvement with Bathsheba and his complicity in the death of her husband—is a symbol of Christ. He, like Jesus, was born in Bethlehem. He was anointed king long before he reigned, just as Jesus was "the anointed" even before the foundation of the earth. His physical victory over Goliath and later enemies point to the ultimate victory of Christ, the "son of David," over death and hell. David was viewed as the prototypical king of Israel, and numerous prophecies and symbols point to the Messiah as the rightful king on David's throne, or as a "second David" (see Psalm 45:6–7; 145:12–13; Isaiah 9:6; 16:5; Jeremiah 33:15–21; Ezekiel 34:23–24; 37:24–25; see also Hebrews 1:8–9; Revelation 22:16).

After David's spiritual fall, he pleaded with the Lord for mercy and for whatever forgiveness and blessing he might still receive. Many of his most poignant psalms express the hope that the Lord would extend mercy to him and not allow him to remain in hell forever (see Psalm 16:7–11). This Davidic hope finds fulfillment in the Atonement of Jesus Christ, which guarantees that all will be resurrected from the dead and all will be redeemed, with only the sons of perdition unworthy to receive any kingdom of glory and spiritual redemption (see D&C 76:31–38). This merciful gift of the resurrection for all mankind is referred to in the scriptures as "the sure mercies of David" (see Acts 13:22–37), another way in which David is a type and shadow of Christ.

*The Brazen Serpent*

During their sojourn through the wilderness amid a period of rebelliousness, the Israelites were afflicted by poisonous serpents that "bit the people; and much people of Israel died." Moses pleaded with the Lord on behalf of his suffering people, and the Lord commanded him to make a serpent of brass and place it on a pole. "And it shall come to pass," said the Lord, "that every one that is bitten, when he looketh upon it, shall live" (Numbers 21:8). Why Jehovah chose to use this unique method of healing is not stated in the Old Testament, but it is explained for us in the Book of Mormon. "A type was raised up in the wilderness," Alma explained, "that whosoever would look upon it might live. And many did look and live. But few understood the meaning of those things, and this because of the hardness of their hearts." (Alma 33:19.)

Later, Nephi son of Helaman testified that this brazen serpent was a type of Christ and how we can be healed both physically and spiritually through his being lifted up upon the cross: "Moses . . . hath spoken concerning the coming of the Messiah.

Yea, did he not bear record that the Son of God should come? And as he lifted up the brazen serpent in the wilderness, even so shall he be lifted up who should come.

And as many as should look upon that serpent should live, even so as many as should look upon the Son of God with faith, having a contrite spirit, might live, even unto that life which is eternal." (Helaman 8:13–15.)

## Manna—Bread from Heaven

One of the most remarkable miracles described in the Old Testament is the manner in which the Lord preserved and led the Israelites as they wandered in the wilderness. This was not a one-time miracle, but rather a forty-year-long manifestation of God's power. For six days each week the Israelites gathered the miraculous manna. They could not stop to plant crops and build mills and granaries, so the Lord provided "bread from heaven" for them while they wandered in the desert (see Exodus 16; Numbers 11:6–9). Without this they would have starved to death. This was a daily, continual reminder of their total dependence upon the Lord for their sustenance (see Deuteronomy 8:2–3). When they finally arrived in the promised land this miraculous manna stopped raining from heaven. As a perpetual reminder of this miracle, however, a jar of manna was placed in the holy ark of the covenant.

Jesus reminded the Jews of something that had been lost from their collective doctrinal memory—that all must eat of the Bread of Life in order to find eternal life. He explicitly stated that manna was merely a symbol of something far greater than mere physical food. He further reminded them that Moses did not provide the miracle of manna, but rather the Father sent this bread from heaven to save them.

Verily, verily, I say unto you, Moses gave you not that bread from heaven; but my Father giveth you the true bread from heaven.

For the bread of God is he which cometh down from heaven, and giveth life unto the world.

Then said they unto him, Lord, evermore give us this bread.

And Jesus said unto them, I am the bread of life: he that cometh to me shall never hunger; and he that believeth on me shall never thirst. . . .

I am that bread of life.

Your fathers did eat manna in the wilderness, and are dead.

This is the bread which cometh down from heaven, that a man may eat thereof, and not die.

I am the living bread which came down from heaven: if any man eat of this bread, he shall live for ever: and the bread that I will give is my flesh, which I will give for the life of the world. . . .

Whoso eateth my flesh, and drinketh my blood, hath eternal life; and I will raise him up at the last day.

For my flesh is meat indeed, and my blood is drink indeed.

He that eateth my flesh, and drinketh my blood, dwelleth in me, and I in him.

As the living Father hath sent me, and I live by the Father: so he that eateth me, even he shall live by me.

This is that bread which came down from heaven: not as your fathers did eat manna, and are dead: he that eateth of this bread shall live for ever. (John 6:32–35, 48–51, 54–58.)

It is clear from Jesus' bread of life discourse that manna was a type for him and his atoning sacrifice, just as the sacramental emblems of bread and water are a "remembrance" of the same. There is also a significant Old Testament link between manna and the sacrament. Not only was a jar of manna kept in the sacred ark of the covenant as a reminder, but also loaves of shewbread and a flask of wine were kept in the temple to serve as types and symbols of the flesh and blood of Christ.

## The Rock and Living Water

Another important Old Testament event that serves as a type of Christ is Moses' miraculous providing of water for the Israelites as they wandered in the desert near Sinai. When the Israelites were suffering from thirst, Jehovah commanded Moses to "smite the rock, and there shall come water out of it, that the people may drink" (Exodus 17:6; see also Numbers 20:7–10). This miracle typifies the "living water" that Christ provides, as he declared unto the Samaritan woman (see John 4:10, 13–14; 7:37–38). Jesus referred to himself as giving "living waters" to the world. He is the very "fountain of living waters" that the prophet Jeremiah centuries earlier had prophesied would come into the world to quench a spiritual thirst in the world by providing everlasting life (see Jeremiah 17:13).

The rock itself is also a significant type of Christ. The Apostle Paul declared that the Israelites "did all drink the same spiritual drink: for they drank of that spiritual Rock that followed them: and that Rock was Christ" (1 Corinthians 10:4). There are many references in the Old Testament to the Messiah being the "Rock of Israel" (see Deuteronomy 32:4,15; 2 Samuel 23:3; Psalm 18:46; Isaiah 8:14; 17:10). "Trust ye in the Lord for ever," Isaiah admonished, "for in the Lord Jehovah is everlasting strength" (Isaiah 26:4). The phrase "everlasting strength" is sometimes translated "eternal rock." This takes on additional significance for us when we think of the Savior's teaching regarding building upon a rock foundation (see Matthew 7:25), which foundation is identified by Helaman in the Book of Mormon as the "rock of our redeemer": "And now, my sons, remember, remember that it is upon the rock of our Redeemer, who is Christ, the Son of God, that ye must build your foundation; that when the devil shall send forth his mighty winds, yea, his shafts in the whirlwind, yea, when all his hail and his mighty storm shall beat upon you, it shall have no power over you to drag you down to the gulf of misery and endless wo, because of the rock upon which ye are built, which is a sure foundation, a foundation whereon if men build they cannot fall," (Helaman 5:12.)

## The Good Shepherd

"The Lord is my shepherd," David declared in the twenty-third psalm. The image of a good shepherd is a familiar Messianic type in the Old Testament (see Genesis 49:24; Psalm 80:1; 95:7; Isaiah 40:11). When the Savior declared, "I am the good shepherd" (John 10:11), he was not just utilizing an interesting literary device but was in reality declaring himself the very fulfillment of this widely known and understood Messianic symbol.

For thus saith the Lord God; Behold, I, even I, will both search my sheep, and seek them out.

As a shepherd seeketh out his flock in the day that he is among his sheep that are scattered; so will I seek out my sheep, and will deliver them out of all places where they have been scattered in the cloudy and dark day.

And I will bring them out from the people, and gather them from the countries, and will bring them to their own land, and feed them upon the mountains of Israel by the rivers, and in all the inhabited places of the country.

I will feed them in a good pasture, and upon the high mountains of Israel shall their fold be: there shall they lie in a good fold, and in a fat pasture shall they feed upon the mountains of Israel.

I will feed my flock, and I will cause them to lie down, saith the Lord God. . . .

Therefore will I save my flock. (Ezekiel 34:11–15, 22; see also 37:24–26; compare to John 10:7–18.)

It is clear that the Apostle Peter understood this type and shadow as he admonished the elders of the church to "feed the flock of God" and minister in the manner of Jesus, who was the "chief shepherd" (see 1 Peter 5:2–4).

## The Scattering and Gathering of Israel

One of the major doctrinal themes of the Old Testament, as evidenced by Nephi's commentary on selected brass plates prophecies in 1 Nephi 19–22, is the scattering and ultimate gathering of the house of Israel. Virtually all of the Old Testament prophets warned of this scattering and prophesied of the gathering in due time (see Deuteronomy 4:27; Isaiah 5:26; 11:11; Jeremiah 29:14; 31:10; Ezekiel 5:10; 37:21–28; Amos 9:9; Zechariah 10:8). From the Book of Mormon we learn that this doctrinal theme is in its own right a type and shadow of the Atonement of Jesus Christ (see 2 Nephi 9:1–12). The scattering and physical bondage that came to the wicked and wayward Israelites represents that spiritual bondage resulting from sin and the estrangement of all mankind from God resulting from the Fall. The promise of gathering not only refers to a gathering to homelands and stakes of Zion but foreshadows a "deliverance" through the Atonement, which gathers us home. This is a physical deliverance for all in the form of resurrection and a spiritual deliverance in the form of salvation for those who return unto the Lord, repent of their sins, and remember their covenants. This major theme not only is instructional in doctrine but also is invitational as it beckons us to be "gathered" unto Christ.

## The Law of Moses

Because of the wickedness and stubbornness of the ancient Israelites, the law of Moses was given to them as a "schoolmaster to bring [them] unto Christ" (Galatians 3:24). Today we often think of the law of Moses only in terms of the complex system of sacrifices and behaviors it prescribed, but there was much more to it than this. Every aspect of the law was to remind the Israelites of Jesus Christ and the requirements of his gospel. Each of the various components of the law, from the sacrificial rites to the health code and laws of purification, were types of Christ. As Abinadi declared:

> And now I say unto you that it was expedient that there should be a law given to the children of Israel, yea, even a very strict law; for they were a stiffnecked people, quick to do iniquity, and slow to remember the Lord their God;
>
> Therefore there was a law given them, yea, a law of performances and of ordinances, a law which they were to observe strictly from day to day, to keep them in remembrance of God and their duty towards him.
>
> But behold, I say unto you, that all these things were types of things to come. (Mosiah 13:29–31.)

The dietary laws, with the companion laws of personal purification, were not intended merely to bring temporal blessings but were immersed in the concept of "holiness to the Lord." What the Israelites ate and what they did in the way of personal hygiene was to be a constant reminder that Jehovah was pure, holy, and sinless and that they should strive to be holy in their spiritual lives, not just healthy and clean in their physical lives (see Leviticus 11).

Three times a year the Israelites were commanded to gather at the tabernacle or temple to worship the Lord and renew their covenants with him. Each of these feasts of ingathering was also to remind them of the redemption that could be theirs through faith and obedience to the Lord. The three events—the Feast of the Passover (*Pesach*); the Feast of Weeks, sometimes called the Feast of the Harvest or Pentacost (*Shavuot*); and the Feast of Tabernacles (*Sukkot*)—were to foreshadow the coming of Christ and typify the atoning sacrifice and the power of salvation.

Not only did Passover commemorate the deliverance of the Israelites from their bondage in Egypt (which was also a type), but it pointed to the ultimate deliverance from bondage that comes to us through Christ. The focal point of the Passover sacrifice was to be a "lamb without blemish" (Exodus 12:5), signifying the pure and perfect life of Christ, the Lamb of God, who was sacrificed for the sins of the world. This lamb was to be sacrificed without any bones broken, a foreshadowing of Jesus' legs not being broken by the Roman guards at the Crucifixion (see John 19:31–36). The blood of the lamb was placed upon the doorposts, just as the children of Israel had marked their homes so that the destroying angel would pass them by as it slayed the firstborn sons of the Egyptians. This foreshadowed the blood of Christ that would preserve the Israelites from death and hell.

Another interesting type in the Passover story is that of the role of the firstborn. In the case of the Father, his firstborn was not spared in order that all others could be (see Colossians 1:13–18; D&C 93:21–22).

The Feast of the Harvest was a festival of thanksgiving for the "firstfruits" of their labors (Leviticus 23:15–17), pointing to the resurrected Christ as the "firstfruits" (see 1 Corinthians 15:20). The Feast of Tabernacles also had significant types and shadows of Christ, such as the hosanna shout as the Israelites waved palm branches as part of their worship of the Lord (see McConkie, *The Promised Messiah*, pp. 433–34; see also Leviticus 23:34; Exodus 23:16; Psalms 113–18; Zechariah 14:16–19). The illumination of the large candelabras (*menorah*) in the temple court, which could be seen from miles around, signified the "light of God" that should illuminate their lives and pointed to Christ as the "Light and the Life of the World" (see John 8:12; 12:46; D&C 11:28; 45:7–9). This feast was held soon after the Day of Atonement, which was perhaps the most important of all the Jewish holidays (see McConkie, *The Promised Messiah*, pp. 435–37; Leviticus 16). On this day the high priest was privileged to enter the sacred Holy of Holies in the house of the Lord, which represented the very presence of God, and there make an atonement for the sins of the people. Sacrifices were slain and the blood of the lamb was sprinkled by the high priest on what was known as "the mercy seat." On this most holy day Israel was to be "ransomed" by a scapegoat upon whom all of the sins of the people were placed, pointing to Christ as our "scapegoat" upon whom all the sins, sorrows, and infirmities of the entire human family were placed.

Numerous other types and shadows are found throughout the law of Moses and within its carnal commandments, but perhaps most explicit of all are the specific symbols associated with its sacrifices. As with all of the types and shadows of the law, these symbols were given so that the ancients could "look forward with steadfastness unto Christ" and "know for what end the law was given" (2 Nephi 25:24, 27). The Apostle Paul spoke of the Mosaic law as but "a shadow of good things to come. . . . For it is not possible that the blood of bulls and of goats should take away sins. . . . But this man [Christ], after he had offered one sacrifice for sins for ever, sat down on the right hand of God." (Hebrews 10:1, 4, 12.)

## SYMBOLS IN SACRIFICES

Animal sacrifice predates the law of Moses by many centuries. In fact, one of the first commandments given to Adam and Eve after they were expelled from the Garden of Eden was the command to worship God through blood sacrifice. This ancient manifestation of the eternal law of sacrifice became a symbol of total faith in and commitment to the Lord—a giving of one's best unto him.

We covenant to live the same law of sacrifice but manifest our obedience today not with a sacrifice of an animal but by offering a broken heart and a contrite spirit and by willingly sacrificing all we have and are to the Lord and the cause of truth. The everlasting law of sacrifice is intended to reveal the nature and mission of Jesus Christ and to ever remind us of his infinite and eternal sacrifice. Adam was taught this Christ-centered symbolism through his own obedience to God's command.

> And [God] gave unto them commandments, that they should worship the Lord their God, and should offer the firstlings of their flocks, for an offering unto the Lord. And Adam was obedient unto the commandments of the Lord.

And after many days an angel of the Lord appeared unto Adam, saying: Why dost thou offer sacrifices unto the Lord? And Adam said unto him: I know not, save the Lord commanded me.

And then the angel spake, saying: This thing is a similitude of the sacrifice of the Only Begotten of the Father, which is full of grace and truth.

Wherefore, thou shalt do all that thou doest in the name of the Son, and thou shalt repent and call upon God in the name of the Son forevermore. (Moses 5:5–8.)

From the time of Adam until after the Savior's resurrection, animal sacrifice was a symbol to point the hearts and minds of the Israelites to Christ and to remind them that through faith and repentance his sacrifice would save them. Though the kinds of sacrifice offered today are different, the purpose remains the same—to point our hearts and minds to the Savior and to remind us to "always remember him" through exercising faith and repentance and by doing the works of Christ. "Certainly, the shedding of the blood of a beast could be beneficial to no man," the Prophet Joseph Smith taught, "except it was done in imitation, or as a type, or explanation of what was to be offered through the gift of God Himself" (*Teachings of the Prophet Joseph Smith*, comp. Joseph Fielding Smith [Salt Lake City: Deseret Book Co., 1976], p. 58). Today, as it was anciently, the ritual or ordinance does not bring the salvation of man or a transformation of his soul, but it serves as a symbol to instruct, edify, and instill "faith unto repentance." Only in this manner does sacrifice possess spiritual power.

Through the centuries as the Israelites became more wicked and were cut off from the enlightenment of the Spirit, the profound spiritual symbolism associated with sacrifice dimmed in their minds. With the law of Moses, the Lord revealed very precise sacrificial rites, all designed to remind them once again of the atoning sacrifice of the Messiah. There were important symbols in even the smallest details of the ritual so that they could not miss the meaning of what they were doing, yet many still missed the point by looking beyond these simple symbols that clearly pointed to Christ.

The burnt offering also reminded Israel that the life of the offerer—not just the animal being offered, was to be above reproach. To emphasize this the law of Moses required that one participate in a symbolic purification bath, or *mikveh*, before worshipping and sacrificing in the house of the Lord. Only through a spiritually pure and clean offerer did the offering become "sweet" unto God. (See Leviticus 1:4–9.) The complete consumption by fire of the animal on the altar also represented the "baptism of fire," or the sanctification that comes by the power of the Holy Ghost when one exercises faith and repentance. Through the Atonement all evil, like dross and refuse, is burned out of our very souls. Elder Bruce R. McConkie taught, "All the fires on all the altars of the past, as they burned the flesh of animals, were signifying that spiritual purification would come by the Holy Ghost, whom the Father would send because of the Son" (*The Promised Messiah*, p. 432).

Another important element of the burnt offerings was that the animal being sacrificed was cut into pieces and each piece was cleansed by the officiating priest. Each part of the animal's body represented different aspects of the offerer's life: the head symbolized thoughts, legs represented the walk of life, the entrails symbolized the affections of the heart and inward motivations of man. This was to remind the offerer of the need to be pure and totally submissive to God, both inwardly and outwardly, just as the supreme sacrifice, the Lamb of God, was "without blemish."

Blood also played a major role in reminding the Israelites of the blood of Christ that would be spilt in behalf of the world. When the animal was brought to the altar, its throat was cut and the priest collected the blood in a bowl. Then, depending on the type of sacrifice, the priest either dabbed the blood on the horns of the altar, splashed it on the four sides, or merely dumped it out at the base of the altar. This manner of "covering" the altar with blood symbolized that all sin (and all of mankind) was "covered" by the blood of the lamb, or Christ.

Blood represented not only the life-giving powers of Christ's Atonement but also death and the consequences of sin that required a reconciliation to God. The blood and death of the animal represented the sins and spiritual estrangement of man. A sacrifice that brought death was required to bring to pass life. It all represented the blood of Christ that made a new life possible. In fact, the Hebrew word from which the English word *atonement* comes means "to cover," signifying that the sin no longer exists, because it has been completely "covered over" by the power of the Redeemer. (See Richard D. Draper, "Sacrifices and Offerings: Foreshadowing of Christ," *Ensign*, September 1980, pp. 20–26; also Andrew Jukes, *The Law of Offerings* [Grand Rapids, Mich.: Kregel Publications, 1976].)

Couched within these sacrificial rites were several other even more detailed symbols of the Savior's suffering, death, and resurrection. For example, one of the Mosaic sacrifices involved the burning of an ox "outside the camp of Israel," illustrating that sin places us "outside" of God and his kingdom, symbolizing spiritual death. The Atonement brings us back "inside" as our spiritual death is overcome through Christ's redemptive power. Another lesser known interpretation of this specific symbol was that Christ was to be crucified outside the city walls (see Hebrews 13:11–13). Similarly, some sacrifices required that the animal be slain on the "north side of the altar," foreshadowing the death of Jesus Christ on Golgotha, which is the north side of Mount Moriah.

Voluntary as well as obligatory sacrificial offerings reminded the Israelites of the destructive nature of sin and of their continual need for repentance. Christ's Atonement "covered" not only sins knowingly committed and faithfully repented of but also sins which are committed in ignorance or by those who are not accountable (see Mosiah 3:11). This points to Christ's redemption of little children who die in infancy (see Moroni 8:5–23; D&C 29:46–50).

Not only were sacrificial ordinances instructional in reminding the Israelites of the future sacrifice of the Son of God, but they also provided the Israelites with an opportunity to renew their covenants to be faithful to their God and to be his "peculiar treasure," or *segullah*. Being faithful and obedient not only in offering sacrifices but in living a life of worthiness helped them to continually remember God and have his Spirit to be with them.

The practice of sacrificing is different today, but it still focuses us on "always remembering" Christ, recommitting ourselves to strive to be more pure and clean, and repenting of our sins. Like the sacrifices of the ancient Israelites, the modern sacrifice of "a broken heart and a contrite spirit" yields the companionship of the Holy Spirit and a remission of sins and "is a similitude of the sacrifice of the Only Begotten of the Father, which is full of grace and truth."

## Messianic Prophecies

Like the individual pieces of a giant jigsaw puzzle, the prophetic words of Old Testament seers may not seem to say much or portray the big picture when taken independently. But from the visions and inspired testimonies of the prophets of old taken together, a panoramic view of the mission of the Messiah emerges. Indeed, the Old Testament testifies of his birth, his ministry of teaching and healing, his suffering and sacrifice, his death and resurrection, and his triumphal return as the King of kings. Truly, "all the holy prophets . . . have prophesied concerning the coming of the Lord" (Mosiah 15:11). On almost every page there are not only types and shadows of his coming and symbols of his supreme sacrifice but also Messianic prophecies and doctrinal teachings about his Atonement, the plan of salvation, and the principles and ordinances of the everlasting gospel. Elder Bruce R. McConkie wrote:

> Whenever there have been prophets, they have spoken of Christ; whenever the Lord has sent teachers, they have taught of Christ; whenever legal administrators have ministered among men, they have performed the ordinances of salvation which are ordained by Christ; whenever the Lord has performed signs and wonders, either by his own voice or by the voice of his servants, such have been witnesses of the goodness and greatness of Christ. . . .
>
> How many Messianic prophecies have there been? In the real and true perspective of things, ten thousand times ten thousand is not a beginning to their number. They are in multitude like the sand upon the seashore. Obviously, all the prophetic utterances about Christ and the plan of salvation were Messianic in nature. But such teachings merely introduce the subject. For instance:
>
> Every proper and perfect prayer uttered by a righteous man, woman, or child, from the day Adam stepped through Eden's portals into his lone and dreary habitation, to the day the angelic hosts acclaimed the birth of God's own Son, was in fact a Messianic prophecy. The mere saying, with sincerity and understanding, of the words of the prayer itself constituted a Messianic affirmation. Why? Because all the prophets, saints, and righteous hosts prayed to the Father in the name of Christ, thus witnessing that they knew that salvation came through him and his atoning blood. Similarly, every true prayer today is a reaffirmation that Jesus is the Lord and that through his blood the believing saints are redeemed.
>
> Every shout of praise and exultation to the Lord Jehovah was Messianic in nature, for those who so acclaimed worshiped the Father in the name of Jehovah-Messiah who would come to redeem his people.

And so with every baptism, every priethood ordination, every partriarchal blessing, every act of administering to the sick, every divine ordinance or performance ordained of God, every sacrifice, symbolism, and similitude; all that God ever gave to his people—all was ordained and established in such a way as to testify of his Son and center the faith of believing people in him and in the redemption he was foreordained to make. (*The Promised Messiah*, pp. 26, 27–28.)

As Elder McConkie so eloquently stated, all of the Messianic prophecies and allusions to Christ in the scriptures in general, and the Old Testament in particular, could not be adequately cited in all the volumes and commentary about scripture, nor could they all be housed in all the libraries of the world. In fact, with our finite and mortal minds we do not even see all of the types and shadows and prophecies of Christ that fill the standard works and are evident all around us. With that in mind, I give only a few examples to illustrate how Christ is taught in the Old Testament with Messianic prophecies. They are not even the "tip of the iceberg" of all of the prophecies and teachings about the Savior found in the Old Testament; indeed, we might liken them to only a single snowflake on the tip of all the snow-capped peaks and icebergs of the world.

## The Birth of Christ

Isaiah prophesied to his people that a "virgin shall conceive, and bear a son, and shall call his name Immanuel" (Isaiah 7:14). Although this prophecy had a specific political application to Isaiah's day, it is clearly a Messianic prophecy concerning the coming of Christ in the meridian of time (see fulfillment in Luke 1:26–30). Although King Herod had to ask his advisers to search the scriptures to see from whence the Messiah would come, most faithful Jews knew that the prophet Micah centuries earlier had declared that the "ruler in Israel" would come out of Bethlehem (see Micah 5:2).

## The Mortal Ministry of Christ

That Jesus would perform mighty miracles was prophesied with Messianic psalms of praise (see Psalm 146:8; 147:3; see also Malachi 4:2; Mosiah 3:5–6). Despite these miracles, the Messiah would be rejected by his own (see Psalm 69:8; Isaiah 49:7; 53:1–3; see fulfillment in Mark 7:1–9). As the Psalmist declared in the first-person voice of the Lord, "All that hate me whisper together against me: against me do they devise my hurt" (Psalm 41:7). Zechariah foresaw and recorded that the Prince of Peace and King of kings would make a triumphal entry into Jerusalem "lowly, and riding upon an ass," even upon "a colt the foal of an ass" (Zechariah 9:9; see fulfillment in Matthew 21:1–5). Similarly, Zechariah prophesied that the Messiah would be betrayed and "sold" for thirty pieces of silver (see Zechariah 11:12–13; see fulfillment in Matthew 26:15; 27:7).

After the betrayal, Jesus was mocked, persecuted, reviled, and scourged. Numerous prophets foresaw these privations and testified of the "suffering servant" of God. Micah spoke of a "rod upon the cheek" (Micah 5:1); a Messianic psalm tells of the wicked persecution and condemnation of the "soul of the righteous" or the "innocent blood" which is Christ (Psalm 94:21); Isaiah describes him as one who would be "stricken, smitten of God, and afflicted" (Isaiah 53:4) and who would "[give his] back to the smiters, and [his] cheeks" to abusers, and "[hide] not [his] face from shame and spitting" (Isaiah 50:6; see also 1 Nephi 19:9; Mosiah 15:5; see fulfillment in Matthew 27:30). Despite the abuse that was heaped upon him, Jesus did not retaliate, just as Isaiah had prophesied: "He was oppressed, and he was afflicted, yet he opened not his mouth" (Isaiah 53:7; see fulfillment in 1 Peter 2:21–25). "Wounded for our transgressions," as Isaiah declared (Isaiah 53:5), and suffering the unspeakable pains of hell "to make reconciliation for iniquity," as the angel Gabriel prophesied to Daniel (Daniel 9:24), Christ fulfilled these Messianic prophecies in Gethsemane and at Golgotha as he "[suffered] the pains of all men, yea, the pains of every living creature, both men, women, and children, who belong to the family of Adam" (2 Nephi 9:21).

## Christ's Death and Resurrection

The Psalmist declared that the Messiah's hands and feet would be pierced (see Psalm 22:16), yet no bones would be broken (see Psalm 34:20), just as the lamb sacrificed and eaten as part of the Passover supper was not to have any bones broken (see Exodus 12:46; see fulfillment in John 19:32–33). Isaiah proclaimed that the Messiah would die with the wicked and make his grave with the rich (see Isaiah 53:9;

see fulfillment in Matthew 27:38, 57–60). After his death and before his resurrection, the Savior continued his mission of redemption in the spirit world. This mission was foreseen by Old Testament prophets who declared that the Messiah would "open the blind eyes, to bring out the prisoners from the prison, and them that sit in darkness out of the prison house" (Isaiah 42:7; see alo Isaiah 49:9; Psalm 146:8; see fulfillment in 1 Peter 3:18–22; D&C 138).

Numerous prophecies and inspired declarations foreshadow the Messiah's ultimate victory over death and the universal resurrection that comes as a result. Job knew that he would be resurrected because of the Atonement of the Redeemer. "For I know that my redeemer liveth, and that he shall stand at the latter day upon the earth," he testified. "And though after my skin worms destroy this body, yet in my flesh shall I see God." (Job 19:25–26; see also Job 14:14–15.) "There is no saviour beside me," declared the Messiah unto the prophet Hosea. ". . . I will ransom them from the power of the grave; I will redeem them from death: O death, I will be thy plagues; O grave, I will be thy destruction" (Hosea 13:4, 14; see fulfillment in 1 Corinthians 15:20–22, 55). The prophet Ezekiel beheld in vision the glorious resurrection that results from Christ's breaking the bands of death (see Ezekiel 37:1–14). Daniel said that those who "sleep in the dust of the earth shall awake, some to everlasting life, and some to shame and everlasting contempt" (Daniel 12:2; compare to John 5:28–29). Even the resurrection of many of the righteous at Jesus' resurrection (see Matthew 27:52–53; see also Alma 40:16–18) was foretold by the prophet Isaiah. "Thy dead men shall live, together with my dead body shall they arise," the Messiah declared. "Awake and sing, ye that dwell in dust: for thy dew is as the dew of herbs, and the earth shall cast out the dead." (Isaiah 26:19.)

So many other prophecies of Christ's mortal ministry and glorious Second Coming could be cited. But one in particular reminds us of our Redeemer's role, his power, and his ultimate triumph over the world. In a prophecy with a double meaning, Isaiah spoke of a ruler in his day within the king's household. At first glance it appears to be a prophecy concerning a political situation that would have no application to us today, but those in tune with the Spirit and familiar with Isaiah's tendency to couch an important prophecy within another will recognize the glorious Messianic message:

And I will clothe him with thy robe, and strengthen him with thy girdle, and I will commit thy government into his hand: and he shall be a father to the inhabitants of Jerusalem, and to the house of Judah.

And the key of the house of David will I lay upon his shoulder; so he shall open, and none shall shut; and he shall shut, and none shall open.

And I will fasten him as a nail in a sure place; and he shall be for a glorious throne to his father's house. (Isaiah 22:21–23.)

Truly the Old Testament is another witness for Christ. In its teachings, its examples, its symbolism, its types and shadows, and its doctrines, the Savior of the world is always the focal point. We have only scratched the surface, both in this chapter and in the entire book, of how Jesus Christ is revealed to us through the pages of the Old Testament. The more we study it, ponder its teachings, and pray about its relevant application to our own lives, the more we will see messages of the Messiah leaping from its pages into our heads and hearts. We will find more types and shadows and Messianic prophecies than we ever imagined possible. All things testify of Christ—over and over again, from one level to a higher one. We can never "harvest" all the messages of Christ from its pages or from any of the scriptures. It may be called the *Old* Testament, but it will become *new* to us each time we prayerfully study it.

The scriptures are an everlasting, never-ending testimony of Jesus Christ and of the glorious truth that "the government shall be [and is] upon his shoulder: and his name shall be [and is] called Wonderful, Counsellor, The mighty God, The everlasting Father, The Prince of Peace" (Isaiah 9:6). The more I understand that the Old Testament is indeed another witness for Christ, the more I am filled with love—even charity, the pure love of Christ—and with a heightened hope in him, the fulfillment of my own Messianic expectation.

He will swallow up death in victory; and the Lord God will wipe away tears from off all faces; and the rebuke of his people shall he take away from off all the earth: for the Lord hath spoken it.

And it shall be said in that day, Lo, this is our God; we have waited for him, and he will save us: this is the Lord: we have waited for him, we will be glad and rejoice in his salvation. (Isaiah 25:8–9.)

The Old Testament is not archaic, irrelevant, or incomprensible. It is interesting and inspiring. As Elder Neal A. Maxwell has said, it demonstrates "relevancy within antiquity." It teaches the gospel of Jesus Christ, not just the law of Moses. It is much, much more than ancient history. It is truly the word of God—the "will of the Lord," the "mind of the Lord," the "voice of the Lord, and the power of God unto salvation" (D&C 68:4). It changes lives. It has mine. Like the Book of Mormon, it leads us to Christ, *if* we will let it. And when we find the Savior within its pages we will be inclined to join our hearts and voices with the ancients in praising the Holy One of Israel.

> *Praise ye the Lord. Praise ye the name of the Lord; praise him, O ye servants of the Lord. Ye that stand in the house of the Lord, in the courts of the house of our God, Praise the Lord; for the Lord is good: sing praises unto his name; for it is pleasant. For the Lord hath chosen Jacob unto himself, and Israel for his peculiar treasure.*
> —Psalm 135:1–4

# Index